Colonial Encounters in Southwest Canaan during the Late Bronze Age and the Early Iron Age

Culture and History of the Ancient Near East

Founding Editor

M.H.E. Weippert

Editor-in-Chief

Jonathan Stökl

Editors

Eckart Frahm
W. Randall Garr
B. Halpern
Theo P.J. van den Hout
Leslie Anne Warden
Irene J. Winter

VOLUME 119

The titles published in this series are listed at *brill.com/chan*

Colonial Encounters in Southwest Canaan during the Late Bronze Age and the Early Iron Age

By

Ido Koch

BRILL

LEIDEN | BOSTON

Library of Congress Cataloging-in-Publication Data

Names: Koch, Ido, author. | Koch, Ido. Tsilah shel Mitsrayim.
Title: Colonial encounters in southwest Canaan during the late bronze age and the early iron age / by Ido Koch.
Description: Leiden ; Boston : Brill, [2021] | Series: Culture and history of the ancient Near East, 1566–2055 ; volume 119 | Includes bibliographical references and index.
Identifiers: LCCN 2020050090 (print) | LCCN 2020050091 (ebook) | ISBN 9789004432826 (hardback) | ISBN 9789004432833 (ebook)
Subjects: LCSH: Palestine—Antiquities. | Canaanites—Antiquities. | Egypt—Antiquities. | Palestine—Relations—Egypt. | Egypt—Relations—Palestine. | Bronze age—Palestine. | Iron age—Palestine. | Excavations (Archaeology)—Palestine. | Israel—Antiquities.
Classification: LCC DS111 .K63 2021 (print) | LCC DS111 (ebook) | DDC 933/.02—dc23
LC record available at https://lccn.loc.gov/2020050090
LC ebook record available at https://lccn.loc.gov/2020050091

Typeface for the Latin, Greek, and Cyrillic scripts: "Brill". See and download: brill.com/brill-typeface.

ISSN 1566-2055
ISBN 978-90-04-43282-6 (hardback)
ISBN 978-90-04-43283-3 (e-book)

Copyright 2021 by Koninklijke Brill NV, Leiden, The Netherlands.
Koninklijke Brill NV incorporates the imprints Brill, Brill Hes & De Graaf, Brill Nijhoff, Brill Rodopi, Brill Sense, Hotei Publishing, mentis Verlag, Verlag Ferdinand Schöningh and Wilhelm Fink Verlag.
All rights reserved. No part of this publication may be reproduced, translated, stored in a retrieval system, or transmitted in any form or by any means, electronic, mechanical, photocopying, recording or otherwise, without prior written permission from the publisher. Requests for re-use and/or translations must be addressed to Koninklijke Brill NV via brill.com or copyright.com.

This book is printed on acid-free paper and produced in a sustainable manner.

Contents

Acknowledgements VII
List of Figures IX

Introduction 1
   1   Egyptian Colonialism and Canaan in Scholarship: An Overview   4
   2   Notes on Nomenclature   8
   3   Chronological Framework   9

1 Dawn   12
   1   Decline and Revitalization of Settlements during the Late Bronze I   13
   2   The Advent of Egyptian-style Objects   16
   3   Reassessing the Levantine–Egyptian Interaction during the Late Bronze I   22

2 The Egyptian Network   25
   1   Modeling the Egyptian Colonial Network   25
   2   Egyptian and Local Centers   27
      2.1 *The Besor Region: Tell el-Ajjul, Gaza and Yurza*   28
      2.2 *The Coastal Plain: Ashkelon and Muḫḫazu*   33
      2.3 *The Shephelah: Gath, Lachish and Beyond*   36
      2.4 *The Ayalon Valley: Gezer*   39
      2.5 *The Yarkon Basin: Jaffa*   40
   3   Local Rulers and the Egyptian Court   43

3 Goddess in Translation: The Fosse Temple at Lachish   45
   1   Introducing the Fosse Temple in Lachish   46
   2   Assessing the Change   49
   3   Hathor and Tiye   50
   4   The Cult in the Fosse Temple in Context   52

4 Ambivalence   54
   1   Building Deposits   55
   2   Conspicuous Consumption   58
   3   The Equestrian Goddess   61
   4   Range of Reactions   67

5 Collapse 71
1. Questioning the Philistine Paradigm 73
2. In Search of the Early Philistines 76

6 Regeneration 81
1. The Yarkon Basin 83
2. The Shephelah and the Coastal Plain 86
3. The Besor Basin, or: The Problem with Gaza 89
4. Retrospective 91

7 Reorientations 92
1. Animal-based Economy and Accumulation of Wealth 92
2. Pottery Production and Communal Feasting 95
3. Religion 97
4. Interpreting Reorientations 100

8 In the Eye of the Beholder 106
1. The Egyptian Connection 108
2. Canaanite Innovations 116
3. Local Glyptic Production during the Iron Age I–IIA 123

Summary: Colonial Encounters in Southwest Canaan in the Late Bronze Age and Early Iron Age 125

Appendix: Chronology of Egyptian Kings 131
Bibliography 133
Index of Place Names 192
Index of Historical Figures 195

Acknowledgements

This book marks the end of the last phase, at least in the coming years, of my journey after the Levantine–Egyptian colonial encounters during the Late Bronze Age and their aftermath during the early Iron Age. Five years have passed since I submitted my PhD dissertation to Tel Aviv University and two years since the Hebrew book based on that PhD was published. Like the Hebrew volume, this revised English edition deals with the limited region between the Tel Aviv and Gaza metropolitan areas. However, it also includes scholarly works published since then and its structure was rearranged in a chronological order that includes additional case studies. Above all, it reflects my individual journey in the study of the effects of colonial rule on subjugated groups—on their structures, practices, and ideas.

Such a journey could not have been possible without the support and advice of dear colleagues, friends, and family. Cordial thanks are extended to my teachers Prof. Nadav Na'aman and Prof. Oded Lipschits. Though our relations have grown, and today I might even be considered their colleague and friend, they remain my mentors, and I am grateful for the many years of inspiration, during which I learnt archaeology and history from two remarkable scholars, for whom I have a great deal of admiration. I thank them for their patience, their encouragement, and their sincere involvement in my professional and personal life.

I am indebted to colleagues and friends from the Department of Archaeology and Ancient Near Eastern Cultures and the Institute of Archaeology at Tel Aviv University. In this regard, I would like to thank Prof. Ran Barkay, Prof. Erez Ben-Yosef, Prof. Shlomo Bunimovitz, Prof. Israel Finkelstein, Prof. Ze'ev Herzog, Ms. Nirit Kedem, Dr. Assaf Kleiman, Dr. Sabine Kleiman, Dr. Dafna Langgut, Ms. Noa Ranzer, Dr. Lidar Sapir-Hen, Dr. Guy Stiebel, Ms. Alexandra Wrathall, Prof. Ran Zadok, and Mr. Omer Ze'evi-Berger. I would like to single out Ms. Helena Roth for her support and thoughtful critiques, Prof. Yuval Gadot, who taught me how to look at the multivocality of archaeology and the complexity of the past, and Dr. Omer Sergi, for countless hours of stimulating discussions on anything and everything.

During the years of writing and revising I had the good fortune to be a guest in two of the most beautiful cities in Europe. My thanks are extended to Prof. Christoph Uehlinger of the University of Zurich, who hosted me as a postdoctoral fellow in 2015–2016 with the generous support of the Swiss Government Excellence Program. This year was a formative one for my academic skills, and for that I am grateful. Heartfelt gratitude is also extended to Prof. Thomas

Römer of the Collège de France, who hosted me on several occasions, offering me sincere friendship and the kindest hospitality.

Thanks to Ms. Miriam Feinberg-Vamosh who translated the major bulk of the text. It was a pleasure to work together. I am indebted to Ms. Myrna Pollak, Ms. Tsipi Kuper-Blau, and Ms. Alexandra Wrathall, who polished various sections and contributed insightful comments and suggestions, who were willing to respond as soon as possible.

Thanks to Dr. Jonathan Stökl, editor of Brill's Culture and History of the Ancient Near East series, who invited me to publish the book in this respected platform. I am grateful to Erika Mandarino, Assistant Editor of Ancient Near East and Jewish Studies at Brill, who assisted in every step of the publication process. Thanks are also extended to the two anonymous reviewers who provided essential critiques that helped me to refine the arguments in each chapter and in the book as a whole.

Finally, I would like to thank my loving family—members of the Koch, Laron, Levitovitch, Cohen and Hoshen families. To Roy, my partner, for endless patience and understanding, long days and short nights, and infinite love. Last but not least, to my parents, Anat and David, to whom I owe so much. Thanks for instilling in me love of the country, for encouraging me to study the past, and for allowing me to talk incessantly since childhood. This book is dedicated to them.

Figures

1   Southwest Canaan: location map   2
2   Scarabs and related artifacts from south Levantine Late Bronze Age I contexts classified according to place of manufacture   18
3   Scarabs from Late Bronze Age I Burials at Tell el-Ajjul classified according to place of manufacture   18
4   Scarabs and related artifacts from south Levantine Late Bronze Age I–IIA contexts classified according to place of manufacture   19
5   Motifs on Middle Bronze Age II local scarabs (nos. 1, 5, 9, 12) compared to motifs on early-mid-18th Dynasty scarabs (nos. 2–4, 6–8, 10, 11): No. 1 Tell el-Ajjul, Tomb 1541 (after Keel 1997: 411 no. 900); 2. Tell el-Ajjul, Tomb 281 (after Keel 1997: 147 no. 123); 3. Tel Beth-Shemesh, surface (after Keel 2010a: 285 no. 160); 4. Tel Gezer, Cave I.A.10 (after Keel 2013a: 439 no. 633); 5. Tell el-Far'ah (S) Tomb 1021C (after Keel 2010b: 205 no. 415); 6. Tell el-Ajjul Tomb 1128 (after Keel 1997: 195 no. 272); 7–8. Tel Gezer Cave 10A (after Keel 2013a: 441 nos. 634 and 635); 9. Tell el-Ajjul Tomb 101 (after Keel 1997: 131 no. 78); 10. Tell el-Ajjul Tomb 1071 (after Keel 1997: 185 no. 240); 11. Tel Lachish Tomb 216 (after Tufnell 1958: Pl. 38 no. 301); 12. Tell el-Ajjul Stratum III-II (after Keel 1997: 473 no. 1076); 13. Tell el-Ajjul Tomb 1026 (after Keel 1997: 175 no. 209); 14. Tel Lachish Tomb 216 (after Tufnell 1958: Pl. 38 no. 307); 15. Tel Batash Stratum VIII (after Brandl 2006: 219 fig. 23)   21
6   Besor region: location map   29
7   Coastal Plain and Shephelah: location map   34
8   Yarkon Basin: location map   41
9   Plan of the three phases of the Fosse Temple (after Koch 2017a: Figure 2)   47
10 Drawing of a decoration of a jug from the Fosse Temple (after Koch 2017a: Figure 3)   48
11 Large-size scarab of Amenhotep III from Jaffa (courtesy of Corpus of Stamp-Seals from the Southern Levant)   51
12 Lamp-and-Bowl deposit from Late Bronze Age Tel Azekah (courtesy of Oded Lipschits)   56
13 Ivory plaques from Tell el-Far'ah (S) (after Koch 2014: Figure 3)   60
14 Ivory plaque from Tel Megiddo Stratum VIIA (after Koch 2014: Figure 4)   60
15 Plan of the "Acropolis Temple", Tel Lachish Level VI (after Ussishkin 2004: 220 fig. 6.4)   62
16 Golden foil, the "Acropolis Temple", Tel Lachish Level VI (after Schroer 2011: 313 no. 869)   63

17	Depictions of naked goddesses grasping flowers—no. 1: Clay plaque, Tel Ḥarasim Stratum V (after Schroer 2011: 307 no. 863); no. 2: Bronze plaque, Akko, "The Persian Garden" (after Ben-Arieh and Edelstein 1977: pl. 6.2); no. 3: Clay plaque, Tel Batash Stratum VIIB (after Panitz-Cohen and Mazar 2006: 252 and photo 104)	64
18	Stele of Qeh (British Museum EA 191) © Trustees of the British Museum	65
19	Depictions of Astarte from Egypt—no. 1: Stone stela, Tell el-Burg (after Hoffmeier and Kitchen 2007: 129 fig. 1b); no. 2: Stone stela, Buhen (after Bibel+Orient Datenbank Online, http://www.bible-orient-museum.ch/bodo/details.php?bomid=4434, accessed 15 February 2016); no. 3: Stone stela, Ramesseum (after Leclant 1960: Fig. 10)	66
20	Scarab, Tell el-Farʿah (S), Tomb 936 (after Keel 2010b: 317 no. 675); 2—Tel Lachish, Tomb 4004 (after Tufnell 1958: pl. 36:316); 3—Tell el-Farʿah (S), Tomb 934 (after Keel 2010b: 265 no. 551); 4—Tel Azekah, Local Level T2–3a (after Koch et al. 2017: Fig. 7.1)	80
21	Settlement patterns of the Late Bronze Age and the Iron Age I (GIS by Omer Zeʾevi-Berger)	82
22	Iron Age Limestone conoids depicting horned animals: 1. Tel Miqne Stratum V (after Keel 2010a: 551 no. 72); 2. Tel Beth-Shemesh Stratum III (after Keel 2010a: 279 no. 144); 3. Tell eṣ-Ṣafi Area T (after Keel 2013a: 121 no. 56); 4. Tel Gezer, 'Fourth Semitic Period' (after Keel 2013a: 185 no. 44)	101
23	Multi-faceted decorated seal-amulet from Tel Gerisa Stratum 6 (after Keel 2013a: 143 no. 7)	107
24	Multi-faceted decorated seal-amulet from Tel Qasile Stratum X(?) (after Mazar 1967: pl. 4–5; Shuval 1990: 73 fig. 2, 123 no. 1)	107
25	Multi-faceted decorated seal-amulet from Tell el-Farʿah (S), Cemetery 800 (after Keel 2010b: 117 no. 210)	107
26	Multi-faceted decorated seal-amulet from Ashkelon, unknown context (after Keel 1997: 721 no. 83)	107
27	Name of Amun-Re on multi-faceted seal-amulets	108
28	Late Iron Age I–Early Iron Age IIA Depictions of Marching Lion: No. 1. Tel Gerisa (Figure 23:1, above); 2. Tel Qasile Stratum X (Figure 24:2, above); 3. Tell el-Farʿah (S) Cemetery 800 (Figure 25:2, above); 4. Ashkelon (Figure 26:2, above); 5. Tell el-Farʿah (S), Tomb 135 (after Keel 2010b: 123 no. 223); 6. Tel Haror, Stratum B1/2 (after Brandl in Keel 2013a: 573 no. 1); 7. Tel Lachish, Tomb 191 (after Tufnell 1953: pl. 45:130); 8. Tel Beth-Shemesh, Tomb 1 (after Keel 2010a: 221 no. 6)	109
29	Late Bronze Age IIB–III Depictions of Marching Lion: No. 1. Tell el-Farʿah (S), Tomb 984 (after Keel 2010b: 367 no. 800); 2. Tell el-Farʿah (S), Tomb 935 (after Keel 2010b: 311 no. 660); 3. Tell Jemmeh, unknown (after Keel 2013a: 59 no. 135);	

4. Tel Azekah, Area S2–Late Bronze Age IIB level (courtesy of Oded Lipschits); 5. Tel Beth-Shemesh, Stratum IV–III (after Keel 2010a: 283 no. 153); 6. Tel Gezer, "2nd Semitic Period" (after Keel 2013a: 297 no. 293); 7. Tel Gezer, Area VI Stratum 6C/B (after Keel 2013b: 447 no. 650); 8. Tel Gerisa, unknown (after Keel 2013a: 153 no. 33)   110

30   Late Bronze Age IIB–III and Iron Age I–Early Iron Age IIA Depictions of Amun-Re's Name Accompanied by Attributes: No. 1. Tel Gerisa, Level 6 (fig. 1, above); 2. Deir el-Balaḥ, unknown (after Keel 2010a: 455 no. 131); 3. Tell el-Farʿah (S), Tomb 981 (after Keel 2010b: 351 no. 758); 4. Deir el-Balaḥ, unknown (after Keel 2010a: 455 no. 132); 5. Tel Beth-Shemesh, Stratum III (after Keel 2010a: 265 no. 111); 6. Tel Akko, unknown (after Keel 1997: 609 no. 225); 7. Tell el-Farʿah (S), unknown (after Keel 2010b: 409 no. 909); 8. Lisht, 20th–21st Dynasty (after: http://www.metmuseum.org/collection/the-collection-online/search/565101?rpp=30&pg=1&ft=09.180.899&pos=1)   111

31   Late Iron Age I–Early Iron Age IIA Depictions of a Winged Deity: No. 1. Tel Qasile (Figure 24:5, above); 2. Tell el-Farʿah (S), Tomb 542 (after Keel 2010b: 93 no. 153); 3. Jerusalem, City of David Strata 9–8 (after Keel 2015: 432 no. 2); 4. Tell el-Farʿah (S), Stratum V/W (after Keel 2010b: 477 no. 919). Late Bronze Age IIB–III Associated Figures: 5. Tell el-Farʿah (S), Tomb 960c (after Keel 2010b: 335 no. 718); 6. Tell el-Farʿah (S), Tomb 902c (after Keel 2010b: 87 no. 138); 7. Tell eṣ-Ṣafi, unknown (after Keel 1990a: 311 fig. 82); 8. Deir el-Balaḥ, Tomb 118 (after Keel 2010a: 406 no. 17)   112

32   Iron Age I–Early Iron Age IIA Depictions of Falcon-Head Deity and a Uraeus: No. 1: Tel Gerisa, Level 6 (Figure 23:4, above); 2: Tel Miqne, Stratum VIA (after Keel 2010a: 549 no. 69); 3: Tell el-Farʿah (S), Tomb 222 (after Keel 2010b: 145 no. 271); 4: Tell el-Farʿah (S), unknown (after Keel 2010a: 421 no. 944); 5: Tell el-Farʿah (S), Tomb 643 (after Keel 2010b: 155 no. 293); 6: Tel Megiddo, Stratum VIA (after Münger 2003: 68 fig. 1:3); 7: Tel Kinrot, Local Stratum S2a (after Münger 2007a: 94 fig. 8); 8: Tel Dothan, unspecified (after Keel 2010a: 497 no. 20); Late Bronze Age IIB–III: 9: el-Ahwat, surface (after Brandl 2012: 249 fig. 14:8); 10: Tel Miqne, unstratified (after Keel 2010a: 547 no. 68)   113

33   Late Bronze Age IIB–III and Iron Age I–Early Iron Age IIA Depictions of Winged Uraeus as Main Motif: No. 1. Tel Gerisa, Level 6 (Figure 23, above); 2: Tell el-Farʿah (S), Tomb 562 (after Keel 2010b: 103 no. 171); 3: Tell el-Farʿah (S), Tomb 960 (after Keel 2010b: 345 no. 743); 4: Tel Beth-Shemesh, Stratum IVB (after Keel 2010a: 279 no. 145); 5: Tell el-Farʿah (S), Area South, Room EF, Stratum E (after Keel 2010b: 387 no. 852); 6: Tel Gezer, unknown (after Keel 2013a: 429 no. 609)   114

34   Late Iron Age I–Early Iron Age IIA Depictions of Anthropomorphic Figures as Main Motifs: No. 1: Tell el-Farʿah (S) (Figure 25:3, above); 2: Ashkelon (Figure 26:3, above); 3: Tel Miqne, Stratum VB (after Keel 2010a: 543 no. 59);

4: Tel Miqne, Stratum VA (after Keel 2010a: 545 no. 65); (after idem, 545 no. 65); 5: Tel Gerisa, Stratum 10(?) (after Keel 2013a: 158 no. 46); 6: Tell el-Farʿah (S), surface (after Keel 2010b: 77 no. 119); 7: Tell el-Ajjul, unknown (after Keel 1997: 443 no. 995)   115

35 Late Bronze Age IIB–III Depictions of Anthropomorphic Figures as Main Motifs: No. 1: Tel Lachish, Tomb 4004 (after Tufnell 1958: pl. 36:316); 2: Tel Lachish, Tomb 4002 (after Tufnell 1958: pl. 39:365); 3: Tell el-Farʿah (S), Tomb 934 (after Keel 2010b: 271 no. 567); 4: Tell el-Farʿah (S), Tomb 935 (after Keel 2010b: 305 no. 647); 5: Deir el-Balaḥ, Tomb 116 (after Keel 2010a: 405 no. 11); 6: Tel Miqne, LBA Tomb (after Keel 2010a: 519 no. 9); 7: Tell el-Farʿah (S), Tomb 934 (after Keel 2010b: 265 no. 551); 8: Tell el-Farʿah (S), Area South, Room EF, Stratum E (after Keel 2010b: 389 no. 855); 9: Ḥ. Eleq (after Keel 2010a: 555 no. 2)   116

36 Depictions of a Bull and Accompanying Elements: Iron Age I–Early Iron Age IIA: 1: Tell el-Farʿah (S), Cemetery 800 (Figure 25:5, above); 2: Tel Qasile (fig. 2, above); 3: Tel Megiddo, Stratum VB (after Loud 1948: pl. 153:225); 4: Tell eṣ-Ṣafi/Gath, Stratum A3 (after Keel 2013a: 117 no. 47). Late Bronze Age IIB–III: No. 5. Tel Gezer, "2nd Semitic Period" (after Keel 2013a: 323 no. 356); 6: Tel Gerisa, unknown context (after Brandl 2008: 147* fig. 8b); 7: Tel Beth-Shemesh, Stratum IV (after Keel 2010a: 285 no. 156); 8: Tel Lachish, Tomb 4004 (after Eggler 2008: fig. 62)   117

37 Late Iron Age I–Early Iron Age IIA Depictions of a Chariot Scene: 1: Ashkelon (Figure 26:5, above); 2: Tel Qasile, Stratum XII (after Mazar 1985a: 19 fig. 6:1); 3: Tell el-Farʿah (S), Tomb 533 609 (after Keel 2010b: 125 no. 224); 4: Tell el-Farʿah (S), Tomb 609 (after Keel 2010b: 131 no. 236); 5: Tell el-Farʿah (S), Tomb 503 (after Keel 2010b: 125 no. 226); 6: Tel Jemmeh, Room KB (after Keel 2013a: 37 no. 83); 7: Tel Gezer, "4th Semitic Period" (after Keel 2013a: 361 no. 448)   118

38 Late Bronze Age IIB–III Depictions of a Chariot Scene: 1: Tell el-Ajjul, Tomb 1116E (after Keel 1997: 205 no. 302); 2: Tell el-Farʿah (S), Tomb 960 (after Keel 2010b: 333 no. 712); 3: Jaffa, unknown (after Lalkin 2008: pl. 30:523); Deir el-Balaḥ, Tomb 116 (after Keel 2010a: 405 no. 11); 5: Tel Gezer, "3rd Semitic Period" (after Keel 2013a: 289 no. 275); 6: Tell el-Farʿah (S), Tomb 606 (after Keel 2010b: 133 no. 240); 7: Tell el-Farʿah (S), Tomb 934 (after Keel 2010b: 269 no. 563); 8: Beth-Zur, Locus 90 (after Keel 2010a: 321 no. 8); 9: Tel Dothan, Tomb 2 (after Keel 2010a: 489 no. 3)   119

39 Iron Age I–Early Iron Age IIA Depictions of Anthropomorphic Figure Standing on an Animal with Long Ears or Horns: 1: Tel Qasile (Figure 24:4, above); 2: Badari, Tomb 5545 (after Brunton 1930: pl. 34:20); 3: Tell Keisan, Stratum 9a (after Shuval 1990: 142 no. 43); 4: Tell en-Naṣbeh, Tomb 32 (after Shuval 1990: 142 no. 44); 5: Tell el-Farʿah (S), Tomb 241 (after Keel 2010b: 183 no. 358); 6: Tel Akko,

Surface (after Keel 1997: 561 no. 84); 7: Tel Akko, Surface (after Keel 1997: 571 no. 111); 8: Tell Abu Salima, unknown (after Petrie 1937: pl. 6:58); 9: Tel Miqne, Stratum V (after Keel 2010a: 549 no. 70); 10: Tell el-Far'ah (S), Tomb 225 934 (after Keel 2010b: 189 no. 374); 11: Tell el-Far'ah (S), Area North, Room VL, Niveau 376', Stratum V/W (after Keel 2010b: 411 no. 919); 12: Tel Lachish, Surface (after Shuval 1990: 144 no. 47); 13: Tell el-Far'ah (S), Tomb 229 (after Keel 2010b: 165 no. 314)   121

40 Late Bronze Age Depictions of Resheph: 1: Tel Gezer, Cave 10A (after Keel 2013a: 439 no. 630); 2: Tel Gezer, Fourth Semitic Period (after Keel 2013a: 352 no. 425); 3: Tel Lachish, Fosse Temple unknown (after Keel and Uehlinger 1998: 77 fig. 85a)   122

41 Iron Age I–Early Iron Age IIA Depictions of an Anthropomorphic Figure Standing on the Back of a Horse: 1: Tel Eton, Tomb 1 (after Keel 2010a: 607 no. 5); 2: Tell el-Ajjul, Tomb 1074 (after Keel 1997: 185 no. 245); 3: Tell el-Far'ah (S), Tomb 509 (after Keel 2010b: 139 no. 356); 4: Ta'anach, unknown (after Keel and Uehlinger 1998: 142 fig. 164b); 5: Tel Beth-Shemesh, Tomb 1 (after Keel 2010a: 233 no. 35); 6: Giveon, Tomb 3 (after Keel 2013a: 469 no. 8); 7: Kadesh Barnea, Substratum 3c (after Münger 2007b: 240 fig. 14.4); 8: Tel Reḥov, Stratum IV (after Keel and Mazar 2009: 58* fig. 2:15)   123

Introduction

Communities located in the southern Levant and the Nile Valley have interacted since time immemorial. As early as the Chalcolithic Period, people moved between, ideas were exchanged, and symbols, concepts and practices were borrowed and localized. By the 16th century BCE relations had changed. The Egyptian rulers of the 18th Dynasty launched campaigns into the Levant, Egyptian soldiers and officials were permanently stationed in several hubs in the southern Levant and a militarized ambience was added to the relations with the local population. It was the beginning of a long period of four centuries during which Egyptian power intensified and developed into a full-blown political hegemony that altered the local landscape and transformed the local society.

This book explores the processes of integration of the southern Levant and Egypt and focuses on local reactions to the Egyptian advent. It traces the mechanisms behind the establishment of Egyptian colonial hegemony over the region and the role of the local population in these processes. It reassesses the impact of Egyptian colonialism on the local society, its structure, its practices and its identity. And it concludes with the fragmentation of the Egyptian hegemony and its consequences for the local society.

As these and other questions require a broad volume of evidence that would constitute a monumental project, a case study was chosen—the southern coast of the southern Levant and its hinterland, a ca. 100-km-long strip bound by and including the modern metropolitan areas of Tel Aviv–Jaffa and Gaza (Figure 1). The advantage of focusing on this region is the abundance of multi-faceted material remains that have been recorded in the numerous excavations conducted in the region beginning with the excavations led by Petrie in late 19th century. The current growth in scholarly interest in the region provides additional, more detailed evidence that allows inquiry at a higher resolution into processes of spatial patterns of human activity, consumption practices, religion, production techniques and many other trends on a regional scale. This book is therefore not a wholescale discussion about the Late Bronze Age southern Levant nor a reconstruction of the Egyptian period in the history of the southern Levant. Rather, it aims to illuminate a specific issue in the social history of the region during the first recorded case of colonialism.

Scholarly interest in a local perspective on a colonial situation is a common, but relatively young, field in the history of academic research. The geopolitical transformations following World War II brought about a shift in the study of ancient empires and their subjects. Postmodern writings led to intense

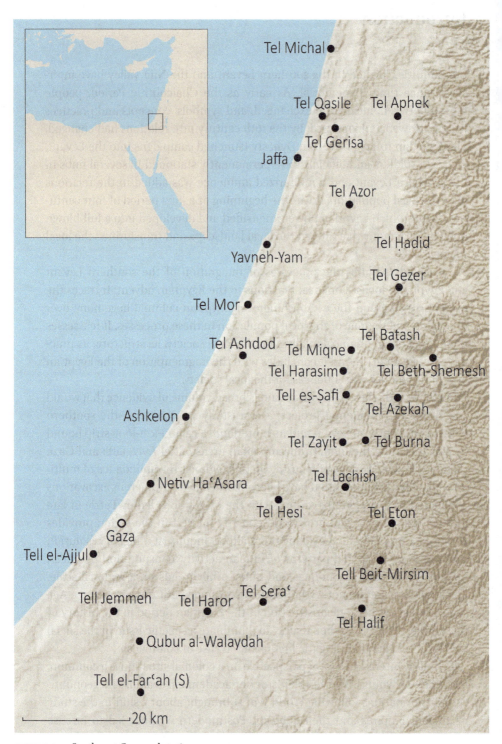

FIGURE 1   Southwest Canaan: location map

discourse on the biased character of the traditional narratives of modern colonial history and contemporary post-colonial situations in the "liberated" states. The "early bird" of such writing, Said's *Orientalism* (1978), dealt with the creation of cultural representation of the colonized and its role in identity formation of the colonizer and in the structuring of the colonial discourse. Though controversial and highly criticized for flaws in methodology and data, *Orientalism* led to an eruption of the discourse termed postcolonialism. This field examined local responses to European colonialism, building on previous writings such as Fanon's *The Wretched of the Earth* (1966) that exposed the scholarly community to the (negative) transformative capacity of colonialism on indigenous identity. Interest increased regarding the misrepresentation of the colonized in the colonial discourse, but also regarding the complexity of colonial encounters, as liminality and ambivalence were considered alongside existing concepts of binarism (Barker et al. 1994; Bhabha 1994). Among the many foci in current postcolonial studies (relevant to the following discussion) are the active role of the colonized in resistance to the colonizer by the appropriation of imperial jargon and symbolism, the reciprocal character of the intercultural exchange with the colonizer ("provincializing the center"), and the (re)negotiation of collective identities of the colonial subjects.[1]

It was not long before postcolonial theory exerted its impact on other fields, one of which is particularly relevant to this book—archaeology. This impact should be understood against the backdrop of wider developments in archaeological theory and practice. By the 1990s the post-processual and interpretive methods of investigation had been accepted by wide circles of archaeologists, which rejected the previous emphasis on generalization, adopting instead subjectivity, high-resolution analysis of specific contexts, and human and non-human agency. One step was the reflective study of the history of archaeology, to be acknowledged as a discipline that developed under the wings of European colonialism and structured by "Classical" education characterized by an admiration for Greek culture and colonization and for Roman imperialism (Dietler 1995; 2005; Gosden 1999: 15–116; García 2007; Lydon and Rizvi 2016). The second step was the growing tendency in the scholarship (Webster and Cooper 1996; Dietler 1997; 2010; Van Dommelen 1997; 2005; 2011; Lyons and Papadopoulos 2002; Given 2004; Gosden 2004; Stein 2005a; Hodos 2006; Dietler and López-Ruiz 2009; Van Dommelen and Rowlands 2012; Mattingly 2014; Khatchadourian 2016) to apply anthropological and postcolonial

---

1 For surveys of postcolonial theory, its history and concepts, see Young (2001); Ashcroft et al. (2004); Young (2005); Sharp (2009); Ashcroft et al. (2013); Loomba (2015); Nayar (2015a, 2015b). See below, in the following chapters, for detailed presentation and application of the various concepts relevant to analysis of material remains.

theoretical concepts to the study of colonial encounters in antiquity, including the material remains of such interactions.

Clearly, applying postcolonial concepts to the field of archaeology requires proper adjustment of several issues. There are problems in defining ancient "cultures" and hence their interaction; there are differences between ancient and European colonialism; and there are difficulties in identifying nations or ethnicities in the pre-Modern world (Hodos 2006: 13–22; cf. Sommer 2012). But at the same time, the mere focus on local reaction to intrusive activity, such as colonialism, provokes questions regarding different modes of responses, from resistance to emulation, the role of local agency and even individual agency, and the multivocality of the material remains that scholars identify as the evidence of ancient empires.

1   Egyptian Colonialism and Canaan in Scholarship: An Overview

This study stands on the shoulders of giants. It is fundamentally based on the intense archaeological exploration of the southern Levant during the last 120 years and is framed by a chronology that was formed by historical study of the period. It differs from most previous studies in its narrative, by presenting a more composite image of local acceptance, ambivalence, appropriation, resistance and rejection in local encounters with the Egyptians. Consequently, it allows further discussion of the aftermath of these relations once the Egyptians had withdrawn from the Levant and the impact of that withdrawal on local society.

An overview of the literature shows that early scholars shared a similar negative image of the Egyptian over their long period of hegemony in the southern Levant. It has been generally assumed that the Egyptian kings established their empire through an aggressive and fierce conquest which resulted in the destruction of the prosperous Middle Bronze Age urban culture. That they imposed an exploitative imperial policy on what remained of the population which resulted in the disruption of local urban life and a long period of political and economic decline (Albright 1949: 101; Kenyon 1960: 209–214; De Vaux 1978: 122; Gonen 1984). Significant to this evaluation was the widely held assumption of the historicity of the biblical narrative regarding the conquest of Canaan by Joshua (Albright 1939), which was interpreted as depicting the replacement of an inferior and corrupt society by the Israelites (Albright 1940: 214).

By the 1970s, and increasingly into the 1980s, new archaeological data became available about the Late Bronze Age in the southern Levant that led to adjustments in the image of the Egyptian empire in Canaan. These adjustments pertained to two major issues during the 1980s and early 1990s. First, the association of every destruction of a Middle Bronze Age horizon with an assumed Egyptian campaign was challenged from the perspective of Egyptology (Redford 1979; Hoffmeier 1989, 1991) and analyses of the archaeological data that indicated a lengthy period of turmoil rather than single events (Bunimovitz 1989; 1995: 320–324; Na'aman 1994: 175–176).[2] Yet the vast majority of studies followed suit in terms of the overall negative image of Egyptian rule, and the entire Late Bronze Age is still viewed as a single process of degeneration that culminated in the "collapse of the Canaanite social structure and its replacement with an entirely new dynamic as new groups emerged in the region at the beginning of the Iron Age" (Gilmour and Kitchen 2012: 4).

The second development was the growing awareness of the prosperity of many sites during the Late Bronze Age IIB (ca. 13th century BCE), chiefly in the southwestern part of Canaan. Moreover, many of these sites feature large assemblages of Egyptian and Egyptian-style artifacts and architectural elements, some adorned with royal names of the 19th and 20th Dynasties. Corroborated by the literary-based historical scenario presented many years earlier by Alt (1944), the archaeological data was interpreted as a reflection of the change in the Egyptian policy towards the southern Levant—the hegemonic rule of the 18th Dynasty was altered by the kings of the 19th Dynasty, who had decided to subjugate southwest Canaan as a whole and to impose direct rule through the transformation of the local towns into Egyptian-governed centers (Na'aman 1981: 185; Weinstein 1981: 17–22). As time passed, sites that featured structures termed "governor residencies" were added to the long list of annexed towns to include the entire region and large portions of the Jezreel Valley that exhibit marked prosperity during the Late Bronze Age IIB–III (Dothan 1982: 294; Oren 1984; Ussishkin 1985: 220–222; 2004: 64; Singer 1986; 1988; 1988–1989; Bunimovitz 1988; 2019: 268–269; Dever 1992: 102; Knapp 1992: 92; Weinstein 1992: 143–144; Stager 1995: 342; Killebrew 2005: 81–83; Morris 2005: 703–704, 713, 768–770; Panitz-Cohen 2014: 548).

Other fields of research during the same time frame explored the variegated nature of the relations between the Egyptians and the local population. These, which mostly dealt with iconography and cult, delved into questions of cultural transmission between Egyptians and locals. On the one hand, Levantine deities were introduced to Egypt during the Late Bronze Age, most visibly in royal contexts (Stadelmann 1967; Helck 1971: 446–473; Keel 1990a: 309–321; Redford 1992: 231–233; Cornelius 1994; Zivie-Coche 1994), while on the other

---

2 See already Kenyon (1973: 176): "There are no certain criteria for connecting the stratigraphical sequence in most sites with the reconquest of Palestine by the Egyptian rulers of the Eighteenth Dynasty."

hand, Egyptian icons and concepts were localized in the Levant and combined with local traditions (Keel 1972; Bunimovitz and Zimhoni 1993; Keel and Uehlinger 1998: 49–108).

The active role of local society during the days of the Egyptian hegemony in the southern Levant was integrated in the larger narratives of the period only through the specific channel of the study of ivory work. By the 1980s it was demonstrated that local workshops manufactured ivories in large numbers and in sophisticated styles that combined elements of both local and foreign, mainly Egyptian, inspiration (Barnett 1982; Leibowitz 1987). These assertions regarding local adaptation of Egyptian iconography and the local production of prestigious artifacts were picked up by Bryan (1996: 37–46), who challenged the consensus regarding the annexation of the southern Levant by the rulers of the 19th Dynasty. She pointed to the limited evidence for Egyptian personnel in these assumed bases (especially when compared to the abundance of evidence from the Egyptian bases in Nubia) and argued for a termination of Egyptian presence by the 13th century BCE. Consequently, Bryan (1996: 77–79) explained the affluence of locally manufactured Egyptian-style objects as reflecting the rise of a local elite that had adapted some elements of pharaonic iconography to represent themselves within a wider socio-economic network that encompassed the eastern Mediterranean.

Bryan's study was highly criticized with regard to its methodology—the chronology of the ivories and their stylistic classification—and its historical conclusions—mainly the arguments for the withdrawal of Egypt by the 19th Dynasty (Lilyquist 1998). Yet her emphasis on local agency was picked up by her student, Higginbotham (1996, 2000), who presented an alternative model for the understanding of the changes in the southern Levant during the Late Bronze Age IIB within the context of the Egyptian empire. The new model followed a center–periphery approach which argues that the political center influences its periphery, and thus the peripheral elite would emulate the culture of the center—such as Roman-period Britain and its Romanized elite (Millet 1990). Accordingly, and based on a comprehensive study of the material remains from the southern Levant, Higginbotham (2000: 129–142) concluded that there was no change in the Egyptian policy and no expansion of its direct holdings; the growing distribution of Egyptian-style objects and architecture reflect, according to Higginbotham, the desire of the local elite—which had been highly integrated in the Egyptian administration since the time of Thutmose III—to emulate Egyptian objects and practices that would enhance their own status and prestige.[3]

---

3 See also Koch 2014: 166–169, and further below.

This challenge to the consensual narrative of Egyptian domination in the southern Levant attracted many negative responses. Its weaknesses were mainly flaws in the treatment of the Egyptian-style material remains (Hasel 1998: 116) and overlooking of the reciprocal character of the Egyptian–Levantine cultural exchange (Oren 2006a: 273). Nevertheless, the basic assumption of the model is important for the consequent analysis of the colonial situation in the southern Levant—that is, crediting the local population (in this case the local elite) with an active role in the creation of the multi-layered material remains of what scholars would interpret as the "Egyptian empire."

The last decade has seen two major developments in the study of the relations between the Egyptians and the local society. One is the complete characterization and analysis of the Egyptian-style pottery from the southern Levant, from its beginnings in the Late Bronze Age I to its termination in the Late Bronze Age III.[4] In a nutshell, the local production of Egyptian-style pottery in several workshops, its typological development in tandem with the developments in Egypt, and its utilitarian, non-prestigious character, led to its recognition as connected to the Egyptian presence in the southern Levant. Large assemblages were thus identified as the remains of communities of officials, soldiers and other Egyptians abroad. It enabled a nuanced discussion of the extent of Egyptian presence from its earliest appearance in the 16th century BCE to its demise in the 12th century BCE. It also illuminated the debatable issue of annexation of Canaan's lowlands by the 19th Dynasty, as most sites assumed to have hosted an Egyptian garrison did not yield Egyptian-style pottery and thus were recognized as local centers (Martin 2011: 263–269).

The second development was the publication of excavations at the several sites that were identified as Egyptian hubs (Barako 2007; Gadot and Yadin 2009; Panitz-Cohen and Mazar 2009; Ben-Shlomo and Van Beek 2014). The number of "governor residencies" was reduced as some of the published structures were identified as estates, thus allowing for a more composite understanding of the structure of the Egyptian holdings in the southern Levant (Gadot 2010; Lehmann et al. 2010; Blakely 2018). Moreover, scholarly attention was diverted to evidence of Egyptian and local collaboration in these colonial installations and to the exposure of the two groups to one another (Cline and Yasur-Landau 2009: 2–4; Gadot 2010: 62; Martin 2011: 152–153; Mazar 2011: 170).

---

4 This pottery had already been noted by Amiran (1969: 187–190) and Weinstein (1981: 21–22), but the primary classification and discussion on the 19th- and 20th-Dynasty pottery were executed by Cohen-Weinberger (1997), Killebrew (1998, 2004; 2005: 67–80) and Higginbotham (2000: 145–170), while Mullins (2006, 2007) and Pierce (2013: 454–531) shed light on the pottery of the 18th Dynasty from the southern Levant. It is especially the corpus compiled and analyzed by Martin (2004, 2005, 2007, 2011) that expanded scholarly perception of this phenomenon, its development and historical context.

The most recent step in the study of the Egyptian–local interaction was taken with the application of colonial encounter theoretical frameworks, similar to the one applied in this book. Braunstein (2011) systematically analyzed the burial practices at the fringe site of Tell el-Farʿah (S), located some 25 km south of Gaza. Ever since the excavation at the site under the direction of Petrie in the late 1920s (Petrie 1930; MacDonald et al. 1932), it has been accepted in scholarship (Oren 1984; Yisraeli 1993; Yannai 2002; Morris 2005: 534–535; Fischer 2011: 34, 64–65, 74) that the Late Bronze Age II habitation includes a "governor residency," a large structure that served the Egyptian administration. Braunstein pointed out the local character of the burials and thus raised questions regarding the identity (or identities) of the deceased—were they Canaanites who manned an Egyptian center, residents of a Canaanite center, or even Egyptians who were buried according to Canaanite practice? Braunstein further inquired as to the meaning given to the Egyptian artifacts—primarily pottery and scarabs—once integrated in their Canaanite context as institutionalizing the colonial situation and reflecting the acceptance of the Egyptian presence. A similar approach has been followed by other scholars dealing with the Late Bronze Age, exploring concepts such as "colonial encounters" (Koch 2018a, 2018b, 2019) and "third space" (Bunimovitz 2019: 273–276).

Lastly, worth mentioning are changes in the study of the relations between Egypt and the Levant in Egyptology. Following the influential research of Loprieno (1988), Egyptologists began exploring the complex relations between the Egyptian court and its clients and subordinates in the Levant and Nubia and the complex demography in Egypt itself. The symbolic depiction of defeated foreigners in Egyptian visual art and literature was contextualized within Egyptian traditions. Its topos was understood vis-à-vis other attestations, visual and textual alike, to have integrated "foreigners" in Egyptian society and administration and their influence on Egyptian religion, economy, and literature (Schneider 2003a; 2010a; Sparks 2004; Booth 2005; Di Biase-Dyson 2013; Anthony 2017). Another (though still preliminary) development is the application of theoretical frameworks for the study of the Egyptian state and its components (Moreno Garcia 2014), and therefore its empire, in the Levant and Nubia, which will allow future studies on "foreigner" participation in the colonial system.

2   Notes on Nomenclature

Several names and terms should be defined in advance before further discussion. The toponym *Levant* is used here to designate the Mediterranean coast and its hinterland between the Taurus Mountains to the north, the Euphrates and the Syrian Desert to the east, and the Sinai Peninsula to the south. The term *southern Levant* is simulated, used to narrow the scope of discussion based on an artificial separation of the Levant approximately south of the Lebanon and Anti-Lebanon mountain ranges. The third toponym used here is *Canaan*, the ancient name of the southern and central portions of the Levant, possibly up to the Homs Gap, that corresponds to the sphere of Egyptian influence during the Late Bronze Age (Rainey 1996; Na'aman 1999); consequently, (1) the term Canaanite is not used as an ethnicon but refers to the local population in the land of Canaan and (2) the southwestern part of the southern Levant is henceforth named *southwest Canaan*.

As for terminology, the jargon in such studies has always been based on the Roman legacy. The Egyptian state during the New Kingdom (ca. 1550–1075 BCE) is traditionally referred to as an *empire*, the accepted term in research to such overarching hegemonic states (Sinopoli 1994: 159–161; Areshian 2013: 10; Steinmetz 2014: 79). It is hard to divorce the term from its Roman homeland and its consequent use in European political ideology (Steinmetz 2014: 78), though nowadays it is applied in research to describe the universal phenomenon of broad, militaristic political frameworks, compartmentalized and multi-cultural, which ruled over extensive territories and restricted the sovereign rights of local peoples subservient to them. The more common term used in this study is *colonialism*, defined by Dietler (2010: 18) as "the projects and practices of control marshaled in interactions between societies linked in asymmetrical relations of power and the process of social and cultural transmission resulting from those practices." Such an understanding of colonialism (cf. Stein 2005b: 24–25; Jordan 2009: 31–33; Steinmetz 2014: 79–80) allows a comparative study of various cases from around the world (Gosden 2004; Stein 2005b), while at the same time "draw(ing) attention to specific colonial situations in particular periods and shift(ing) the focus from the supraregional colonial enterprise to the locally experienced contacts and consequences on the ground" (Van Dommelen 2012: 398).

3 Chronological Framework

The examination in this book of the archaeological data from southwest Canaan in the Late Bronze and early Iron Age first of all requires the presentation of the dating system used to define the chronology of each of these periods. Absolute chronology is a matter of debate among scholars, and this is not the place to elaborate on this matter. The absolute chronology of the

TABLE 1   Chronological framework

Transition	Chronology (all dates BCE)
Middle Bronze Age III/Late Bronze Age I	First half the 16th century
Late Bronze Age I/Late Bronze Age IIA	Mid-15th century
Late Bronze Age IIA/Late Bronze Age IIB	Mid-13th century
Late Bronze Age IIB/Late Bronze Age III	Early 12th century
Late Bronze Age III/Early Iron Age I	Late 12th–early 11th century
Early Iron Age I/Late Iron Age I	Second half of the 11th century
Late Iron Age I/Early Iron Age IIA	Middle of the 10th century

Egyptian rulers follows Schneider (2010b) and Aston (2012–2013) and is presented in the Appendix. Table 1 presents the archaeological horizons and their chronology based on the stratigraphy of Tel Megiddo, the only site to date to provide a complete sequence of the Late Bronze Age and the Iron Age I (Toffolo et al. 2014).

The application of the Tel Megiddo chronology to southwest Canaan requires some modifications: "Late Bronze Age III" corresponds in this book to "Iron Age IA" in Mazar (2015) and "transitional Bronze–Iron Age" in Martin (2011);[5] its long timespan (the entire 12th century BCE) allows the inclusion of the last phase of Egyptian presence in the region, the latter elements of the typical Late Bronze Age fossils (e.g., settlement pattern, pottery forms and decorations, and Egyptian-style innovations in production, cult and other aspects), and the initial appearance of the Aegean/Cypriot-inspired innovations such as local production of Aegean-style pottery.[6] The Early Iron Age I corresponds to the so-called "Bichrome Phase" in southwest Canaan, which differs from the earlier phases by way of changes in settlement patterns and the introduction of innovations in production and consumption of pottery and other object groups (such as seals). The late Iron Age I corresponds to the advanced phase of the Iron Age I, known for the "debased" phase of bichrome pottery.

---

5   Note that the term "transitional Bronze–Iron Age" is applied by Greenberg (2019: 274–275) to include the Iron Age I as well.
6   The monochrome Aegean-style pottery produced in the southern Levant (more below, Chapter 7) has traditionally been compared to Late Helladic IIIC Early–Middle and/or Late Cypriot IIIA assemblages (Dothan and Zukerman 2015); both horizons are securely dated within the 12th century BCE (Manning 2006–2007). Note that Sherratt (2006) compared the earliest vessels from Tel Ashdod to Late Cypriot IIC types.

Clearly, these classifications are artificial and static assemblies of sites that existed in "archaeological periods"—which are a modern scholarly projection onto the past—rather than a precise reflection of a particular historical reality (Lucas 2004). Some of the sites may have been founded at the beginning of a "period" and abandoned shortly thereafter, while others may have been established at the end of that period and existed mainly in the period that followed. Moreover, new data could change the precise chronological framework at any phase (Knapp and Manning 2016: 134). These dates and periodization should thus be regarded as assisting the understanding of the archaeological processes and not as a fixed historical framework.

CHAPTER 1

Dawn

The mechanisms that brought about the consolidation of Egyptian hegemony over the southern Levant during the 18th Dynasty are shrouded in the meager information provided by written sources.[1] Beginning with the first Egyptian campaign beyond the Nile Valley, led by Ahmose against the city of Sharḥan[2] (Morris 2005: 28–29), the Egyptian king and his successors (Amenhotep I, Thutmose I, Thutmose II and Hatshepsut) documented their expeditions to the northern Levant, from Byblos to the Euphrates River (Hoffmeier 2004: 123, 127–128; Morris 2005: 27–34; Ahrens 2015; Höflmayer 2015: 195–197 with literature). The most valuable sources are related to the time of Thutmose III, who was challenged by the political transformation in the northern Levant and especially the expansion of the Kingdom of Kadesh. Thutmose III set out to Canaan at the head of his army, defeated a local alliance near Megiddo and overcame the Levantine rulers south of Kadesh (Redford 2003). Following his victory, he established Egypt's domination over the Levant (see details in Morris 2005: 115–126; 2018: 141–162). His successors, Amenhotep II and Thutmose IV, continued to embark on military campaigns in the northern Levant until an alliance was formed, sealed by a marriage between the ruling houses of Egypt and Mitanni, during the reign of Amenhotep III (1386–1348 BCE) (Morris 2005: 126–136; Kahn 2011a; Dodson 2014: 9–10, 36–37 with literature).

Given such modest written evidence, much ink has been spilled in scholarly debate regarding the historical reconstruction of this period. Some scholars have associated the handful of Egyptian campaigns aimed in the northern Levant (Ahmose through Thutmose II) with the destructive end of the Middle Bronze Age in the southern Levant to a coherent process in which the country was aggressively subjugated and the Egyptian empire was created (Weinstein 1981: 1–10; Dever 1990; Weinstein 1991). Other scholars have argued against such association, pointing to the limited information that precludes any reconstruction of Egyptian policy regarding the southern Levant until the first campaign of Thutmose III, followed by several campaigns of Amenhotep II and Thutmose IV (Redford 1979; Hoffmeier 1989, 1991; Na'aman 1994; Bunimovitz

---

1 A previous version of this chapter was published as Koch 2019.
2 For vocalization of the toponym, see Rainey 1993.

1995: 322; Redford 2003: 185–194; Hoffmeier 2004). Consequently, a more nuanced version of the traditional perspective suggests that the Egyptians expanded their hegemony through sporadic, mostly undocumented campaigns that spanned the Late Bronze Age I (Morris 2005: 27–38; Burke 2010: 51–53).

A development in the study of the chronology of the southern Levant brought about a major challenge to the correlation of the Late Bronze Age I with assumed Egyptian campaigns. Since the early stages of scholarship, it has been the consensus that the south Levantine archaeological periodization during the second millennium BCE corresponded to the reign of Egyptian kings, and consequently, the Late Bronze Age IA begun with the commencement of the New Kingdom, ca. 1550 BCE (Albright 1949: 96). An Ultra-Low Chronology of the second millennium BCE was suggested based on the stratigraphy of Tell ed-Daba', arguing that the Middle Bronze Age lasted well into the days of the 18th Dynasty (Bietak et al. 2008; Bietak 2015). Except recently published radiocarbon evidence now suggests otherwise. Radiocarbon dates from sites such as Ashkelon, Tel Ifshar, Tel Kabri, Tel Burak, and Tell el-Hayyat support a High Chronology for the Middle Bronze Age in the southern Levant (Höflmayer et al. 2016a; Höflmayer et al. 2016b; Bruins and van der Plicht 2017; Höflmayer 2017; Greenberg 2019: 263–264), dating the Middle Bronze Age II to III transition to ca. 1700 BCE. That means an extension of the Middle Bronze Age III (ca. 1700–1550 BCE) or an earlier beginning of the Late Bronze Age I (ca. 1600 BCE or somewhat later). The main implication is that the destructions of the Middle Bronze Age III could have occurred during the 17th–early 16th century BCE, long before a single Egyptian soldier stepped foot on Levantine soil. While the new high chronological framework is still preliminary and debatable (Ben-Tor 2018), it brought to light the methodological flaws in the conventional correlation of archaeological periods with historical figures and events. Consequently, and until detailed radiocarbon sequence of the Late Bronze Age I is published, there should be much caution in the "find-a-pharaoh" discourse (Sherratt 2011: 8–9) of historically labeling destruction layers from the southern Levant.

1 Decline and Revitalization of Settlements during the Late Bronze I

The often-assumed destruction wave that terminated the dense network of socially segmented cities and towns during the latter part of the Middle Bronze Age III was at its simplest, a long and complicated process. Some settlements, such as Tel Aphek Stratum X15 (Gadot and Yadin 2009: 39), Tel Beth-Shemesh

(Bunimovitz and Lederman 2008: 1645; 2013), and Tell el-Ajjul[3] (Horizon H5 of the recent excavation) (Fischer and Sadeq 2002: 125–130), were destroyed; others, such as Tel Haror (Oren 1993a: 582) and Tel Jemmeh (Ben-Shlomo and Van Beek 2014: 1054) were abandoned. The fortified settlement at Tel Lachish was destroyed and to a limited extent resettled, during the Middle Bronze Age III (Level P-3) (Ussishkin 2004: 160–164); the massive rampart and gate of the large center at Ashkelon were abandoned (Stager et al. 2008: 236) and the settlement nucleated to the inner mound,[4] whereas the small settlement at Tel Seraʿ may have continued unimpaired (Oren 1993b: 1330).

The resettlement process was a long one. Some sites were resettled shortly after destruction/abandonment; others were reestablished some decades later. Beginning in the south, the settlement at Tel Seraʿ was joined during the Late Bronze Age IA by reestablished settlements at Tell el-Ajjul (Horizons 4–3) (Fischer and Sadeq 2002: 119–125), Tel Haror (Oren 1993a: 582), Tel Nagila (Stratum VI) (Uziel 2008: 115–201; Uziel and Avissar-Lewis 2013), and possibly also Tel Ḥesi (City II) (Fargo 1993: 631); farther to the east, a rather modest settlement at Tel Ḥalif (Stratum XI) developed in the Late Bronze Age I (Strata XI–X) (Seger 1983: 4; Seger et al. 1990: 18–19). Of these, Tell el-Ajjul and Tel Ḥalif were destroyed during the Late Bronze Age IB and were resettled, Tel Haror and Tel Seraʿ (Stratum XI) and possibly also Tel Ḥesi (City III) were settled uninterruptedly, and Tel Nagila went into decline and was eventually abandoned.

Not much is known about the Late Bronze Age I–IIA settlement at Ashkelon (Stager et al. 2008: 301–303; Brody 2016), previously the largest settlement in southwest Canaan. A settlement at Tel Ashdod developed through the Late Bronze Age I–IIA (Strata XX–XVII) (Dothan and Porath 1993: 27–36) and a small settlement appeared at neighboring Tel Mor (Stratum XI) (Barako 2007: 11, 15; cf. Martin 2011: 189–191). Farther north, the Middle Bronze Age earthen ramparts and a gate at Yavneh-Yam were apparently used in the Late Bronze Age I–IIA (Fischer 2008: 2073; Uziel 2008: 54–114), and additional information

---

3   The findings from Petrie's excavation at Tell el-Ajjul (Petrie 1931, 1932, 1933, 1934) were roundly criticized and no consensus emerged among scholars as to the history of the site (Albright 1938a; Kempinski 1974; Sparks 2005; Kopetzky 2011: 207, 209; Winter 2018). Until a complete reevaluation of the finds is conducted, their interpretation regarding the settlement sequence at the site and its chronology cannot be concluded.

4   There appears to be no evidence of the settlement's continuation on the northern tell of Ashkelon in the Late Bronze Age and Iron Age I (Finkelstein 2007: 520; Yasur-Landau 2007: 615): the fortifications from the Iron Age IIB (Phase 8 on the northern mound) were built directly over the glacis from the Middle Bronze Age II (Phase 10) (Stager et al. 2008: 236).

of occupation comes from the nearby tombs uncovered north and south of the site (Ory 1948; Yannai et al. 2013).

Turning eastward, a cluster of Late Bronze Age I settlements include Tel Miqne, which also nucleated to the upper mound, where settlement remains (Stratum X) were found covered by a layer of ash (Dothan and Gitin 1993: 1052; Killebrew 1996; Dothan and Gitin 2008: 1953), Tel Batash, where a sequence of three settlements were established and destroyed through the Late Bronze Age I (Strata X–VIII) (Mazar 1997: 23–26, 41–72; Panitz-Cohen and Mazar 2006: 123–132; Mazar and Panitz-Cohen 2019: 89–97), and possibly also Tel Ḥarasim (Stratum VI) (Givon 2008: 1766). Late Bronze Age IA sherds from Tel Lachish (Singer-Avitz 2004: 1021; Ussishkin 2004: 188) and Tel Gezer (Mazar 1989: 61; Finkelstein 2002a: 280) indicate limited activity at both sites that intensified during the Late Bronze Age IB, when a temple was built at the foot of the western slope of the former (Fosse Temple I) (Tufnell et al. 1940: 21–24, 36–37; cf. Singer-Avitz 2004: 1024–1026) while a burial cave located on the slope of the latter yielded evidence for the prosperity of its residents during the Late Bronze Age IB–IIA (Seger and Lance 1988). More limited information attests to a Late Bronze Age I settlement at Tel Beth-Shemesh (Stratum IVA) (Bunimovitz and Lederman 1993: 250) and at Tell eṣ-Ṣafi (Maeir 2012a: 16–17).

Farther north, Jaffa (Kaplan and Ritter-Kaplan 1993: 657; Herzog 2008: 1791; Burke et al. 2017) and Tel Gerisa (Herzog 1993a: 482) were settled during the Late Bronze Age I and were joined by a new settlement at Tel Azor, which was destroyed and rebuilt shortly afterwards (Ad et al. 2014). It appears that also Jaffa suffered a destruction during the Late Bronze Age IB (Burke et al. 2017: 93), though it was shortly rebuilt during the Late Bronze IIA, featuring public buildings such as a gate and a temple (Herzog 2008: 1791; Martin 2011: 238–240; Burke et al. 2017: 105–107). The harbor at Tel Michal (Stratum XVI) was reestablished during the Late Bronze Age I, and was again destroyed and renewed during the Late Bronze Age IIA (Stratum XV) (Herzog 1993b: 1037). Contrary to that, Tel Aphek remained abandoned for a long period until the renewal of settlement sometime in the Late Bronze Age IB–IIA (Strata X14–X13) (Gadot 2003: 185; Gadot and Yadin 2009: 39, 42–49, 583).

The transition to the Late Bronze Age IIA in the region was accompanied by several destructions, (at Tel Azor, Tel Miqne, Tel Batash, Tell el-Ajjul, and Tel Ḥalif) but the following years saw a growing number of settlements and more substantial remains. In some cases, accumulation of wealth is evident by the construction of large buildings, such as at Jaffa (Level V) (Kaplan and Ritter-Kaplan 1993: 657; Herzog 2008: 1791), Tel Beth-Shemesh (Level 9) (Brandl et al. 2013; Bunimovitz et al. 2013), and Tel Gezer (Stratum XVI) (Dever 1986: 36–46; 1993: 502–503); or the refurbishment of others i.e., the Fosse Temple at

Tel Lachish (Tufnell et al. 1940: 22, 24, 37–38). Remains dating to this period were found also at (from north to south) Tel Azekah (Yasur-Landau et al. 2014), Tel Zayit (Tappy 2008: 2082), Tel Burna (Cassuto et al. 2015), Netiv Ha'Asarah (Shavit and Yasur-Landau 2005), Tell Beit-Mirsim (Stratum C_1) (Albright 1932: 37–52; 1938b: 61–79), and Tell Jemmeh (Ben-Shlomo and Van Beek 2014: 1054–1055).

To conclude, southwest Canaan was resettled in a long process in which clusters of settlements developed through the Late Bronze Age IA–IB: in the Besor Basin, along the coast, the inner coastal plain and the western Shephelah, and in the Yarkon Basin. Overall, the Late Bronze Age IIA was a period of stability when most existing settlements advanced in their development and were joined by additional settlements through the region south of the Yarkon Basin. There were some destructions as well. There were four short-lived settlements at Tel Batash, for example, with four destructions hitting local populations during the Late Bronze Age I–IIA; Tell el-Ajjul and Tel Ḥalif were destroyed in the Late Bronze Age IB, while Tel Gezer and Tel Beth-Shemesh were destroyed in the Late Bronze Age IIA. But overall, the Late Bronze Age I–IIA is characterized by long recovery from the turmoil of the Middle Bronze Age III.

2   The Advent of Egyptian-style Objects

Southwest Canaan and Egypt were closely interconnected much before the rise of Ahmose and his ambitious campaigns. Material remains reflecting these contacts go back as early as the Chalcolithic Period and the Early Bronze Age (Van den Brink and Levy 2001; Sowada 2009; Höflmayer and Eichmann 2014; Mączyńska 2014; Schneider 2015), reaching an unprecedented peak during the Middle Bronze Age (Marcus 2007; Ahrens 2011a, 2011b; Flammini 2011; Mourad 2015; Cohen 2017). These contacts brought about the movement of objects, people, and ideas on both sides. This peak of interaction during the Levantine Middle Bronze Age is best represented by the establishment of Levantine communities in the Nile Delta (Bader 2011, 2013; Mourad 2015) and the initial dissemination of Egyptian artistic conventions throughout the Levant and the appropriation of Egyptian scarabs, followed by the emergence of a prosperous local production that elaborated on Egyptian pictorial concepts (from good-luck formulae to figures of deities or their attributes) and developed a rich local pictorial sphere (Goldwasser 2006; Ben-Tor 2007; 2011a; Schroer 2008). It can therefore be argued that the mutual acquaintance and previous interactions between societies in southwest Canaan and Egypt formed the background of the complex image each region and society had of the other, which would not have been negative by definition.

The material remains from the Late Bronze Age southern Levant include a new characteristic of the Levantine–Egyptian interaction unparalleled in other periods: a gradually expanding large-scale local production of Egyptian-style pottery. It began at Tell el-Ajjul with local production of pottery types indicative of the early 18th Dynasty (Kopetzky 2011: 201–207), and expanded with mid-18th Dynasty types to Jaffa (Stratum VI late) (Burke and Lords 2010; Burke et al. 2017: 92–98) and Tel Beth-Shean (Strata XIB and R-1b) (Mullins 2006, 2007; Martin 2011: 123–155). As outlined in the Introduction, these geographically isolated assemblages are domestic in character, consisting mainly of utilitarian vessels used in food preparation and eating. They were interpreted, therefore, as the remains of Egyptian activity at these sites—most probably soldiers and officials (Burke and Lords 2010: 27–28; Martin 2011: 240, 260). Moreover, the production of such utilitarian vessels where local substitutes were available suggests that ritual symbolic necessities were being met, augmenting the functional ones (Greenberg 2019: 290–291). Consequently, it has been suggested that this change in pottery production and consumption at a handful of sites indicates that a limited Egyptian presence in the Levant began during the early-18th Dynasty and later intensified during the mid-18th Dynasty, probably following the first campaign of Thutmose III (Höflmayer 2015: 201). Sporadic finds of a handful of Egyptian-style bowls and slender ovoid jars at Tel Seraʿ (Strata XIID–XI) and a single slender ovoid jar from the Fosse Temple I at Tel Lachish (Martin 2011: 219, 223), probably reflect some sort of interaction between locals and the Egyptian communities along the coast.

Another sort-of remnant of the Levantine–Egyptian interaction were Egyptian scarabs and related seal-amulets i.e., plaques and cowroids. These gradually spread during the Late Bronze Age I and were widely consumed by the Late Bronze Age IIA, replacing the aforementioned prosperous local production that was established during the Middle Bronze Age III (Lalkin 2008: 205–209; Ben-Tor 2011b: 202–207). Not surprisingly, the greatest number of Egyptian seal-amulets comes from Tell el-Ajjul, with 30 Egyptian seal-amulets, compared to five from all the rest of Canaan—four from Tel Megiddo and a single seal-amulet from Taanach (Figure 2).[5] Moreover, it is only at Tell el-Ajjul,

---

5 These include Tell el-Ajjul Tombs 257, 281, 290, 291, 327, 329, 346, 360, 375, 1007, 1020, 1026, 1030, 1032, 1037, 1039, 1041, 1055, 1071, 1073, 1104, 1117, 1128, 1147, 1510, 1532, 1904, 1918, 2126 (Keel 1997); Tel Batash Strata X–IX (Brandl 2006: 214–218); Tel Beth-Shean Strata R-2–1 and Tombs 42 and 59 (Keel 2010a); Tel Hadar Stratum V (Keel 2013a: 508–509 no. 1); Tel Ḥalif Stratum X (Keel 2013a: 536–537 no. 10); Tel Lachish Fosse Temple I (Tufnell et al. 1940: pl. 32A no. 1); Tel Megiddo Stratum IX, Level F-10, and Tombs 37K4, 1100C, 2117, 2123, 3018E (Guy 1938; Loud 1948; Lalkin 2006); Tel Michal Stratum XVI (Giveon 1989); Tel Seraʿ Stratum XII and Taanach Stratum I (Lalkin 2008).

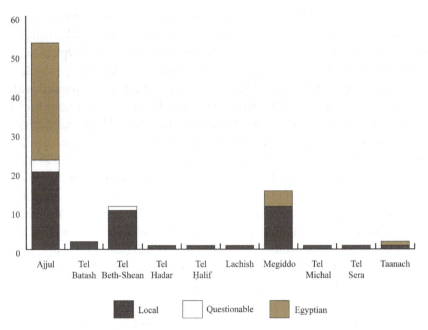

FIGURE 2   Scarabs and other seal-amulets from south Levantine Late Bronze Age I contexts classified according to place of manufacture

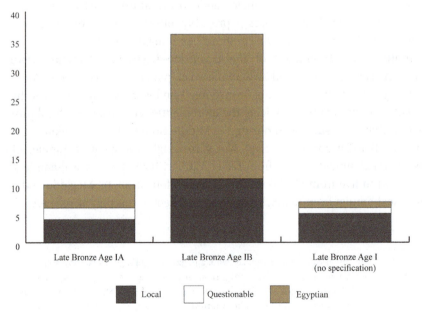

FIGURE 3   Scarabs and other seal-amulets from Late Bronze Age I Burials at Tell el-Ajjul classified according to place of manufacture

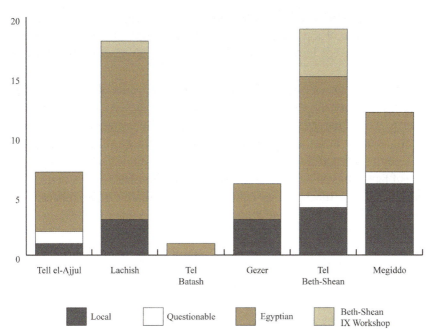

FIGURE 4   Scarabs and other seal-amulets from south Levantine Late Bronze Age I–IIA contexts classified according to place of manufacture

and more specifically, in the burials,[6] that a gradual increase in consumption of Egyptian seal-amulets from the Late Bronze Age IA to the Late Bronze Age IB is visible (Figure 3): from similar numbers as the locally produced seal-amulets during the Late Bronze Age IA to ca. 75% of the total items in the Late Bronze Age IB. When one includes seal-amulets from assemblages generally dated to the Late Bronze Age I, with no distinction of sub-phases, the Egyptian imports constitute about two thirds of the entire assemblage.

The broad distribution of Egyptian scarabs and other stamp-amulets beyond Tell el-Ajjul is attested to at a somewhat later horizon, from assemblages that include material remains dating to both the Late Bronze Age I and the Late Bronze Age IIA (Figure 4).[7] These assemblages indicate the widespread consumption of Egyptian scarabs in southwest Canaan, at Tel Beth-Shean and to

---

6   The dating of the burials at Tell el-Ajjul follows Gonen 1979, 1981, 1992.
7   These include Tell el-Ajjul Tombs 1062X, 1068, 1083 (Keel 1997); Tel Batash Stratum VIII (Brandl 2006); Tel Beth-Shean Stratum IX and Tomb 27 (Keel 2010a); Tel Gezer Cave 110A (Keel 2013a); Tel Lachish Fosse Temple I/II transition (Tufnell et al. 1940) and Tombs 216 and 501 (Tufnell 1958); and Tel Megiddo Stratum VIII and Tombs 1145B and 877C1 (Guy 1938; Loud 1948).

a lesser extent also at Tel Megiddo. The case of Tel Beth-Shean is of special interest because of the evidence of a local workshop that produced scarabs in molds that were formed on the basis of Egyptian scarabs (Ben-Tor and Keel 2012).

The distribution of imported seal-amulets in Canaan and their consumption by locals reflect Egyptian agency, like traders or Egyptian officials *en route* to Levantine locales, but also the interactions between locals and Egyptians based at Tell el-Ajjul that brought about the growing prestige given to these imported artifacts by the Canaanite population. Moreover, the presence of Egyptian seal-amulets in burials dated to this phase attests to the integration of these artifacts in local cultural settings. It therefore also reflects local agency—local individuals and groups that welcomed this specific innovation (originating from Egypt) and appropriated it to fit local context.

How innovative was this process? In other words, what was the place of these Egyptian seal-amulets in the daily lives of their owners? The point of departure is the long history of scarabs in the southern Levant since the Middle Bronze Age: the importation of Middle Kingdom and Second Intermediate Period scarabs, followed by a prosperous local production and widespread distribution of numerous amulets across the region. The clear majority of the scarabs dating to both the Middle and Late Bronze Ages, Egyptian and local alike, were found in burials (Lalkin 2008: 186–204; Ben-Tor 2011a: 32), sometimes consisting of a ring or a necklace placed on the body of its owner or beside it. A similar practice in Egypt was common since the First Intermediate Period conveying a personal connection between the artifacts and the owner. Egyptian texts illuminate the meaning of the practice, which was part of a ritual that include incantations and a symbolic entanglement of amulets, beads, and seashells into necklaces that function as a charm, the materialization of divine protection (Dubiel 2012: 67–69; cf. Cortebeeck 2016). The amulets found in tombs are themselves therefore relics of their owners' life. Consequently, it can be concluded that the Egyptian imports during the Late Bronze Age I were entangled with local charm practices.

The change in the case of the amulets used during the Late Bronze Age I was, therefore, not connected to the function of the scarabs but rather to their source—being imported from Egypt. The distinct character of the 18th Dynasty iconography includes a predominant component of royal concepts (Ben-Tor 2011b: 205), but upon their acquisition by locals, these artifacts were detached from their Egyptian context and were read according to the existing pictorial conventions in southwest Canaan that had developed during the Middle Bronze Age II–III from previous Egyptian prototypes.

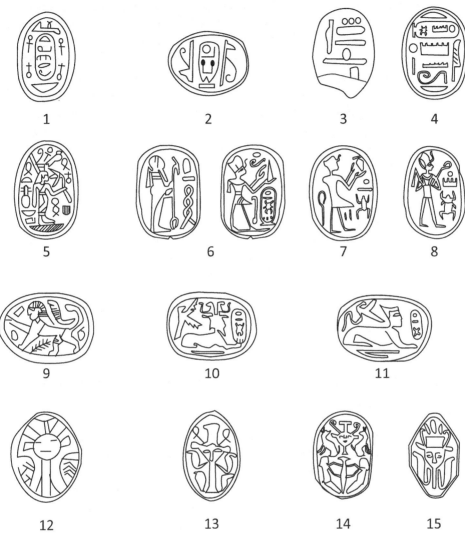

FIGURE 5 Motifs on Middle Bronze Age II local scarabs (nos. 1, 5, 9, 12) compared to motifs on early–mid-18th Dynasty scarabs (nos. 2–4, 6–8, 10, 11): No. 1 Tell el-Ajjul, Tomb 1541 (after Keel 1997: 411 no. 900); 2. Tell el-Ajjul, Tomb 281 (after Keel 1997: 147 no. 123); 3. Tel Beth-Shemesh, surface (after Keel 2010a: 285 no. 160); 4. Tel Gezer, Cave I.A.10 (after Keel 2013a: 439 no. 633); 5. Tell el-Far'ah (S) Tomb 1021C (after Keel 2010b: 205 no. 415); 6. Tell el-Ajjul Tomb 1128 (after Keel 1997: 195 no. 272); 7–8. Tel Gezer Cave 10A (after Keel 2013a: 441 nos. 634 and 635); 9. Tell el-Ajjul Tomb 101 (after Keel 1997: 131 no. 78); 10. Tell el-Ajjul Tomb 1071 (after Keel 1997: 185 no. 240); 11. Tel Lachish Tomb 216 (after Tufnell 1958: Pl. 38 no. 301); 12. Tell el-Ajjul Stratum III–II (after Keel 1997: 473 no. 1076); 13. Tell el-Ajjul Tomb 1026 (after Keel 1997: 175 no. 209); 14. Tel Lachish Tomb 216 (after Tufnell 1958: Pl. 38 no. 307); 15. Tel Batash Stratum VIII (after Brandl 2006: 219 fig. 23)

Good-luck formulas as well as royal and divine names may have been understood similarly. A precedent for this was already set by Middle Kingdom predecessors, who contributed to the development of Canaanite hieroglyph formulae i.e., the common *anra* combination (Figure 5: nos. 1–4). Royal figures might have been perceived by their owners as intermediaries between the common people and the divine sphere (Figure 5: nos. 5–8) or as protective figures (Figure 5: nos. 9–11) (Cooney and Tyrrell 2005: 6–8). The most direct appropriation was probably the 'Hathor Head' (Figure 5: nos. 12–15) that was localized in the region and applied for Levantine deities (Schroer 1989: 181–182; Ben-Tor 2007), and hence it is conceivable to suggest a similar process during the Late Bronze Age.

Egyptian iconography was embraced by the locals, and its appropriation may have included the development of new meanings based upon local pictorial conventions. Over the centuries, this process had a dual outcome: (1) the consumption of the Egyptian amulets was shared by Egyptians and locals for both the living and the dead, thus creating similarities in their appearances; and (2) this medium became a channel through which further Egyptian pictorial concepts and even complete scenes were appropriated and localized by Canaanite artisans.

3 Reassessing the Levantine–Egyptian Interaction during the Late Bronze I

The Late Bronze I–IIA was a period of revitalization of the settlement pattern in most parts of the region with evidence for social segmentation during the Late Bronze Age IIA. There were a handful of destructions. Another aspect of the settlement pattern is the nucleation of the previous large centers of Ashkelon and Tel Miqne and the apparent growth of prosperity at neighboring sites during the Late Bronze Age IIA which suggest a change in distribution of wealth and the rise of an altered social structure. The local centers grew in those locales that had been important in the Middle Bronze Age II (and which were built upon again in subsequent periods). The return to the location of the previous fuci of power might have been associated with their physical appearance: standing tall because of the construction projects from the Middle Bronze Age II that molded the landscape and manifested the local elite's control over its surroundings (Uziel 2010).

Contemporaneous to this revitalization process, Egyptian presence was established at Tell el-Ajjul and Jaffa (and farther north at Tel Beth-Shean). The

Egyptian activity at Tell el-Ajjul during the early 18th Dynasty[8] was an enclave on the southwestern corner of the Levant: The closest Egyptian site during the early to mid-18th Dynasty was Tell el-Habua, guarding a corridor leading from northern Sinai to the eastern Delta (Hoffmeier and Moshier 2013: 498–501). Evidence for mid-18th Dynasty presence in northern Sinai is found together with late-18th Dynasty remains at two sites: Bir el-Abd, located ca. 75 km east of Tell Habua, and in and around Ḥaruva (Oren 1993c: 1389–1391; 2006b), located some 35 km southwest of modern Rafah and 12 km east of al-Arish.

Tell el-Ajjul could have functioned as a stronghold aimed to block unexpected invasions by Egypt, a base serving the Egyptian armies, and a harbor involved in Egyptian maritime activity.[9] The latter two explanations would also fit Jaffa during the Late Bronze Age IB onwards. Tell el-Ajjul might thus have served the Egyptian armies in the campaigns aimed at the northern Levant at least once during the reign of each king until Thutmose III. These armies might have met with local resistance but the rather limited destructions in southwest Canaan during the Late Bronze Age I suggest that the more common local reaction was to pay homage.

Tell el-Ajjul was most likely the hub from which Egyptian-style pottery and amulets were distributed across the region. This glimpse into the south Levantine–Egyptian interactions during this period allows further speculation regarding the scope of such interactions. The synchronism of the emergence of foci of power in Canaan and the development of Egyptian presence in the region suggests a connection between the two processes. These might have included the exchange of agricultural commodities between coastal centers and communities farther inland that benefited from these transactions. New paths of interaction were formed, creating a middle ground (Gosden 2004) which facilitated the spread of Egyptian ideas (see more in the following chapters) on the one hand, and the accumulation of wealth by local agents on the other. The gradual growth of sites in the region during the Late Bronze Age I

---

8 Common scholarly wisdom identifies Tell el-Ajjul with Sharḥan, captured by Ahmose (Kempinski 1974; Morris 2005: 28–29 n. 7) but not without critique (Rainey 1993; Redford 2003: 11–12).

9 Egyptian sources refer to the navy since the Middle Kingdom (Spalinger 2005: 5–6); the navy is referred to in written sources dating to the days of Kamose ("The Kamose Stela") and Ahmose (Darnell and Manassa 2007: 65–67), and predominantly from the days of Thutmose III onwards, when "the navy appears most prominently as a means of troop transport and supply, whose efficacy greatly contributed to Egyptian imperial expansion" (Manassa 2013: 2). For a possible later reference to marine units, from the reign of Seti I, see Goldwasser and Oren (2015).

from Tel Haror in the south, through Tel Lachish and Tell eṣ-Ṣafi to Tel Gezer in the north, might be a manifestation of such a process.

The frequent Egyptian campaigns to northern Canaan and farther to the northern Levant during the days of Thutmose III and his successors possibly strengthened the importance of the harbors in southwest Canaan. At the same time, there is only meager evidence for any clash between the Egyptians and the locals in this region. On the contrary, relations deepened, as was suggested regarding the consumption of Egyptian artifacts decorated with royal iconography that might have been localized in southwest Canaan. The main outcome was that this practice was shared by both Egyptians and southern Levantines for both the living and the dead.

It may therefore be posited that the gradual growth of many settlements in the Late Bronze Age I–IIA was linked to the development of an Egyptian presence along the coast. The growing demand for agricultural products at Tell el-Ajjul and Jaffa led to a complex process in which the concentration of power aligned with control of economic surpluses in which elites (who lived in nearby centers and could provide that produce) profited and became established. A complex and manifold relationship thus developed between the representatives of the royal Egyptian court and local rulers, who influenced and encouraged the prosperity of both sides. Clearly, the superiority of the Egyptian military dictated the senior position of the Egyptians in this relationship.

CHAPTER 2

The Egyptian Network

1   Modeling the Egyptian Colonial Network

The common designation of a polity as an empire is usually translated into a mental map of a large territorial entity, and is visualized in maps as large masses with lines demarcating their borders. This convenient means of depicting territorial bulks has achieved an elaborate style and a nuanced attention to topographic features such as uninhabited deserts or mountain peaks. Yet this approach can hardly be accepted as a reflection of a historical moment in time. This static delineation of boundaries and exclusion is a legacy of the early-modern European mindset of territorial nation states that was later applied in the colonial division of the world (Diener and Hagen 2010; Strandsbjerg 2010; Ashcroft et al. 2013: 39–40). Being a fundamental component in the conception of statehood, European scholarship understood ancient states as territorial entities as well. But by empowering the dominant state as a large territorial bulk that swallowed local polities, tribes, and "no-man's-lands," scholars construct a spatial realty that (1) implies that an ancient government had the ability to exert its power in equal capacity over a well-defined territory during its entire existence (just like the ideal modern state); (2) restricts the peculiarities of any given period and space—all conquests were alike and all provinces were equally dominated and stable; and (3) minimizes the viewer's ability to conceive of restructurings of processes and boundaries (Smith 2005: 832–38, 845; Parker 2013: 126).

Indeed, recent scholarship tends to emphasize the structural complexity of ancient states, with a marked tendency towards models of networks.[1] Such a model allows for an understanding of a polity as having complex, sometimes flexible boundaries (Smith 2005; Parker 2006; Smith 2007) that might include several noncontiguous territorial islands bound through reciprocal, familial, religious, and additional mechanisms (Van Valkenburgh and Osborne 2013: 11–12). Each polity controlled its lands through a range of methods, from direct

---

1   See Mann (1986: 1) and the later review by Schortman (2014). For various applications of the network model see Parker (2002, 2003, 2006, 2013, 2015) on the Neo-Assyrian Empire, Campbell (2009) on the Late Shang in China, Glatz (2009) on Late Bronze Age Anatolia, Sugandi (2013) on the Mauryan Empire, Zori et al. (2017) on the Inka, and Smith (2017) on Pre-Columbian Mesoamerica.

exploitation by the central government to client-patron relations. The components of a polity were thus connected to the central hub, but also to each other in continuous interactions that developed cohesion. Moving to the macro level, a polity might have expanded into an overarching system by thickening its network: the establishment of new hubs—such as administrative centers, colonies, trading posts, and ritual centers—and through incorporating other networks by means of force or allegiance (Smith 2005: 838). Manifestations of such a relationship depended on many variables, such as the parties' previous knowledge of each other, the balance of power between them and the cultural and administrative traditions of the local elites (Sinopoli 1994: 163–164).

Understanding the Egyptian state as such, one should acknowledge the various components of what scholarship designates as "the Egyptian empire". Its main territorial bulk was its core, the Nile Valley north of the first cataract all the way to the Mediterranean. It was unified several times during its history, allowing its rulers to expand their influence beyond the Nile Valley. During the early days of the "New Kingdom," the Egyptian court focused its efforts on two regions. The first was Nubia, which (for various historical reasons and due to its geographical location just upstream on the Nile) was incorporated into the empire by means of conquest and colonization (Smith 2003, 2013; Spencer et al. 2017). The second was the northern Levant where Egypt renewed its influence, as was suggested in the previous chapter, with the establishment of harbors along the Levantine coast and a few inland bases meant to secure transportation between the Egyptian heartland and its foci of interest farther to the north. Beyond these hubs and their immediate vicinity, neighboring influential groups either paid annual tributes, remained resistant to the imperial interests, or were located outside of the hegemonic sphere but collaborated with Egypt's interest.

Empires are, therefore, not a homogenous territorial entity, and hence the Egyptian empire is a designation of a varied range of exertion of power by the kings and by their administration and other agents in multiple types of ecological niches and cultural settings. As argued by Bradley J. Parker (2013: 139):

> [T]he nature of imperial control, and the methods by which imperial power was applied outside of an imperial core, probably varied considerably, producing what is essentially a network of territorially and hegemonically controlled imperial domains. Imperial power was, in most cases, disseminated through regional centers. These centers acted as nodes in networks that linked pieces of the imperial mosaic, some of which might be significantly dispersed, to the imperial core … Since the

degree of imperial control probably became more diffuse with distance from nodes in imperial networks ... imperial domains should not be seen as bounded by static impervious borders.

The network model presents a more detailed understanding of mechanisms developed to exert central authority in conjunction with the peculiarities of the interconnectedness between various parts of the system. Related to the issue of colonial encounters, the network model emphasizes the distinctiveness of the encounters in the imperial heartland (where the empire's impact is archaeologically visible in all aspects of material remains) relative to those taking place in the provincial center, in a local town, and elsewhere. These encounters are all grouped under the same all-encompassing structure of an empire and its many branches and hubs, but they evolve from differing degrees of connectivity and their outcomes are different.

2   Egyptian and Local Centers

The Egyptian network in southwest Canaan included Egyptian centers and local centers,[2] identified based mainly on Egyptian written sources and the el-Amarna correspondence. Egyptian sources during the period between the conquest of Sharḥan in the 15th century BCE and the campaign of Thutmose III are silent regarding southwest Canaan. Several locales, such as Yurza, are mentioned in the sources related to the first campaign of Thutmose III (Ahituv 1984: 202–203), but they contain no information about the character of the settlements. The earliest information about the region dates to the mid-18th Dynasty—an administrative document (Papyrus Hermitage A1116), describing the appointment of emissaries (maryannu) from centers in Canaan to Egypt, who received portions of grain and beer in the Egyptian court (Na'aman 1994:

---

[2] I chose the term "center" rather than the common designation "city-state." This is mainly because the word "city" (in Sumerian *uru*; Akkadian *ālu*) is used in Semitic languages to describe all sorts of settlements, from large urban centers to the smallest villages; one cannot glean anything from it about the status or size of the various center (Yoffee 2009: 280; Pfoh 2016: 98–106). Each site must be discussed separately before defining it as a city, and the data from the Late Bronze Age does not support a general description of the political centers as urban settlements. There are difficulties in defining the term "state" and hence the difficulty in employing it to describe the social frameworks that existed in Canaan (Savage and Falconer 2003: 31–33; Burke 2008: 119–121), where evidence points to a patrimonial structure, based on (sometimes symbolic) familial connections and the status of the family patriarchs (Schloen 2001; Pfoh 2016: 123–167).

183; Morris 2005: 37). Of these, only Ashkelon was in the southern part of Canaan, although Lachish is listed elsewhere in the document (Webster et al. 2019). It seems that the settlements mentioned were the residences of prominent locals, who were at the time in contact with the Egyptian royal court (Na'aman 1997: 613–614).

The most extensive information about the political segmentation of Canaan during the Egyptian period comes from the el-Amarna letters, an unknown portion of the diplomatic correspondence of the Egyptian court during 20 years, including the last decade of Amenhotep III, the reign of Amenhotep IV/Akhenaten, and the first years of Tutankhamun (Cohen and Westbrook 2000; Mynářová 2007, 2014). The correspondence includes letters sent to the Egyptian court from the "great kings" of the era—mainly the kings of Hatti, Babylonia, Mittani, and Assyria—and from Levantine rulers subordinated to the Egyptian king. From the early stages of research, the information embedded in the correspondence has been used to reconstruct the political disposition of the Egyptian network in the Levant: the location of the Egyptian and local centers, the identity of the local rulers, and their ties with the Egyptian administration (Na'aman 1975 with extensive literature; 1997; Finkelstein 1996a). A major development in the reconstruction of the political disposition based on the el-Amarna correspondence was achieved by the petrographic analysis of the letters (Goren et al. 2004). The results enabled the identification of the origin of letters sent by local rulers, making it possible to map out the centers that were in existence at this time (followed by Na'aman 2011a; Finkelstein 2014; Koch 2016).

2.1 The Besor Region: Tell el-Ajjul, Gaza and Yurza

The Besor region (Figure 6) includes the expanses of loess soil around Naḥal (Hebrew for intermittent stream) Besor and Naḥal Gerar, the adjacent coast, and the band of dunes south of Naḥal Shiqma. The maximal delineation would also include the wide region (of about 2,700 sq km) from the southwestern Hebron Hills and the northern Negev Highland, covering the Lahav Hills and the Beersheba Valley.

Tell el-Ajjul was apparently the largest and most well-established center in the Besor region in the Middle Bronze Age.[3] By a process that is not described

---

3 Despite the elusive information gained from the excavation directed by Petrie at Tell el-Ajjul, it can be concluded that during the Middle Bronze III the settlement covered an area of some 12 hectares. A fine-tuned stratigraphic sequence emerges from the brief excavations directed by Fischer and Sadeq (2002). Accordingly, the earliest remains (Phase 8) included a number of stone walls and floors covered with a thick layer of ash, dated to the Middle Bronze Age II. The settlement was renewed after a short hiatus (Phases 7–6), leaving behind brick walls,

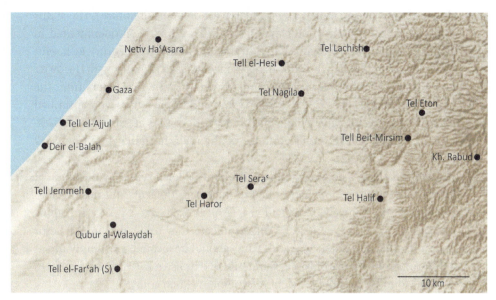

FIGURE 6   Besor region: location map

in written sources and is difficult to reconstruct considering the lack of information about Gaza itself,[4] Tell el-Ajjul lost power to Gaza during the period of Egyptian presence. Yet it clearly continued to exist in the Late Bronze Age II, as attested by Egyptian-style pottery from the later phases of the 18th Dynasty, and, in diminishing quantities, until the time of the 19th and perhaps even the 20th Dynasty (Kopetzky 2011: 201–209). Gaza, in turn, became the important center of the Besor region, maintaining its status, with some gaps, for millennia to come (Humbert et al. 2000; Di Segni 2004; Na'aman 2004).

Few Egyptian sources mention Gaza. The earliest is in the inscriptions of Thutmose III, who seized it and called it "Town-of-the-Ruler's Seizure"

---

floors and installations, developed (Phase 5) and among its remains were large structures, including a number of sub-phases, the latest of which was destroyed in the Middle Bronze–Late Bronze transition. The builders of the settlement that was renewed after some time constructed large buildings making use of the walls of the ruined structures of the previous phase. Two sub-phases were discerned in these buildings (Phases 3–4), which were dated to the Late Bronze Age IA–B. This settlement was also destroyed in a fire. The remains from the next phase (Phase 2) included a number of brick walls, floors, tombs and installations, dated to the Late Bronze Age IIA.

4   The mound of Gaza (Tall al-Kharruba) is in the heart of the modern city and archaeological data about it are scant. Probes conducted by Phythian-Adams (1923) revealed remains from the Late Bronze Age and the Iron Age I–II. A more recent survey revealed remains from Late Antiquity onwards (Clarke et al. 2004).

(Redford 2003: 13–14; Morris 2005: 54–56 with previous literature). The status of Gaza as an Egyptian center may possibly have first been documented in Taanach Letter no. 6, which is dated to the end of the 15th century BCE, sent by an Egyptian official who cites his presence in Gaza (Rainey 1999; Horowitz and Oshima 2006: 141–142). Gaza is mentioned in only two letters from the el-Amarna archive (nos. 289 and 296), yet 15 additional letters were inscribed and sent from its vicinity in the name of local rulers, thus attesting to the presence of scribes and to the importance of the town in the Egyptian network (Goren et al. 2004: 322–324).[5]

Egyptian sources do attest to the existence of a local center by the name of Yurza in the Besor region, mentioned in the inscriptions of Thutmose III and the el-Amarna archive (EA 314 and 315) (Aḥituv 1984: 202–203). Petrographic analysis of the letters sent from Yurza indicate they originated in the Besor region (Goren et al. 2004: 299–301). Yurza should be located, most probably, at Tel Haror, on the banks of Naḥal Gerar, site of extensive Late Bronze Age I–IIB remains found across the 10-hectare settlement (Koch 2016).[6]

---

5 The sources from the 19th and 20th dynasties do not describe Gaza directly, though it might have been called "Pa-Canaan," as in the descriptions of the first campaign of Seti I (Morris 2005: 345–347; Hasel 2009). The narrator of Papyrus Anastasi I (27: 8), dated to the time of Ramesses II and describing various sites in the Egyptian sphere of influence in the Levant, writes of the city of Raphia, its fortifications and its geographical location in relation to Gaza (Fischer-Elfert 1986: 231). Gaza is mentioned twice in Papyrus Anastasi III (6:1–5) as the place of residence of officials active along the "Ways of Horus"—the roads that crossed northern Sinai and connected Canaan to Egypt (Morris 2005: 478–486). The Ostracon Michaelides 85 (unprovenanced) portrays the preparations for celebrations in Gaza held in honor of the goddess Anat (Morris 2005: 489–491). Gaza is ostensibly mentioned in only one source from the 20th Dynasty, Papyrus Harris I (9:1–3), describing the acts of Ramesses III, including the establishment of a temple to Amun in Canaan; according to a number of scholars that temple was in Gaza (Uehlinger 1988; Wimmer 1990: 1086–1088; Morris 2005: 727–729) but this suggestion has been criticized (Higginbotham 2000: 58–59; Hasel 2009: 12–13).

6 Tel Haror features a low terrace of about 15 hectares. On the northern end of the terrace is the upper tell, about 1.5 hectares. From various preliminary publications (Oren 1992, 1993a, 1995; Oren and Yekutieli 1996; Brandl et al. 2015) it emerges that the settlement at Tel Haror was established in the Middle Bronze Age and its remains include large structures covering an area of some 4 hectares and surrounded by an earthen rampart that created the site's present-day shape. According to the excavators, the settlement was hit at the end of the Middle Bronze Age and was renewed some time thereafter, but on a smaller scale. Its remains include a number of sub-phases from the Late Bronze Age I–IIB, which ended in a major conflagration. Remains of the settlement from the Late Bronze Age III include a few segments of a large structure; the results of the excavation are unclear as to the end of the settlement, but it seems that it was replaced by a new settlement, whose remains included structures with stone foundations, many lined silos and refuse pits, in which an assemblage of Iron Age I pottery was found. The traditional identification of Yurza at Tell Jemmeh (Maisler 1952; Goren et al. 2004: 299–301) is not consistent with the lack of evidence

The settlement system in the region of Gaza in the Late Bonze Age IIA, partly corresponding to the late 18th Dynasty and hence to the 30-year Amarna Period, was rather modest. Yurza/Tel Haror included some large-scale architecture (Oren 1993a: 582; 1995), a cultic complex was built at Tel Seraʿ above the large structure that dominated the site since the Middle Bronze III (Oren 1993b: 1330), and more limited remains were found at Tell el-Ajjul and the resettled Tell Jemmeh and Netiv Haʿasarah (above). Evidence of Egyptian presence—that is, the consumption of various types of Egyptian-style pottery in large numbers—was still confined to Tell el-Ajjul, with a handful of specimens known from Tel Seraʿ as well (Martin 2011: 223). There was, apparently, no marked change in the material manifestation of the relations between the Egyptians and the locals during the 18th Dynasty except for the rise of Gaza as the main hub instead of Tell el-Ajjul.

The Late Bronze Age IIB was a period of further development. The settlement at Tel Haror grew and included domestic units and refuse pits, where imported Egyptian, Cypriot and Helladic wares were found alongside an ostracon inscribed in hieratic script (below). Large courtyard houses were built at Tell Jemmeh (Ben-Shlomo and Van Beek 2014). A new phase of the cultic enclosure was built at Tel Seraʿ (Stratum X) alongside a new large structure that featured Egyptian architectural concepts (Oren 1993b: 1330–1331; Reade et al. 2017), where numerous Egyptian-style bowls were found (Martin 2011: 222, 224–225).

In addition, new settlements were established across the region. In one of these, at Deir el-Balaḥ, a large complex that featured Egyptian construction techniques developed in several phases,[7] and locally produced Egyptian-style pottery exhibiting a rich variety of types was consumed in great quantity (Martin 2011: 209–215). Sometime later, settlement was reestablished at Tell el-Farʿah (S), known mainly from a large structure built according to an Egyptian square ground plan and the cemeteries around the mound, where dozens of Egyptian-style vessels and amulets were uncovered (Yannai 2002;

---

of a settlement in the Late Bronze Age I at that site (Ben-Shlomo and Van Beek 2014: 79–81, 1054), which contradicts the reference to Yurza in the sources from the time of Thutmose III. For a critique of Rainey's proposal (1993: 185) identifying Yurza at Tel Ḥesi, see Goren et al. (2004: 301).

7 The excavator's chronology and stratigraphy of Deir el-Balaḥ (Dothan 1979; Dothan and Brandl 2010) has been revised in recent years (Killebrew et al. 2006; Martin 2011: 214–215). The most important argument against the excavators' original dating is the absence of Late Bronze Age IIA and 18th-Dynasty ceramic forms. It is possible to reconstruct a large multi-room structure established during the LB IIB (Strata IX and VI–IV), with later phases lasting well into the LB III (Strata VIII–VII).

Fischer 2011; Martin 2011: 234–235). A similar structure was built at Tel Hesi, located further to the east, along Naḥal Shiqma (Blakely 2018). Further to this, rural settlements were established during this period.[8]

Yurza/Tel Haror was destroyed in the Late Bronze Age IIB (Oren 1993a: 582), like many centers beyond the region of Gaza (below). Unlike in other parts of Canaan, however, the destruction of Tel Haror was an isolated event; on the contrary, the archaeological records of the region of Gaza show development, and no other violent episode is known. The Egyptian complex at Deir el-Balaḥ further developed, and a square Egyptian-style structure, similar to that from Tell el-Farʿah (S), was built at Tel Seraʿ (Stratum IX), where the consumption of Egyptian-style pottery grew (Oren 1993b; Martin 2011: 222–223, 225–227). Development can also be seen at Tell Jemmeh, where further structures were built and a handful of Egyptian-style vessels were found (ibid., 241–242), and at the small rural site of Qubur al-Walaydah (Stratum VIII), which was adorned with a brick structure that might reflect Egyptian inspiration (Lehmann et al. 2010: 142–148; Wimmer and Lehmann 2014). Rural settlements were established during this period as well (Oren and Mazar 1993; Shavit 2003: Site no. 208).

This picture of Egyptian influence expanding in the region of Gaza is complemented by the presence of bowls bearing Egyptian Hieratic inscriptions that deal with the Egyptian administration—a typical trait of southwest Canaan dated mainly to the 20th Dynasty.[9] The majority of these inscriptions mention the collection of large quantities of grain, inscriptions from Yurza/Tel Haror, Gath/Tell eṣ-Ṣafi and Lachish name "foreign rulers,"[10] and the

---

8   Additional Late Bronze IIB settlements were explored at Netiv HaʿAsarah, Tel Ridan (Vitto and Edelstein 1993) and Rafah along the coast (Margovsky 1971), and Qubur al-Walaydah between Tell Jemmeh and Tell el-Farʿah (S) (Lehmann et al. 2010: 141).

9   These inscriptions were found at Tel Seraʿ, Tel Haror, Tell el-Farʿah (S), Deir el-Balaḥ, Tel Lachish, Tell eṣ-Ṣafi and Qubur al-Walaydah (Wimmer 2019: 144 with literature). A few hieratic inscriptions, including three from Tel Beth-Shean and one from Ashkelon, deal with subjects unrelated to the Egyptian administration (Wimmer 2008). The spatial distribution of the hieratic inscriptions in southwest Canaan compared to the royal monuments in northern Canaan possibly reflects the Egyptian presence in the former compared to the need to promote propaganda in the latter, and see Levy (2017).

10 The symbol wr (A19) is translated as "foreign ruler" (Sweeney 2004: 1608; Wimmer and Maeir 2007: 42). The fragmentary inscription from Tel Haror includes a toponym that Görg (in Wimmer and Maeir 2007: 42 n. 9) proposed reconstructing as "[Q3 ḏ3]-tj," i.e., Gaza. Four inscriptions from Lachish mention foreign rulers, but none has survived intact: One inscription from Lachish mentions one such lord, from whose name only the first syllable survived ("Ya-"), along with his place of residence, which is unclear, but perhaps could be read as Lachish (Wimmer 2019: 139–140). Another inscription from Lachish mentions another ruler, whose place of residence, according to Wimmer and Maeir (2007: 42 n. 8), should be read as "Jj-pw" (Jaffa). Inscriptions nos. 2 and 4 mention other rulers, whose

inscriptions from Tel Seraʿ note the receipt of grain by temples. This is ostensible evidence of a system of amassing grain in the region around Gaza in the best of the Egyptian tradition of dedicating agricultural holdings to subsidize temple activities (Wimmer 2010: 226 with previous literature).[11]

The material remains thus attest to the development and consolidation of an Egyptian-oriented network of colonizers and locals, individuals serving the imperial administration or collaborating with it. It gradually grew and expanded during the Late Bronze Age IIB, when the small Egyptian enclave was connected through roads along the northern coast of the Sinai Peninsula to the Egyptian heartland, and additional installations were built around it along the coast and further inland. Regrettably, the relation between the intensification of the Egyptian presence along the coast, the destruction of Yurza/Tel Haror and the expansion of the Egyptian-style pottery and architecture is still unclear.[12] Nonetheless, it can be concluded that the region of Gaza prospered during the Late Bronze Age. The destructions at Tell el-Ajjul in the Late Bronze I–IIA and Yurza/Tel Haror in the Late Bronze IIB were isolated events, while neighboring settlements evolved concomitantly with a growing number of Egyptian-style pottery vessels and Egyptian-style structures. By the Late Bronze Age III the entire region had been integrated within the Egyptian network and was administered by imperial installations spread across it. In other words, the region reached a settlement prosperity in settlement as a result of the Egyptian colonization.

2.2   *The Coastal Plain: Ashkelon and Muḫḫazu*

For purposes of this discussion, the Coastal Plain (Figure 7) is artificially delimited between Naḥal Shiqma in the south and the Yarkon Basin in the north. It includes six kurkar (local vernacular for calcareous sandstone) ridges

---

names and place of residence did not survive (Sweeney 2004: 1607–1610). Wimmer and Maeir (2007: 41–42) read the inscription from Tell eṣ-Ṣafi as [...]-*jr*⁽ʔ⁾ *wr Ḏ₃-p*[₃-...], translating it as "[...]el⁽ʔ⁾ prince of Ṣf(t)." They interpreted it, on the basis of similarly structured inscriptions from Tel Lachish and Tel Seraʿ, as mentioning a ruler of *Ṣft* whose name included the theophoric "El." In their opinion, this is evidence of the name *Ṣft* used during ancient times alongside the more accepted name of the town—Gath.

11 Possible additional evidence of the importance of the temple in Gaza is the inscription on three scarabs—one from Tel Beth-Shemesh and two from Tell el-Farʿah (S)—"to the temple of Ramses lord of Heliopolis," which, in Uehlinger's opinion (1988: 9–15), shows the existence of estates serving the temple. For a critique of this suggestion, see Brandl (2004: 59).

12 As no detailed publication is available it is difficult to suggest a more nuanced chronology of the material remains beyond the term Late Bronze Age IIB, a term that encompasses most of the 13th and the very early 12th century BCE.

FIGURE 7   Coastal Plain and Shephelah: location map

(10–20 m above sea level in the west and about 100 m above sea level in the east); the western part is covered with dunes while the eastern part is partly covered with red sand dunes and mainly by alluvial plains of the various streams that were exploited for cultivating field crops and orchards (Ravikovitch 1969: 26–27; Dan et al. 2002).

Ashkelon and Yavneh-Yam were the two main settlements along the coast during the Middle Bronze Age. Both were fashioned with an earthen rampart encompassing a wide area and a gate (Stager 2002; Stager et al. 2008: 218–236; Uziel 2008: 54–114). Both the rampart and the gate at Yavneh-Yam were used in the Late Bronze Age I–IIA as well. At both sites, the limited extent of excavation has apparently precluded the uncovering of remains from the Late Bronze Age IIA, documented in sherds found at the site. Remains of the settlement in Ashkelon's upper mound included floors, parts of walls and tombs dated beginning in the Middle Bronze Age II and continuing until the Late Bronze Age II (Stratum XIX) (Stager et al. 2008: 301–303; Brody 2016; Toffolo et al. 2018). At Yavneh-Yam, pottery was collected from the Late Bronze Age II, the same period as tombs uncovered north and south of the site (Fischer 2008: 2073; Yannai et al. 2013).

Historical information about these two centers comes from several sources. Ashkelon is known from Papyrus Hermitage A1116, attesting to a convoy of the local elite during the time of Amenhotep II (above), and from el-Amarna letters (EA 301–306, 321–326 and 370) that reveal the ties between the rulers of Ashkelon and the Egyptian court (Goren et al. 2004: 294–299). In another letter, sent by Abdi-Ḫeba of Jerusalem (EA 287), an unnamed lord from Ashkelon is accused of conspiring with lords from Gezer and Lachish against him. The inscriptions commemorating Merneptah's military campaign against Gezer and Ashkelon also provide such information about the connections between these two places (Hasel 1994; Morris 2005: 276–282; Kahn 2012: 258–263).

Yavneh-Yam has been identified as Muḫḫazu (Stieglitz 1974; Goren et al. 2004: 270), mentioned in inscriptions of Thutmose III, in a single el-Amarna letter (EA 298) and in an inscription of Ramesses II from Amara West. In addition, petrographic examination of two letters (EA 294, 296) indicates that they originated on the coastal plain between modern-day Ashdod and Caesarea (Goren et al. 2004: 292–294; Koch 2016: 95–97).[13]

Thus it would emerge that the two local centers along the coastal plain were Ashkelon in the south and Yavneh-Yam in the north. These are the same sites that were regional power centers in the Middle Bronze Age II and are mentioned in Egyptian sources from the time of Thutmose III (Muḫḫazu), Amenhotep II (Ashkelon), and in the el-Amarna letters (Ashkelon, Muḫḫazu).[14]

---

13   EA 294 contains the complaint of the ruler about problems the nearby ʿapiru were causing the people he had sent to serve in Jaffa. EA 296 documents attempts by the local ruler to improve his image to the king by mentioning that he had joined the Egyptian administration and enumerating his previous offices, as well as that he had fulfilled his task of protecting "the gate of Gaza" and "the gate of Jaffa" (Naʾaman 1997: 615).

14   Although in recent years other scholars have accepted the identification of the second center at Tel Ashdod, certain doubts remain, as Ashdod is not mentioned in Egyptian sources, and a previous attempt to identify the town's original name has been contested (Rainey 2003: 163*–164*). The latest appearances of both toponyms date to the 19th Dynasty, in sources from the time of Ramesses II (Muḫḫazu) and Merneptah (Ashkelon).

Between the two centers, around the mouth of Naḥal Lachish and the coast nearby, the Egyptians established another coastal estate. The first installation was Tel Mor, located on a kurkar hill near the right bank of Naḥal Lachish, about 1.5 km from its estuary. Several phases of Egyptian presence spanned the Late Bronze Age IIA–III.[15] The second installation was built on a kurkar hill near the beach, close to the site of Ashdod-Yam: a large, multi-room complex (about 0.1 hectare in size) and agricultural installations for wine production. The site was dated to the Late Bronze Age IIB and revealed a great deal of Egyptian-style pottery from the 19th Dynasty (Nahshoni et al. 2013). It seems that the Egyptian reliance on harbors is further exemplified by these two little sites.[16]

2.3 The Shephelah: Gath, Lachish and Beyond

The Shephelah is the common Hebrew name for the hills south of Ayalon Valley (separately dealt with below), east of the coastal plain, west of the central hill country and north of the Beersheba Valley, from 100 m above sea level in the west to 500 m above sea level in the east, with a number of particularly high peaks, mainly in the southeast. The hills are mainly chalk overlaid by a nari crust, covered with rendzina and dark brown soils good for horticulture and grazing (Dan 1988: 56). Intermittent streams that drain the central hill country flow between the hills of the Shephelah create narrow valleys covered with colluvial soils (good for orchard cultivation) near the slopes of the Judean Highland and alluvial soils in the west. These streams are grouped in three basins: Naḥal Sorek, Naḥal Lachish (including Naḥal Ha'Elah and Naḥal Guvrin), and Naḥal Shiqma.

Most settlements were in the western part of the Shephelah, where the hills are moderate and the valleys are wider. The largest of these mounds during the Middle Bronze Age to the Iron Age were Tel Miqne, Tell eṣ-Ṣafi, and Tel Lachish. As was presented in the previous chapter, Late Bronze Tel Miqne was a faint shadow of the large urban center once covering the entire mound.[17]

---

15 At some point a rectangular structure was built on the site (Stratum IX), the remains of which included a limited amount of Egyptian-style pottery (Barako 2007: 15–19, 45, 173; Martin 2011: 190–191). More substantial evidence for Egyptian presence is seen in the remnants of the next settlement (Stratum VIII) that included a large structure with thick walls that were damaged and renovated after some time (Stratum VII) and a number of smaller structures to the east (Barako 2007: 20–26, 45, 151; Martin 2011: 191–192).

16 Note a third site, located on the coast south of Ashdod Yam, in which sounding documented remains of a structure from the Late Bronze Age that was interpreted as a fort (Berman and Barda 2005: Site no. 48).

17 Preliminary publications of the excavations do not shed light on the date of renewal of the Late Bronze Age II settlement. It can be summarized that the settlement (Strata X–VIIIB)

Tell eṣ-Ṣafi, the site of ancient Gath, is located on a spur near the left bank of Naḥal Ha'Elah. The site consists of a U-shaped, 15-hectare upper mound, whose southern part is higher, and an extensive lower city surrounding the upper tell on the east and north. Late Bronze Age II settlement remains were found on the upper mound alone, including a large structure of the "courtyard house" type, uncovered on the northeastern slope, which was destroyed or abandoned in the Late Bronze Age IIB (Shai et al. 2011; Maeir 2012a: 18, 224–229, 252, 258–259; Shai et al. 2017; Maeir et al. 2019).

The seven-hectare square site of Tell ad-Duwer/Lachish is located in the southwestern part of the region on a hill near the left bank of Naḥal Lachish. The various archaeological expeditions unearthed the remains of a settlement that gradually developed during the Late Bronze Age IA until the Late Bronze Age IIB,[18] when it was destroyed (Ussishkin 2004: 60–62).

Turning to the written sources, the status of the rulers of Lachish (and their ability to communicate with the Egyptian court) is reflected in the aforementioned Papyrus Hermitage 1116a. The relations between the rulers of Lachish and the Egyptian court were allegedly maintained in the following decades, as reflected in the letters sent from Lachish and found at el-Amarna (EA 329, 330–332, and probably also EA 311).[19] Sometime before the "Amarna Period" another center emerged at Gath. Shuwardata from Gath was involved in a web of interaction that includes alliance with Milki-Ilu the ruler of Gezer, and had complex relations with Abdi-Ḥeba of Jerusalem. This struggle, described in detail (EA 279, 280, 289, 290), reveals that Shuwardata claimed the town of Qiltu—identified with biblical Keilah, modern al-Qila, situated in the upper

---

was confined to the 4-hectare upper mound and left behind remnants of dwellings and installations, among them a number of sub-phases, the last of which was destroyed in a major conflagration dated to the Late Bronze Age IIB (Killebrew 1996: 23–27; 2013: 80–83).

18 The Late Bronze Age IIA settlement remains include a temple at the foot of the mound ("The Fosse Temple"; established during the Late Bronze IB) (Tufnell et al. 1940: 37–38). Additional remains, dated to the Late Bronze Age IIA–B, include several construction phases unearthed on the western slope of the mound (Phases S-3-1) and fragments of structures uncovered in the center of the mound (Ussishkin 2004: 188–191, 323–343, 1033–1045; Streit et al. 2018: 261–266). Cemeteries surrounding the site were in use throughout that period (Tufnell 1958: 65–66). Remains of the next phase (Level VII) included structures on the northern slope, in the center of the mound (Phase P-1) and on the western slope (Tufnell 1958: 49, 51–61; Ussishkin 2004: 191–201, 344–351). The Fosse Temple was renovated at this time, and the cemeteries around the site continued in use (Tufnell et al. 1940: 38; Tufnell 1958: 66–68).

19 It is not clear whether the letter sent by a low-ranking official (EA 333) and reports of the conspiracy between the lords of Lachish and the head of a nearby town to attack "the land of the king" reflects a real event or the tension between the imperial agents and the local rulers who preferred to report directly to the Egyptian court.

Elah Valley (Naʾaman 2010a: 92–95). In a letter sent by Abdi-Ḫeba of Jerusalem (EA 287), unnamed lords from Ashkelon and Lachish are also mentioned as part of this coalition. Other letters describe the great threat to the status of the lords of Lachish and the lords of Gath alike: they had to defend their possessions from the threat of warrior bands named ʿapiru (EA 288 and 335, among others) (Naʾaman 2011a: 289–292).[20]

Were these the only centers in the Shephelah? This issue has been debated for two decades now (Finkelstein 1996a; 2014; Naʾaman 1997, 2011a). The petrographic analysis of the el-Amarna letters (Goren et al. 2004: 286, 290–291) has shed some light on this issue. Two letters (EA 275 and 276) sent by an individual called Yaḫzib-Hadda, whose exact residence is not attested, were made of clay that originated in one of the valleys in the eastern Shephelah; another letter (EA 277) is assigned to the same group. Still another letter (EA 229), of similar provenience, was sent by a ruler whose name was partly preserved—Abdi-na[…]. It is significant that two letters sent by rulers of Gath (EA 64 and EA 278) have a similar provenience, probably sent from a locale under their hegemony (Goren et al. 2004: 291; Naʾaman 2011a: 283 n. 6). It was therefore proposed that Yaḫzib-Hadda and Abdi-na[…] were either lords of local centers located in the valleys of the eastern Shephelah, most plausibly Tel Beth-Shemesh (Naʾaman 2011a: 283–284) and/or Tell Beit-Mirsim, or alternatively were lords from Gath who governed for a short time (Finkelstein 2014: 267).

The probability that a local lord was based at Tel Beth-Shemesh during the Amarna Period finds support in the unearthed remains from this three-hectare site located on a spur dominating the eastern portions of the fertile Sorek Valley. The Late Bronze IIA Level 9 includes remains of several structures, predominantly a large structure on the northern slope that partly reused the walls of the previous settlement, in which luxuries imported commodities were found (Bunimovitz et al. 2013; Weiss et al. 2019). The settlement was destroyed in a major conflagration. Remains of the next settlement (Stratum 8) included longitudinal halls paved with stream pebbles, which were dated to the Late Bronze Age IIB (Bunimovitz et al. 2013: 53; Lederman and Bunimovitz 2014: 63). The end of this settlement is unclear.

Another possible seat of local lords is Tell Beit-Mirsim, a three-hectare site located at the foot of the Hebron Hills, on a hill overlooking the upper Shiqma

---

20   The term ʿapiru (Sumerian logogram SA.GAZ in the el-Amarna letters) was originally used as a designation for uprooted or migrating individuals or groups. This seems to be the meaning in many letters from el-Amarna, while in some cases, the term became a derogatory appellation for rivals of local rulers, presented as opposition to the Egyptian interests (Naʾaman 1986: 272–276; Fleming 2012: 43–45).

Basin.[21] The Late Bronze Age II settlement at the site, which was renewed after a long hiatus, left behind extensive structures of the "courtyard type," silos and an oil extraction installation. Two phases were discerned in this settlement (Strata C_2–C_1), both of which were destroyed in a fire, the last of which was dated to the Late Bronze Age IIB (Albright 1932: 37–52; 1938b: 61–79).

2.4   The Ayalon Valley: Gezer

The Ayalon Valley is a well-defined ecological niche, bound by the hills of the Shephelah to its south and west and the central hill country to its north and east. In the northwestern corner it joins the Coastal Plain. It was a prime traffic route connecting these three regions, including on its northeast, the well-documented topographic corridor ascending on the long, narrow spurs of the moderate hills of the al-Jib Plateau (part of the Ramallah anticline) (Magen and Finkelstein 1993: 19–20). The fertile valley was cultivated since time immemorial, while the hills to the south and north are covered with terra rossa and mountainous redzina soils that were exploited mainly for orchards and grazing.

The regional center of the Ayalon Valley during the second and first millennia BCE was Gezer, located on one of the hills bounding the valley on the west that separate the valley from the alluvial plain of Naḥal Sorek. Elongated in form, and featuring two hills with a saddle in between, the mound is about 13 hectares in size. The remains dating to the Late Bronze Age attest to a gradual growth of the settlement, beginning with modest activity sometime after the end of the Middle Bronze Age city and reaching its zenith in the Late Bronze Age IIA before its end.[22] The next settlement was more modest and was destroyed in the Late Bronze Age IIB.[23]

---

21   Another possibility is that Tell Beit-Mirsim and nearby settlements were within the sphere of Lachish or that Egyptian influence in the area was quite limited and therefore no significant centers were established.

22   The earliest significant remains in Late Bronze Age Tel Gezer include a burial cave uncovered on the slope of the mound, which was dated to the Late Bronze Age IB–IIA (Seger and Lance 1988). More substantial remains were dated to the Late Bronze IIA (Stratum XVI), including a segment of a large structure on a high point at the western part of the mound and a pillared structure on the southern edge. Both were dismantled during the Late Bronze Age IIA (Dever 1986: 36–46; Ortiz and Wolff 2017: 68–72). The claim of the excavators (Dever 1986: 36–46; 1993) that the settlement was enclosed by a perimeter wall has been criticized in several studies (e.g., Bunimovitz 1983; Finkelstein 1994; Yannai 1994) and has been refuted by the results of the renewed excavations (Ortiz and Wolff 2017: 72; 2019: 79, 81).

23   Scant remains of Stratum XV include structures, floors, an oil-extraction installation and pits. That settlement was apparently partially destroyed during the Late Bronze Age IIB (Dever et al. 1970: 22–24; Dever et al. 1974: 48–50; Dever 1986: 46–51). The few remains from the next phase (Stratum XIV) show a short-lived settlement, apparently from the Late Bronze Age III (Dever et al. 1970: 23–24; Dever et al. 1974: 50–52). The renewed

Written sources document the history of Gezer at four chronological junctures: In the Thutmose III inscriptions it is mentioned as one of the settlements in the region, a stele of Thutmose IV that refers to people from Gezer who were deported to Egypt (Morris 2005: 134), and the el-Amarna correspondence that attest to the presence of influential lords.[24]

From the el-Amarna correspondence we may glean information about the web of interactions (alliances and rivalries) between the lords of Gezer and their neighbors, from Gath-Carmel (modern Jatt in the Sharon Plain) and Shechem to the north, Jerusalem to the east, Gath to the south, and beyond. Much information was given about the struggle of Milki-Ilu from Gezer and his allies against Abdi-Ḫeba of Jerusalem over rural settlements located in the contact zone of the valleys of Ayalon, Ha'Elah and the central hill country (Na'aman 2011a: 289–292; Finkelstein 2014: 265–271). We also learn about the threat by 'apiru bands against three settlements situated to the east of Gezer (EA 273, 274).[25] It may therefore be proposed that the rulers of Gezer had some influence over settlements nearby and in the more distant settlements in the Ayalon Valley, which were their rural hinterland.[26]

2.5 The Yarkon Basin: Jaffa

This unit (Figure 8) includes the alluvial plain of the Yarkon River and its northern tributaries (Naḥal Qaneh, Naḥal Rabba and Naḥal Shiloh), the alluvial plain of lower Naḥal Ayalon and the hills surrounding both of these plains on the north, east and south, with a total area of about 100 sq km. The alluvial plains converge in two narrow strips—in the northward-tending bed of Naḥal Ayalon toward its confluence with the Yarkon River and at the foot of the central hill country to the east. This portion of the central hill country consists of low limestone hills covered with soils good mainly for orchards and grazing. The western half of the area is covered with red sand, kurkar and dunes

---

excavations at the site unearthed further remains that were dated to the same horizon (Ortiz and Wolff 2019: 74–79).

24 See Chapter 4 on the inscriptions from the time of Merneptah mentioning a punitive campaign the latter undertook against Gezer.

25 In these letters sent from Gezer, the term most probably refers to warrior bands based in the sparsely inhabited hills north and east of the Ayalon Valley, strategically located spots from which to launch attacks against the rural hinterland of Gezer (EA 273, 274, 292 ["there is hostility from the hill country against me"; translation by Rainey 2015: 1129] and 297).

26 Nevertheless, in my opinion we must reject the theory that the rulers of Gezer imposed their hegemony over the cluster of settlements on the banks of lower Naḥal Sorek (Finkelstein 1996b: 229 fig. 1). It is not based on the written sources, considering that the only inscription mentioning Muḫḫazu (EA 298), identified in this area (Stieglitz 1974), does not attest to Gezer as ruling there, and see below.

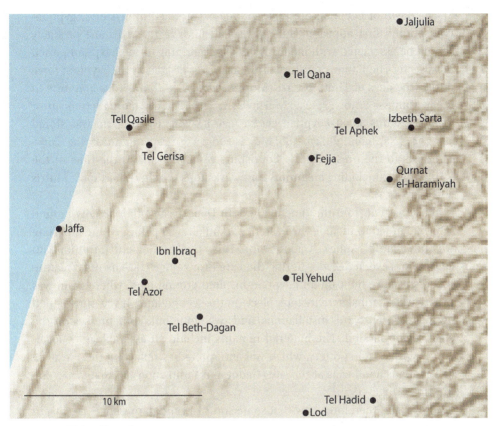

FIGURE 8   Yarkon Basin: location map

along the coast, interrupted by the narrow bands of the Yarkon River and Naḥal Ayalon and their moderate banks (Gadot 2003: 30–34; Ayalon 2009: 27–29).

The main site in the Yarkon Basin during the Late Bronze Age was Jaffa. The published preliminary results of the many excavations conducted at Jaffa attest to the establishment of a well-built settlement in the Late Bronze Age IIA (Level V) that was fashioned with a gate and a temple. Remains of the next period (Level IVB) included a brick fortification wall and a gate built of kurkar, adorned with titles of Ramesses II. The gate was destroyed in a fire and rebuilt (Level IVA), perhaps more than once, and continued in use until the end of the settlement in the 12th century.[27] The southern slope of the mound was used for burial during the Late Bronze Age IIB (Re'em 2010).

---

27   For summaries of the Late Bronze Age remains at Jaffa see Herzog (2008); Burke and Lords (2010); Martin (2011: 238–240); Burke et al. (2017).

The dawn of Egyptian presence in Jaffa is shrouded in mystery. Egyptian-type pottery first appeared during the Late Bronze IB, and most probably should be associated with memories of the beginning of the Egyptian period at this site: The Ramesside story of the takeover of Jaffa by an Egyptian force during the days of Thutmose III (Morris 2005: 138 with previous literature in n. 89; Manassa 2010: 253–256; Martin 2011: 240). The el-Amarna letters attest to Jaffa's status as an Egyptian center (see EA 296) where grain was stored (EA 294) (Na'aman 1981: 179–180; Morris 2005: 253). Papyrus Anastasi I (26:3–9) attests to the presence of a flourishing center in Jaffa at the time of the 19th Dynasty, including an armory and workshops (Fischer-Elfert 1986; Morris 2005: 470–471).

It seems that from the time of the 19th Dynasty Egyptian activity around Jaffa expanded to include the eastern Yarkon alluvial plains, where an estate was built at Tel Aphek (Gadot 2010). This small settlement (Stratum X12) existed for several decades during the Late Bronze Age IIB. The main feature was a structure built on an Egyptian-inspired ground plan, where grain was stored and a scribal activity took place on the second floor. It was surrounded by a paved courtyard, installations, and two stone-built winepresses on the edge of the mound. The material remains include an assemblage of local- and Egyptian-style pottery, which was interpreted as reflecting the presence of Egyptians and locals at the site (Gadot and Yadin 2009: 55, 59–66, 582–86; Martin 2011: 180–187).

These data therefore show that some sort of Egyptian presence had begun at Jaffa as early as the middle 18th Dynasty. Egyptian-style architecture and pottery from the Late Bronze IIA and IIB levels at Jaffa complemented by evidence in written sources indicate firm and stable Egyptian possession. Moreover, the Egyptians gradually intensified their influence and expanded eastward so that by the time of the 19th Dynasty there was an Egyptian holding (albeit short-lived) at Tel Aphek. In quite broad strokes it may be proposed that a parallel process took place in both the Besor region and the Yarkon basin—expansion of Egyptian activity at the end of the 18th Dynasty and mainly in the 19th Dynasty, from the centers along the coast eastward into the hinterland.[28] This development came to an end during the Late Bronze IIB and the Egyptian presence at Jaffa was terminated sometime during the Late Bronze Age III.

---

28 Jaffa's association with the settlements in its agricultural hinterland is also known from the first millennium BCE, as documented in inscriptions from the time of the Assyrian King Sennacherib about Ashkelon's rule over those settlements; see Na'aman (2009: 352).

3 Local Rulers and the Egyptian Court

The revitalization of the social landscape of southwest Canaan reached its peak during the Late Bronze IIA. By then, the contemporaneous process of Egyptian establishment at Tell el-Ajjul–Gaza and Jaffa and emergence of a local elite led to the integration of major portions of the region within an Egyptian-oriented network. Thus, while Egyptian royal sources are infused with a military perspective towards the southern Levant, the archaeology of southwest Canaan and the information embedded in the el-Amarna correspondence suggest a more complex situation of negotiation and collaboration that brought about the integration of Egypt into local daily life and the expansion of Egyptian hegemony over the region. That these ties intensified as the years passed can be seen from the increasing number of Egyptian sources mentioning Canaanite settlements, and the ever-greater appearance of Canaanites in Egyptian administrative lists.

The content of the el-Amarna letters reflects the nature of the relationships between the royal court and the local rulers (Na'aman 2000; Pfoh 2016, 2019). To begin with, the letters sent from the rulers in southwest Canaan to Egypt reflect their perception of their status at the royal Egyptian court, while only the two letters sent from Egypt, one to Gezer (EA 369) and one to Ashkelon (EA 370), and the letter found at Tell el-Hesi (EA 333), mentioning events at Lachish, reflect the Egyptian perspective.[29] From the dozens of letters emerges an image of the local rulers as "'men of prestige' with political authority … they had to protect the community they represented to the outside world and they had to assure the well-being of the people living in it by appealing to that … silent and distant overlord that was the Pharaoh" (Pfoh 2019: 252). Indeed, the kings of the 18th Dynasty did not change their policy—they did not augment Egyptian presence in Canaan and their involvement in internal matters was usually restricted to cases where Egyptian interests were at risk.

In their letters, the local rulers repeatedly stressed their loyalty and perseverance in their main mission—protection of the "king's land"—and sometimes their role in the Egyptian administration before they achieved their current position. Remarkably, the rulers from southwest Canaan chose submissive wording, more so than their companions farther to the north, probably a manifestation of their geographical (and perhaps also social) proximity to Egypt and to points of control in Gaza and Jaffa (Morris 2006). But the goal of

---

29 An example of the Egyptian perspective is in the use of the term "man of the city X" (*awîl* ^{uru}X) as a title for local lords (EA 369) as opposed to the term "mayor" (*ḫazānūtu*) (see EA 370), which reflects a closer connection to the Egyptian administration.

the correspondence was to win Egyptian recognition of their status, Egyptian patronage in their constant struggles against their neighbors, and Egyptian protection in their defense from marauding ʿapiru bands.

Egyptian hegemony can be seen in the way the local lords were required to pledge a loyalty oath and were commanded to appear at the royal court, as well as in the status of the Egyptian emissaries and their demands from local rulers. It can also be seen in the role of the king and his officials[30] as arbitrators of local conflicts (mainly when they threatened Egyptian interests in Canaan),[31] in the offerings the local rulers sent to Egypt (Morris 2018: 127–137), and in the soldiers and the curvée labor they provided to Egyptian holdings (e.g., EA 365). But to some extent, these relations were more complex than the often-assumed Manichaean suzerain–subjugated character, as reflected in the exchange of rare gifts with the royal Egyptian court (e.g., EA 369) (Naʾaman 1981: 178–179; 2002b).

Many hegemonic states established their rule in areas that were important to their military and economic interests, while subjugating neighboring areas to their influence in a manner that was neither uniform nor continuous, in a lengthy process that included forging alliances and agreements with local elites (Goldstone and Haldon 2009: 18–19; Parker 2013: 136–139). Of course, such political frameworks were established by force of arms, and in many cases destroyed political and social frameworks. But they always relied on the cooperation of local elites, which were to some extent autonomous and in keeping with the political and cultural circumstances in each place (Sinopoli 2001: 456–457). We may interpret the moves of the local elites as perpetuation of Egyptian hegemony, but at the same time, they established their own rule, expanded their ties and integrated themselves into a broader economic network. Moreover, at times when the central government was weak, such processes led to the empowerment of the local elites even to the extent of attaining their political independence (Sinopoli 2001: 452).

---

30   Based on the limited information about Egyptian officials (Jeske 2019), it seems that their responsibilities were flexible and changing. Some of them may be identified as coming from a Canaanite background and while fulfilling their office in Canaan they may have lived in one of the Egyptian centers along the coast (Morris 2005: 255–256, with earlier literature). The officials monitored the local rulers, they were their liaisons with the Egyptian administration (see EA 333) and sometimes arrived at the head of a garrison to protect them in their town or in a nearby settlement (see EA 292: 26–40; see also EA 284–287, 289).

31   See, for example, the Egyptian involvement during the "Labʾayu affair" (Finkelstein and Naʾaman 2005: 179–180).

CHAPTER 3

Goddess in Translation: The Fosse Temple at Lachish

Lachish is a special case for the study of southwest Canaanite–Egyptian colonial encounters.[1] The five expeditions at the site unearthed vast remains dating to the Late Bronze Age, providing diverse paths of exploration. One path is based on the work of the expedition headed by James L. Starkey, which unearthed next to the mound remains of a structure that was named the "Fosse Temple" (Tufnell et al. 1940). To this day it is the sole published cult place from Late Bronze Age southwest Canaan.[2]

The theoretical framework to deal with the Fosse Temple follows current approaches practiced in the archaeology of religion. These approaches (Jaffe 2015: 5–9 with extensive literature; Rüpke 2015) have gradually rejected the traditional images of religion as a static and stable structure—sometimes considered the fundamental element in social identity—and favor its current understanding as a flexible network of agents (humans and objects alike) and structures, that constantly changes under various circumstances (Hazard 2013; Tweed 2015; Bräunlein 2016). For the most part, those changes are understood as shaped and reshaped in accordance with and in response to changing situations (Shaw 2013: 1–3). This includes translation and appropriation of religious beliefs and practices, their entanglement in the local context with new meanings, and the reshaping of existing concepts and practices to be understood within a wider social context (Bender and Cadge 2006; Clack 2011: 227–229; Äikäs and Salmi 2013: 75–77).

Religion can be manipulated to gain capital, a process best seen in its common subjugation to royal monopoly that emphasizes the ruler as representative of the gods and sometimes magnified by such means as deifying the ruler per se (Brisch 2008; De Maret 2011; Brisch 2013; Porter 2014).[3] In the case of hegemonic states, such ideologies developed to justify the broad reach of their rule, the ruler's function in bringing order to the chaos of existence and

---

1 A previous version of this chapter was published as Koch 2017a.
2 A thorough study of temples and sanctuaries from the Levant is beyond the scope of this discussion. For survey of finds and scholarship and updated discussions, see Mierse (2012), Hundley (2013: 105–136) and papers in Kamlah (2012).
3 For Late Bronze Age examples of temples in the service of the ruling ideology, see the case of Hazor as discussed by Zuckerman (2012).

the preeminence of the hegemonic power over client groups (Sinopoli 1994: 167–169; Parker 2011; Areshian 2013: 7–10). At the same time, religion is used and manipulated by individuals to position themselves in their society, and by a society itself as means for grouping or reshaping group identity (Day 2011; Rebillard 2015; Rüpke 2016).

Moving back to Lachish, the Fosse Temple was founded during the Late Bronze Age IB and developed in three consecutive phases until its destruction in the Late Bronze Age IIB. These are the same years during which Lachish grew and was established as the seat of powerful lords with close connections to the Egyptian court. The Fosse Temple thus stands as a prime case study for examination of the reflection of social changes in religious transformations. In other words, the tracing of changes in local religion has the potential of exploring the means employed by a group to comprehend the colonial situation.

1   Introducing the Fosse Temple in Lachish

The Fosse Temple is a modest structure uncovered next to the western slope of Tel Lachish. It was completely excavated by Starkey's team, leaving no visible trace. Yet the detailed publication by Tufnell and her colleagues (1940) allows the studying of its stratigraphy, dating, and the various types of artifacts. The excavators traced three architectural phases in the temple (Figure 9):

- The first phase dates to the Late Bronze Age IB (Tufnell et al. 1940: 21, 24, 83; Singer-Avitz 2004: 1024–1026). The optimum reconstruction of the meager remains of this phase includes an asymmetric long room, with pillars arranged in a row, a raised platform along the southern wall and two auxiliary side-rooms (Tufnell et al. 1940: 36–37 and pl. 66). Remains from this period are rarely visible on the mound itself.
- The second phase was built on a new, expanded plan and according to glyptic and imported ware, it dates to the late 18th Dynasty/the Late Bronze IIA (Tufnell et al. 1940: 22, 24). The square central hall had four pillars with several benches located along the northern, eastern and western walls; the southern wall had a raised platform, and the entire complex was flanked by two or three auxiliary rooms (Tufnell et al. 1940: 37–38 and pl. 67). Like in the previous phase, remains from this period are rarely found on the mound.
- The third phase functioned during the Late Bronze IIB until its destruction together with the town itself (Tufnell et al. 1940: 22; Ussishkin 2004: 60–61). The plan of this phase is almost identical to the previous plan and should be understood as a gradual outgrowth of the existing structure (Tufnell et al. 1940: 38, 40–42 and pl. 68; Bietak 2002: 60). The earliest known stratified

remains from the mound date to this period, including several construction phases unearthed on the western slope of the mound (Phases S-3–S-1, Level VII), in the center of the mound (Phase P-1) and on the northern slope, as well as continuous burial around the town.[4]

The few finds attributed to the first phase provide only limited information regarding the earliest cult in the Fosse Temple: a gold pendant, which has a clear association with the worship of the local goddess (Tufnell et al. 1940: pl. 26 no. 15; Schroer 2011: 288) and a bronze figurine of a male deity with a tall hat (Tufnell et al. 1940: pl. 26 no. 31–32). Notable evidence is the pits filled with a large number of bowls found around the structure, and particularly from the later phases of the temple, probably the remains of communal banquets. It is possible that the location of the temple outside the town attests to its cult, perhaps housing a deity with some association to nature or agriculture.[5]

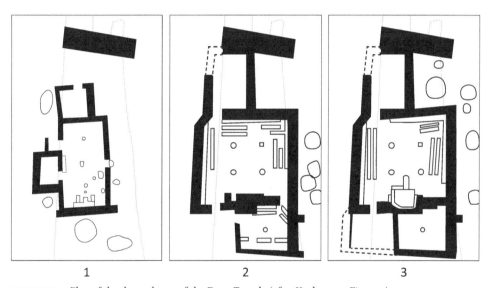

FIGURE 9   Plan of the three phases of the Fosse Temple (after Koch 2017a: Figure 2)

---

4 Tufnell 1958: 49, 51–61, 65–68; Ussishkin 2004: 188–201, 323–351, 1033–1045.
5 Various explanations for the location of the temple have been suggested and rejected (see Ussishkin 2004: 58–59 for earlier interpretations). In light of the common practice of founding cult places near a natural feature (Van Andringa 2015: 31), I would suggest that the location of the Fosse Temple might indeed reflect some association to nature, agriculture, or even a sacred tree or trees. The cult of sacred trees is known in the Levant from the Chalcolithic period to modern times (Na'aman and Lissovsky 2008: 190–198). The temple's compound may have had a sacred tree or trees, possibly in the western area, where a handful of empty pits were found (see, e.g., Tufnell et al. 1940: pl. 67 no. 151). That the structure was built after the commencement of activity at that spot during the Late Bronze Age IA might support

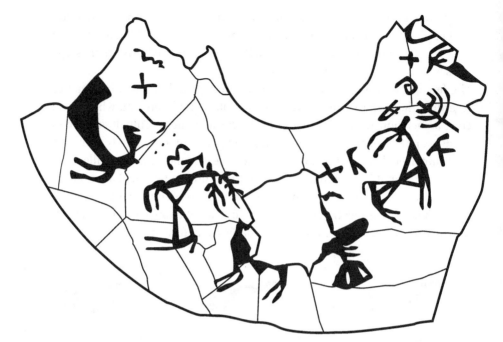

FIGURE 10   Drawing of a decoration of a jug from the Fosse Temple (after Koch 2017a: Figure 3)

Much more is known regarding the second phase: The plan of the temple is different from the earlier phase and from other temples in Canaan and resembles structures from 18th Dynasty Egypt (Bietak 2002: 63–74). In addition, the assemblage found within the temple and in the pits around it contains a mixture of artifacts made in local tradition that show affiliation with local goddesses, in this case the goddess *Elat* (Figure 10),[6] alongside artifacts imported

such interpretation, in which meager cultic activity was followed by the construction of a temple.

6   Canaanite-style artifacts from the second phase include pendants decorated with a stylized tree or the figure of a goddess (Tufnell et al. 1940: pl. 26 nos. 4, 6), a goblet decorated with female genitalia accompanied by two ibexes (Tufnell et al. 1940: pl. 47A and 47B no. 229), and a bronze figurine of a male deity from a nearby structure (Tufnell et al. 1940: pl. 26 no. 33). Artifacts from the third phase include ivories decorated with rosette and stylized tree (Tufnell et al. 1940: pl. 19 nos. 16–18, pl. 20 no. 31), ivory figures of horned animals (Tufnell et al. 1940: pl. 17 nos. 11–14), ivory scepters, some decorated with pomegranate heads (Tufnell et al. 1940: pl. 20 nos. 23–28), a star-shaped golden pendant (Tufnell et al. 1940: pl. 26 no. 9). Canaanite-style artifacts from the nearby pits include gold pendants decorated with the figure of a goddess and a stylized tree, stars or rosettes (Tufnell et al. 1940: pl. 26 nos. 5, 7, 10–14), and pottery vessels decorated with female genitalia (Tufnell et al. 1940: pl. 61 no. 4), animals accompanying a palm tree (Tufnell et al. 1940: pl. 48 nos. 246–250) and the famous jug

from Egypt (or perhaps locally made in Egyptian style) mainly associated with the cult of Hathor.[7]

2 Assessing the Change

The changes observed in the transition from the first to the second phases in the Fosse Temple reflect a change in the cult at Lachish. Refurbishing of temples is probably intended to stop erosion, but structural modification is a means to accommodate changes in the community, such as political needs of the ruler or even the change of the ruling ideologies (Van Andringa 2015: 33–34).[8] Moreover, temples were regularly equipped with images, decorations, vessels, and other sorts of paraphernalia that were originally deposited or brought by visitors as votive offerings (Frevel 2008). These were accumulated over the years, used, interpreted and reinterpreted by the participants in the rituals, in a mechanism that constantly reshaped the cult (Van Andringa 2015: 35–38; Von Hesberg 2015: 320–323).

How different was the cult following the change? Looking back in hindsight, it is evident that Canaanites acquired Egyptian artifacts associated with Hathor as early as the Middle Bronze Age, and her images were adapted to represent Canaanite goddesses (Schroer 1989: 196–197; Ben-Tor 2007: 181–182).

---

    decorated with animals accompanying a scared tree and an inscription dedicating it to the goddess Elat. It seems that some of the artifacts of the latter phase originated in the second phase, as attested to by the presence of Amenhotep III scarabs on the altar dated to the 13th century BCE (Tufnell et al. 1940: 68–70 and pl. 32B nos. 36–39).

7 See Egyptian faience necklace with amulets in the form of Hathor heads, lotus buds, and rosettes (Tufnell et al. 1940: pl. 14), an ivory cosmetic bottle (Tufnell et al. 1940: pl. 15), ivory cat and waterfowl figurines (Tufnell et al. 1940: pl. 17 nos. 9, 10), an ivory artifact decorated with a waterfowl figure (Tufnell et al. 1940: pl. 19 no. 19), Egyptian faience bowls decorated with Hathor head (Tufnell et al. 1940: pl. 22 no. 58), an additional bowl found on the altar and other vessels (Tufnell et al. 1940: pl. 22 nos. 55–57). Similar faience bowls were found in the temple at Timna (Schulman 1988: 129 and fig. 42) and possibly at the so-called Lion Temple in Jaffa (Sweeney 2003: 61–62 and fig. 5). For the Egyptian origin of these bowls and their association with the cult of Hathor, see Pinch (1993); Keel and Uehlinger (1998: 76); Strandberg (2009: 148–152); Schroer (2011: 218–220). Egyptian imports from the pits include a Hathor amulet (Tufnell et al. 1940: pl. 21 no. 46) and additional faience vessels decorated with waterfowls and lotus buds (Tufnell et al. 1940: pl. 23 nos. 61, 64–67).

8 In this regard, see the transformation of temples in northern Canaan during the Late Bronze Age I–IIA at Tel Hazor and Pella, where cultic complexes dedicated to the storm god were built. The excavators of both sites understood the construction of these enclosures as attesting to the beginning of a transformation in the ideology of the elite (and perhaps also a change in the composition of the elite itself), which placed that deity and his cult at the foundation of its rule (Bourke 2012: 170–171; Zuckerman 2012: 117, 122).

In this regard, the affiliation of the Fosse Temple cult with an Egyptian cult associated with Hathor is analogous to the veneration of the goddess at Byblos and her association with the main deity of the city—Baʿalat Gubla ("The Lady of Byblos") (Zernecke 2013; Quack 2015: 257–259; Kilani 2020: 53–57, 219–222). The background against which this process at Byblos is to be understood are the strong ties between Byblians and Egyptians (established already during the Old Kingdom), and the adoption and adaptation of Egyptian cultural traits by its elite for millennia (Espinel 2002; Flammini 2010, 2011). Another famous example of such translation is the Levantine participation in the Egyptian cult of Hathor "Lady of Turquoise" at Serabit el-Khadim and her consequent identification with West-Semitic "Baalat" (Wimmer 1990: 1066–1068 with earlier literature).[9]

The case of Lachish thus continues a trend of the Egyptian–Levantine relations since the third millennium BCE, but it should be borne in mind that each case has its own socio-political circumstances. In what follows, I would like to suggest a possible scenario of the circumstances that led to the change in Lachish.

3   Hathor and Tiye

A possible explanation for the connection between the Fosse Temple cult and the Egyptian cult may be found in the glyptic items unearthed by the British expedition. These include two scarabs bearing the name of Amenhotep III, a plaque bearing his name found in the foundation of the second phase, and a scarab bearing the name of Tiye, his consort, found on the floor of the building. This unique assemblage led the excavators to associate the renovation of the building with the days of that king (Tufnell et al. 1940: 49 and pl. 32A/B nos. 2–4 and 7). Moreover, three medium-sized scarabs and a large "lion-hunt" scarab were found on top of the altar of the third phase, probably reflecting their centrality in the local cult (idem, pl. 32A/B nos. 36–39).

Noteworthy are the large scarabs, known from other sites in the southern Levant, such as Beth-Shean, Tel Beth-Shemesh, and Jaffa (Figure 11)—a novelty of the days of Amenhotep III, commemorating a lion-hunt, Tiye as the beloved

---

9 Compare also the prolonged process of translation of Hathor imagery in Cyprus during the Late Cypriot period that, based on her association with copper mining, led to the integration of her symbolism within the iconography of the local goddesses. Significantly, the integrated figure is attested in the Cypro-Geometric III period onwards (Carbillet 2011). Reference courtesy of V. Boschloos.

FIGURE 11   Large-size scarab of Amenhotep III from Jaffa
COURTESY OF CORPUS OF STAMP-SEALS FROM THE SOUTHERN LEVANT

consort and the construction of a lake dedicated to Tiye, among other scenes (Berman in Kozloff and Bryan 1992: 70–72; Baines 2003; Kozloff 2012: 108–109). These scarabs are characterized by uniformity in style and production, and might have been produced in a single workshop, possibly in the late third– early fourth decades of Amenhotep III's reign, contemporaneously with and in direct relation to his monumental construction activities (Brandl et al. 2013).

Amenhotep III is well known for his palaces and temples, either newly erected or built in place of previous buildings (Kozloff and Bryan 1992: 72–124; Bryan 1997; Johnson 1998; O'Connor 1998; Kozloff 2012: 120–147, 168–176). Most of these temples were dedicated to the king himself or to his personification as one of the Egyptian deities, such as the temple "Nb-Ma'at-Re' united with Ptah" at Memphis (Morkot 1990; Kozloff 2012: 176–180). The temple complex at Thebes includes the mortuary temple of Amenhotep III, where statues of deities surrounded his own statue (Johnson 1998: 66–75). Temples were also built in the Egyptian holdings at Nubia, like the temple at Soleb, north of the third cataract, where Amenhotep III was worshiped as "Nb-Ma'at-Re' Lord of Nubia" (Kozloff and Bryan 1992: 105–110; Johnson 1998: 79; Kozloff 2012: 169–172). Additional temples were dedicated to Tiye, the best known of which were located at Malkata, Thebes, and Sedinga, near Soleb, where she was worshiped as Hathor (Kozloff and Bryan 1992: 110; Kozloff 2012: 172–174).[10]

These building projects were mostly erected during the third decade of Amenhotep III's reign, in preparation for his first jubilee festival (Ḥeb-Sed) which was celebrated at Thebes, during which he accorded divine attributes to himself and his consort Tiye, making them both living gods (Kozloff and Bryan 1992: 39–41; Johnson 1998: 86–89; Grover 2008; Kozloff 2012: 182–196). One

---

10   See also fragments of statuettes of Tiye from the temple of Hathor at Serabit el-Khadim, depicting her with traditional attributes of the goddess (Petrie 1906: Fig. 133; Dijkstra 2015: 165–176), which might indicate her local worship as Hathor.

possible representation of the festival is a bracelet depicting Amenhotep III and Tiye seated on their thrones, with their two daughters playing Hathor's sistrum, emphasizing the royal couple's divinity (Grover 2008: 11–12).

Tiye, long acknowledged as one of the most prominent consorts in Egyptian history (Kozloff and Bryan 1992: 43; Schoske 2008; Kozloff 2012: 102–103), played a central role in the festival, during which she was presented as Hathor, with Hathor's traditional attributes, thus creating an icon of queenship used by later royal consorts in Egypt (Kozloff and Bryan 1992: 171–177, 202–203, 212; Johnson 1996: 72–77; Grover 2008: 8–9; Troy 2008: 158–163). Other representations depict Tiye as a sphinx trampling enemies or as an anthropomorphic figure seated with adversaries at her feet—both previously associated solely with the king; their adaptation to a feminine character attests to Tiye's prominence in the Egyptian court (Carney 2001: 33–34, 37–38).

4 The Cult in the Fosse Temple in Context

In light of the above, it is possible to suggest the following scenario. The cult in the Fosse Temple was dedicated to a local goddess—probably Elat—who was associated during the Late Bronze IIA with Egyptian Hathor. Hathor, in turn, was linked to the royal cult of Tiye, who was deified by her husband, Amenhotep III. One can assume that the introduction of the new cult was an initiative of the Egyptian administration, as a means to strengthen the loyalty of the local population, similar to parallel phenomena in colonial experiences. Yet caution is needed, for the persistence of the royal cult in local context outside of its homeland (see the existence of the Fosse Temple long after the death of Tiye; Phase III of the temple), seems to reflect the active role of the Canaanite population in this process.[11]

More important, the incorporation of elements from the cult of Hathor into the local cult at Lachish reflects a process of cross-cultural discourse that is deeply embedded in the interconnectedness characterizing the Late Bronze Age. The translation of foreign gods into local ones was a common phenomenon during this period of intense interregional connectivity, reflected in various texts from Hatti, Egypt, Ugarit and elsewhere, encompassing diplomacy, myths and ritual (Smith 2010: 37–90 with extensive literature; Singer 2013a). Fine examples related to Canaan are the appearance of West Semitic deities in the Nile Delta during the second millennium BCE following constant

---

11   See, for example, the case of the cult of the Roman emperor developed by cities in Anatolia (Alcock 2005: 328 with further literature).

Levantine migrations and their adoption by the Egyptian court during the New Kingdom (Schneider 2003b; Tazawa 2009; Münnich 2013; Quack 2015; Wilson-Wright 2016).

The association of the local goddess of Lachish with Hathor/Tiye is, therefore, an example of a colonial encounter. In this respect, the translation of Hathor to Elat—and thus the probable practice of some sort of royal cult associated with Tiye—reflects the intense relationships between the Canaanites from Lachish and the Egyptian court. Rather than indicating an Egyptian policy or an Egyptianization of the local population, it is an attestation to the means of the locals to incorporate Egypt within its own world. It was only long after the death of Amenhotep III and Tiye that the cult in the Fosse Temple ended, following the destruction of the town by the 13th century BCE.

CHAPTER 4

Ambivalence

The 18th Dynasty ended, according to conventional periodization, during the reign of Horemheb (Dodson 2009; Manassa Darnell 2015). The latter appointed as his successor one of his army commanders, Paramesse (Ramesses I), who ruled for less than two years, but his descendants would rule Egypt for a century in what is termed the 19th Dynasty. The days of this royal house were marked by two trends that altered the relations between the Egyptian court and its Levantine client.

On the one hand, the rulers of the 19th Dynasty led multiple military campaigns across the Levant. The ultimate threat came from the north, where the Hittites defeated Mitanni, Egypt's ally, took over the Mitanni holdings in Syria and faced off directly against Egypt itself (Bryce 2005: 154–220; Cordani 2011; Stavi 2015). Following several successes by Seti I, Ramesses II, his son and heir, conducted several military campaigns to counter the expansion of Muwatalli II the Hittite. Despite intensive propaganda showcasing his victories, it seems that Ramesses II lost to Muwatalli II at the great battle next to the city of Kadesh, and was forced a few years later to form a peace treaty (Bryce 2005: 227–241; Morris 2005: 354–366, 372–376 with literature). Other problems were closer to Egypt. Among the many campaigns, some were aimed at the southern Levant, with the objective of pacifying the growing local resistance, resulting in destructions and deportations (Na'aman 2011b: 45–49 with extensive literature). Most relevant to this discussion is Merneptah's campaign in the fifth year of his reign, which included the submission of Ashkelon, Gezer and Yenoam, and one tribal group—Israel (Hasel 1994; Morris 2005: 276–282; Kahn 2012: 258–263).

On the other hand, the 19th Dynasty originated and ruled from the Delta, where Egyptian–Levantine discourse had been progressing since the early second millennium BCE. Their residence, known as Pr-Ramesses, "The House of Ramesses," was established in proximity to several 18th Dynasty installations, at the site of Avaris, the capital of the Hyksos kingdom (Bietak and Forstner-Müller 2011). A prominent deity in the newly established capital was Seth, whose cult had for centuries incorporated pictorial elements of Levantine storm gods (Schneider 2003b; Allon 2007; Tazawa 2009: 154–160). Moreover, the proximity of the new court to the Levant made communication and transportation accessible,[1] especially for its officials in southwest Canaan, the closest neighbors of the Delta to the east. Thus, the integration of southwest Canaan within the colonial network, which steadily grew during the 18th Dynasty, had the potential to intensify within a few decades.

1   Building Deposits

One of the earliest studies on localization of Egyptian practices in Canaan was the thorough treatment of a practice by Bunimovitz and Zimhoni (1993): the placing in the Late Bronze Age IIB until the Iron Age I of a set of two bowls concealing an oil lamp under a wall or a floor, or on a floor adjacent to a wall (Figure 12). Bunimovitz and Zimhoni pointed to the chronology of the practice and its distribution in southwest Canaan and at Pella—the regions closest to the Egyptian presence. In light of the absence of a preceding Canaanite tradition, they suggested that this practice was a Canaanite translation of a well-established Egyptian tradition that involved placing votive offering in or beneath the foundation of new buildings (Bunimovitz and Zimhoni 1993: 123–124).

New finds from recent years contribute to a better understanding of the chronology and distribution of this practice (as originally assembled by Bunimovitz and Zimhoni 1993: 120–121). Apparently, soon after its introduction in the Late Bronze Age IIB, the practice became a common tradition that was performed over a prolonged period until its demise in the Iron Age IIA: The introduction of the specific set of two bowls concealing an oil lamp took place in at least six settlements in southwest Canaan during the Late Bronze Age IIB.[2] Deposits dated to the Late Bronze Age III were found at additional sites in southwest Canaan, and farther north at Tel Beth-Shean, Tel Reḥov and

---

1   And see the building projects along Sinai's northern coast, "the Ways of Horus", during the reign of Seti I and Ramesses II (Morris 2018: 189–191 with literature).

2   Deir el-Balaḥ Stratum VIII or VII (Dothan and Brandl 2010: 76, 81; Dothan and Nahmias-Lotan 2010), Tel Aphek Stratum XII (Gadot and Yadin 2009: 55, fig. 8.58:15–17), Tel Lachish Level VIIA in Area S and Level P-1 (Bunimovitz and Zimhoni 2004: 1147–1149 nos. 1–3, 6–8), Ashkelon Phase 22 in Grid 38 (see preliminary reports online http://digashkelon.com/preliminary-reports), Tell eṣ-Ṣafi Stratum E4B (Maeir 2012a: 226 and pl. 10.22B, 10.23A–B, 10.24B), and Tel Beth-Shemesh Stratum IV (Bunimovitz and Lederman 2016: 219 and fig. 6.80:1–2). Additional sets are reported, yet to be published, from Tel Gerisa (Bunimovitz and Zimhoni 1993: 118–119) and from a New Kingdom fortress next to Haruva (northeast of present-day al-Arish) (Bunimovitz and Zimhoni 1993: 108).

FIGURE 12   Lamp-and-Bowl deposit from Late Bronze Age Tel Azekah
COURTESY OF ODED LIPSCHITS

Ṭabaqat Faḥl.[3] By the Iron Age I the practice of lamp-and-bowl deposits was limited once again to southwest Canaan,[4] and its latest evidence come from Iron Age IIA Tel Azekah and possibly Tel Beth-Shemesh.[5]

---

3   Tel Lachish Level VI in Area S (Bunimovitz and Zimhoni 2004: 1148 nos. 4–5), Tel Gezer Stratum 5A in Field I and Stratum 6B in Field VI (Dever et al. 1970: 23, plan IV, pls. 9A–B, 28: 12–14; Dever 1986: 76, plan XVI, pls. 22:12–13 and 18–19, 95B and 96A), Tel Azekah Level T2–3 (Here, Figure 12), Tell Jemmeh Stratum JK (Petrie 1928: 6, pls. 6, 49, 51) and Phase 1 in Field I (Ben-Shlomo and Van Beek 2014: 316 figs. 6.150–6.151), Tel Beth-Shean Strata N-3 and S-4 (Panitz-Cohen and Mazar 2009: 78 and photos 3.8 and 3.9, 125–126 and photos 4.49 and 4.50), Pella/Ṭabaqat Faḥl Phase 1 in Area III (McNicoll et al. 1982: 56, fig. 7a, pl. 123:1–10), and reported sets from Tel Seraʿ Stratum IX (Bunimovitz and Zimhoni 1993: 110) and Tel Reḥov Stratum D-7 (Mazar 1999: 14).
4   Tel Gezer Strata 5C–B in Field VI (Dever 1986: pls. 36: 1–4), Tel Miqne Strata VIB and VC (Mazow 2005: 437–438; Dothan et al. 2016: 23 and photos 2.16 and 2.32), Tel Beth-Shemesh Stratum III and Level 6 (Bunimovitz and Lederman 2016: 163, 218–220 and figs. 6.67, 6.68, 6.79:1–5, 6.80:5–14 and 18–20), and Ashkelon Phase 9 in Grid 50 (Stager et al. 2008: 306) and Phases 20b–17a in Grid 38 (Aja 2009: 381–385). One of the two deposits found by Petrie at Tell el-Ḥesi includes a bell-shaped bowl (Petrie 1891: pl. 8:128) that should probably be associated with the Joint Archaeological Expedition Stratum VIII dated to the Iron Age I.
5   Two lamp-and-bowl deposits were found at Tel Azekah in the foundations of an Iron Age IIA structure in Area T2 (courtesy of O. Lipschits and Y. Gadot). A lamp and a chalice found in

It is thus clear that ever since its commencement, the practice had well-known traits—its composition and its association with structures. The variants are few. Regarding the composition, the bowls that function as serving dishes might signify the set as an offering, while the upper bowl concealed the offering. The lamp was most probably offered in association with light. Light (and darkness) is both a matter of itself and a provider of sight to humans. Anthropologists consider light to be a major component of social interaction, illuminating and defining spaces and orchestrating movement (Bille and Sørensen 2007). Light can be contained within matter, such as brilliant objects that "could have been conceived as material manifestations of light, and of the social relationships and spiritual qualities which light embodies" (Saunders in Bille and Sørensen 2007: 268). Light is perceived and used differently in different cultural settings. In second millennium BCE southwest Asia and Egypt, light was often associated with gods and their actions.

The context of these offerings is telling—placed most commonly within structures, beneath or above floors. In some cases they may have functioned as foundation deposits, although this would have been the exception rather than the rule. It seems therefore more appropriate to view them as building deposits—intended to communicate with family ancestors or non-human entities. The repeated placing of the offerings under walls or floors, or on floors adjacent to walls, indicates that the essential message of the ritual remained the same—an offering connected to the building it resided within. Such offerings have been interpreted in various ways (Maeir et al. 2015: 428–429). One way explains them as offerings to ancestors or deities that perhaps contained aromatic oil, incense or some other attractive tribute. Another interpretation emphasizes the sociality between humans, spaces and objects and the transformative capacity of the objects themselves. In this light, once incorporated into the architecture the vessels became part of the structure that can manipulate non-human powers to strengthen and maintain positive relations between the inhabitants and the hosting building (Nakamura 2004: 18–19; Herva 2005: 218–224).

As was pointed out by Bunimovitz and Zimhoni (1993: 123–124), the absence of systematic burial of deposits in Late Bronze Age southern Levant implies that the placing of lamp-and-bowl offerings was an innovation.[6] The inspiration could thus have been Egyptian foundation rites that during the 19th and

---

the destruction layer of Tel Beth-Shemesh Level 3 were interpreted as a version of lamp-and-bowl deposit (Bunimovitz and Lederman 2016: 219 and figs. 6.79:6–8).

6 Contrary to Müller (2018: 188), other sorts of ritual deposition, with no clear pattern, are sporadically attested (e.g., the ivory assemblage from Tel Megiddo Stratum VIIA; Feldman 2009).

20th Dynasties included the placing of a few tools and pottery vessels together with amulets (such as scarabs), jewelry, and inscribed bricks (Weinstein 2001: 560). The Canaanite version was thus a localization of an Egyptian practice, the placing of foundation deposits, which involved reinterpretation of the procedure—breaking its inherent association with the laying of a foundation, and substituting utilitarian pottery vessels in place of prestige items, thus giving the ritual new meaning.[7] These lamp-and-bowl offerings serve as a clear marker of which regions were influenced most by Egyptian activity in Canaan and may likewise be taken as evidence of a specific ritual shared by communities within this interconnected colonial setting.

2   Conspicuous Consumption

Among the remains from Late Bronze Age Tel Lachish there is a unique feature: a relatively large assemblage of 373 bird bones, 256 of which were identified according to taxa (Croft 2004: 2257 table 33.2, 2305 table 33.25). "Relatively" since it comprises about 2 percent of the terrestrial faunal assemblage (ca. 19,550 bones, 18,200 of which are domesticated Bovidae—sheep, goats, and cattle); but "large" since an overview of the faunal remains from Late Bronze strata in the southern Levant shows that most sites yielded only a dozen bird bones and usually much fewer.[8]

The bird bones from Late Bronze Age Tel Lachish are clustered within two groups: (1) wild species, of which gamebirds (mainly chukar) constitute one third of the assemblage (86 bones); and (2) domesticated species—goose (72

---

[7] Other scholars argue against this association, based on the occurrence of foundation deposits across southwest Asia during the third and second millennia BCE (DePietro 2012: 111–118; Müller 2018: 186–188). Note, however, that other sorts of ritual deposition have no clear pattern and are documented sporadically (e.g., the ivory assemblage from Tel Megiddo Stratum VIIA; Feldman 2009). Nevertheless, even if the connection to the Egyptian heartland itself is not accepted, the distribution of the lamp-and-bowl deposits in Egyptian installations and in the local centers around them is of interest.

[8] These include Tell eṣ-Ṣafi (Lev-Tov 2012: 591–593), Tel Miqne Stratum VIII (Lev-Tov 2010: 94 table 7.2), Tel Aphek Strata XII–XI (Horwitz 2009: 528, 545 table 21.1, 548 table 21.7), Tel Michal Strata XVI–XV (Hellwing and Feig 1989: 242 and table 22.4), Tomb 1 at Tel Dothan (Lev-Tov and Maher 2001), Shiloh Stratum VI (Hellwing et al. 1993: Tables 15.3 and 15.5), Hesban Level 19 (Boessneck 1995: 134), Tel Yoqneam Strata XX–XIX (Horwitz et al. 2005: 399–400 and table v.26), Tel Qashish Strata VI–V (Horwitz 2003: 431–432 and table 37), Tel Hazor (Lev-Tov and McGeough 2007: 96 table 5–1), and the 'Mycenaean' tomb at Tel Dan (Horwitz 2002). The sole site that exhibits a different pattern is Tel Ḥalif (Seger et al. 1990: 26–27 and table 8), where 56 bird bones were collected from the Late Bronze layers, but no information is given regarding the various species.

bones) and pigeons and doves (27 bones) (Croft 2004: 2304). Of the domesticated group, pigeons and doves had been bred since the third millennium (the latest) (Gilbert and Shapiro 2014), and indeed the distribution of their bones at Lachish includes all periods studied, while goose bones appear in great numbers solely in the Late Bronze Age.

There is no doubt that the consumption of goose meat in Lachish commenced because of the intense interaction with the Nile Valley. The intimacy of the Egyptians with the Nile and its fauna is reflected in numerous representations of various waterfowl species, including the goose, as early as the Old Kingdom (see papers in Bailleul-LeSuer 2012). In this context, the goose (Anser sp.) was domesticated in a process whose exact date and span are debated but it seems safe to conclude that by the 18th Dynasty goose-keeping had already become routine (Boessneck 1986; Houlihan 1986: 54–65; Boessneck and von den Driesch 1992: 36–38; Houlihan 2001: 189–191; Albarella 2005: 252–253).[9] Besides its meat, the goose was valued for its fat, which constitutes almost half of the bird's mass, known by the 18th Dynasty (e.g., Papyrus Ebers) as an important ingredient in remedies against headaches, treatments for erectile dysfunction and for healing mosquito bites and other ailments (Nunn 2002: 72, 150, 161 and 199). Another feature of the goose was its down, used for stuffing cushions, etc.; though evidence for this comes from a much later period (Pliny the Elder, Naturalis Historia, X 27), this aspect of goose economy may well have been known earlier.[10]

The introduction of geese to Lachish may be understood in light of depictions on ivory plaques unearthed at nearby Tell el-Farʻah (S) and at Tel Megiddo to the north. Petrie's excavations at Tell el-Farʻah (S) yielded three ivory plaques (Figure 13). They depict three scenes: fowling and fishing in the marsh, a procession of servants carrying the hunted animals, and a banquet in which the ruler is shown sitting on a throne, accompanied by his spouse, courtiers, dancers and musicians. The uniqueness of these depictions, probably due to their Canaanite provenance, is the combination of marsh and banquet scenes, otherwise unknown in Egypt, where these motifs have a separate tradition of depiction (Lilyquist 1998: 26, 28; Ziffer 2005: 150). Another

---

9   It should be noted that while the goose had been documented in Mesopotamia as early as the Old Babylonian period (Akkadian *kurkû*), it is known as a wild fowl and there is no attestation to its domesticated nature (cf. CAD K: 651b–652b). It is only from the Neo-Assyrian period onward that sources mention domesticated waterfowl as tributes from vassal kingdoms and as exotic food for royal feasts.

10 Down stuffing was found in pillows from the KV 63 cache, dated to just after the reign of Tutankhamun, but the type of bird from which it came is unclear (Ertman et al. 2006: 25). Reference courtesy of Deborah Sweeney.

FIGURE 13   Ivory plaques from Tell el-Farʻah (S) (after Koch 2014: Figure 3)

FIGURE 14   Ivory plaque from Tel Megiddo Stratum VIIA (after Koch 2014: Figure 4)

depiction of a banquet with waterfowl is engraved on ivory plaques from Tel Megiddo Stratum VIIA (Figure 14). The plaques show three scenes: the ruler driving his chariot in a battle, a return from the battle, a procession of servants carrying geese, and the banquet itself. Its Levantine background is embedded in the narrative of the return from the battle scene, known from other Near Eastern banquet scenes (Ziffer 2005: 151–154).

The depiction of geese in the context of feasts is meaningful. A feast differs from mundane consumption of food by its communal and symbolic character. Seating order and timing, sequence and style of consumption, differentiated cuisine and tableware, and various other elements all reflect, structure, and maintain social relations, identities, and memories (Dietler and Hayden 2001; Dietler 2007; 2011: 180–187; DeFrance 2009: 141–143; Twiss 2012: 363–365 with literature; Hayden 2014; O'Connor 2015). As for the Levantine kinship-based society, textual sources describe the existence of cultic feasts, where social stratification was emphasized according to the portions of the distributed meat, the type of consumed animals and other factors (Lev-Tov and McGeough 2007). Zuckerman (2007) presented a comprehensive assemblage of data regarding possible feasting at Hazor, including the architecture of two ceremonial precincts, alongside pottery (mainly serving vessels), thousands of animal bones (mostly oxen and sheep) concentrated at specific loci, and prestige objects that were visibly consumed. Imported objects were highly appreciated, such decorated Aegean serving vessels—but only those that fit the traditional, ideological traits regarding the character of the feasting itself (Yasur-Landau 2005: 172–180).

In this context, and keeping in mind the absence of domesticated fowl from the southern Levant, the goose at Lachish (and perhaps also Megiddo) is to be understood as an extravagant, luxury food, desired by many but conspicuously consumed by few (DeFrance 2009: 127–128). It is therefore suggested that the local elite incorporated goose meat into their feast menus as a manifestation of their economic wherewithal and their connections with Egypt, and hence of their superior status in relation to their immediate environment.

3   The Equestrian Goddess

Another sphere of Egyptian influence in southwest Canaan is evident in the local cult of Lachish during the Late Bronze Age III. As summarized in Chapter 2, Lachish gradually developed during the Late Bronze Age I–IIB until its destruction. It was rebuilt shortly afterward (Level VI), and remains of this settlement were found across the mound covered by a thick destruction debris that was dated to the Late Bronze III.[11] The finds from this level provide a vivid image of the community and its entangled practices, which included Egyptian derived charms, domestic cult and culinary practice outlined above, and the incorporation of Egyptian derived architectural elements in a temple built on the mound and a nearby mudbrick granary (Ussishkin 2004: 215–315). Joined during the Late Bronze III was a burial in hieroglyph inscribed anthropoid clay coffins was practiced (Tufnell 1958: 131–132, 248–249 and pls. 45–46).[12] This custom is likewise known from Deir el-Balaḥ (Lipton 2010)—a colonial hub— and Tell el-Farʿah (S) (Petrie 1930: 6–9, Pls. XIX, XXIV), whose material remains

---

11   Tufnell 1958: 49–61; Ussishkin 2004: 62–64, 70–71, 215–281, 297–305, 352–361, 624–631, 1051–1055, 1584–1588; Weissbein et al. 2016.
12   Tufnell et al. 1958: 131–132, 248–249 and pls. 45–46; Ussishkin 2004: 64.

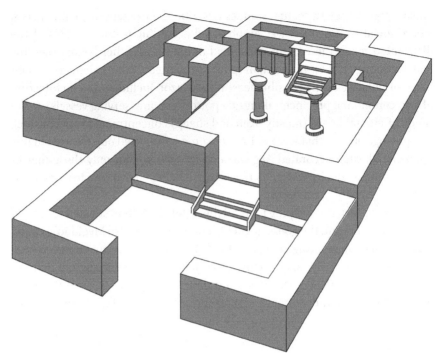

FIGURE 15   Plan of the "Acropolis Temple", Tel Lachish Level VI (after Ussishkin 2004: 220 fig. 6.4)

feature a marked Egyptian influence, and from Tel Beth-Shean (Oren 1973: 101–150)—the main Egyptian foothold in northern Canaan, Tel Shadud, in the center of the Jezreel Valley (Van den Brink et al. 2017), and possibly also from Pella/Ṭabaqat Faḥl (Yassine 1975: 60 and n. 11, 62). As previously mentioned, Braunstein's systematic analysis of the burial practices at Tell el-Farʻah (S) concluded that such burials were the result of local incorporation and adaptation of Egyptian-style artifacts into the local tradition.

The inhabitants of the new Lachish did not rebuild the traditional cult site at the foot of the mound (the Fosse Temple) but rather founded their own temples, on the top of the mound. In the one that was published, a complex comingling of local and Egyptian features can be observed. The temple was laid out according to local conventions (Figure 15), and ornamented with architectural details typical of Egyptian aesthetics, such as blue-colored plaster walls and octagonal pillar bases (Ussishkin 2004: 215–281).

Due to looting of the temple before its destruction, no firm conclusion regarding the local cult can be drawn; yet scholars have suggested some of its meager finds as reflect Egyptian influence, these include two objects depicting

FIGURE 16
Golden foil, the "Acropolis Temple", Tel Lachish Level VI (after Schroer 2011: 313 no. 869)

images of deities. The first is a stone slab incised with multiple lines, some joined together to form an anthropomorphic male figure wearing a tall crown with a streamer and waving a spear with both hands, which has been interpreted as the figure of a storm god, perhaps Ba'al (Cornelius 1994: 163; Lipiński 1996: 260). The second is a golden foil depicting a naked anthropomorphic female (Figure 16) wearing an elaborate crown, which includes horns and feathers, who is holding lotus flowers in both hands and standing on a horse with a crown of long feathers. This image embodies, in my opinion, a long bidirectional process of Egyptian-Canaanite cultural interaction.

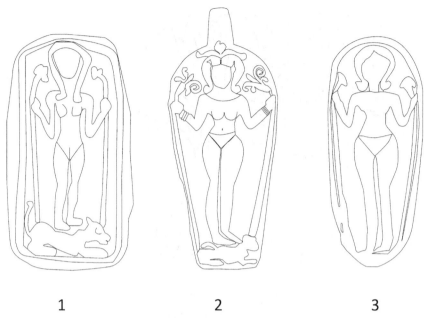

FIGURE 17 Depictions of naked goddesses grasping flowers—no. 1: Clay plaque, Tel Ḥarasim Stratum V (after Schroer 2011: 307 no. 863); no. 2: Bronze plaque, Akko, "The Persian Garden" (after Ben-Arieh and Edelstein 1977: pl. 6.2); no. 3: Clay plaque, Tel Batash Stratum VIIB (after Panitz-Cohen and Mazar 2006: 252 and photo 104)

The stance of the figure, her attributes and the horse are typical of depictions of goddesses: the frontal nakedness of the figure and her pose grasping flowers resemble local goddess depictions, while the equestrian aspect associates her with Egyptian depictions of Astarte (Clamer 2004: 1314–1320; Cornelius 2004: 51; Schroer 2011: 312). Frontal depictions of a naked goddess wearing a Hathor wig and holding flowers in her hands were popular in the southern Levant during the Late Bronze II, especially in southwest Canaan (Figure 17). They derive from north-Levantine–Anatolian depictions of a naked goddess with a tall crown, grasping horned animals (Cornelius 2004: 56–57 with previous literature).[13] The earliest appearance of such depiction in southern Levant is dated to the Late Bronze IIA: A bronze plaque found at a tomb located in the present-day Acre (Fig. 17:2) depicts a figure holding long-stemmed flowers and standing atop a lion (Ben-Arieh and Edelstein 1977: 29–30 and pl. VI: 1–2). Another example dating to the Late Bronze IIA is a clay plaque from Tel Batash Stratum VIIB (Fig. 17:3), depicting a similar figure without the lion

---

13 Frontal depictions of naked female figures are known from second millennium BCE Egypt (Budin 2015), yet their relations to Middle Bronze Age Levantine depictions is not clear.

FIGURE 18   Stele of Qeh (British Museum EA 191)
© TRUSTEES OF THE BRITISH MUSEUM

pedestal (Panitz-Cohen and Mazar 2006: 251–252 and Photo 104). Both specimens are firmly dated to Late Bronze Age IIA based on associated pottery and accompanying glyptic items bearing the names of Amenhotep III and Tiye. A similar posture is found on a plaque from a contemporaneous context at Tel Beth-Shemesh Level 9, where a male-looking anthropomorphic figure is depicted facing right while grasping long-stemmed lotus flowers (Ziffer et al. 2009).

Frontal depictions of a naked goddess holding attributes in her hands were appropriated in Egypt for a goddess called *qdš(t)* (Figure 18). Sporadically mentioned in Egyptian textual sources as early as the days of Amenhotep III, these images of *qdš(t)* are all dated (at the earliest) to the 19th Dynasty and are restricted to two regions—Memphis and the workers' colony at Deir el-Medina; they are not associated with royal ideology (Tazawa 2009: 96–101, 153, 163–167). Therefore, it is plausible to suggest a scenario of cultural transmission, in which the adaptation of a north-Levantine-Anatolian motif became common in the southern Levant during the 14th–13th centuries BCE, from where it subsequently diffused into Egypt during the 13th century BCE via intercultural discourse.

FIGURE 19   Depictions of Astarte from Egypt—no. 1: Stone stela, Tell el-Burg (after Hoffmeier and Kitchen 2007: 129 fig. 1b); no. 2: Stone stela, Buhen (after Bibel+Orient Datenbank Online, http://www.bible-orient-museum.ch/bodo/details.php?bomid=4434, accessed 15 February 2016); no. 3: Stone stela, Ramesseum (after Leclant 1960: Fig. 10)

On other side of the coin is the equestrian nature of the figure depicted on the golden foil.[14] Goddesses with horses are only known from New Kingdom Egyptian iconography—in various forms of Astarte associated with horses (Figure 19). The earliest documented attestation of an equestrian Astarte in Egypt is probably the stele from Tell el-Borg on the eastern frontier, dating to the mid-18th Dynasty (Hoffmeier and Kitchen 2007). Her worship, most probably as tutelar deity of horse trainers, spread across royal and military contexts during the later parts of the New Kingdom (Wilson-Wright 2016: 27–61). It seems, therefore, that this equestrian aspect of female deity appeared in the southern Levant due to Egyptian royal propaganda, or through interaction among individuals—horse trainers or military elite—in the opposite direction of transmission to the naked goddess some 100 years earlier.

Summing up the above, the figure depicted on the golden foil from Lachish can either be described as an indigenous naked goddess-type enthroned with some Egyptian-derived attributes associated with Astarte or as Astarte adapted to local conventions for depicting a goddess. The absence of written sources impedes an answer. In any case, the entanglement of these various pictorial components reflects centuries-old intercultural interaction that almost certainly included the adoption of various cultic traditions. This Levantine image of an equestrian deity—standing above rather than riding the horse—was commonly depicted on amulets centuries after the withdrawal of Egypt from

---

14   The second occurrence of such a combination is depicted in an unprovenanced mold from Tel Qarnayim, near Tel Beth-Shean, where the naked goddess is depicted standing above a horse and accompanied by two smaller anthropomorphic figures (Ben-Arieh 1983).

the region (below, Chapter 8), thus attesting to its thorough assimilation into the local imagery.

4 Range of Reactions

The discussion above reveals the protectorate encounters between the locals and the wider colonial network that shaped major aspects of the local life: the inclusion of Egyptian amulets, translation of goddesses, the development of a colonial domestic cult, conspicuous consumption of waterfowl, construction according to Egyptian ground plans, burial in anthropoids coffins, and the acceptance of divine images.

The colonial experience continuously fluctuates between a range of reactions to the Other, from attraction to repulsion. Following Bhabha (1994), the complexity of the relationship between the colonizer and the colonized can be defined as ambivalent because, as summarized by Ashcroft et al. (2013: 10), "the colonized subject is never simply and completely opposed to the colonizer. Rather than assuming that some colonized subjects are 'complicit' and some 'resistant,' ambivalence suggests that complicity and resistance exist in a fluctuating relation within the colonial subject. Ambivalence also characterizes the way in which colonial discourse relates to the colonized subject, for it may be both exploitative and nurturing, or represent itself as nurturing, at the same time."

A range of reactions can be characterized as resistance. Resistance can lead to violent uprising. Clearly, a large-scale revolt was dangerous. If it fails, a revolt might bring death upon the conspirators and a more repressive regime for those who remain. There were many attempts at active resistance, as the campaigns led by Seti I, Ramesses II and Merneptah attest. The cases of Gezer and Ashkelon are noteworthy, but there was undoubtedly more widespread passive resistance. Passive resistance may materialize in everyday life as the cohesion of local traditions and the elaboration of contacts with alternative modes of interactions than those with the hegemonic center (Sharp 2009: 74–75, 128; Glatz 2013: 23–26, 29–43; Smith 2013: 87–94; González-Ruibal 2014: 16–22 with literature).

The other side of the spectrum is attraction. Some studies interpreted attraction as the locals' fascination with Egyptian culture. The theoretical framework from which this interpretation emerged is center–periphery, arguing that the political center influences its periphery, and thus the common model shows how a peripheral elite would emulate the culture of the center (Millet 1990). In the case of the southern Levant and Egypt (Higginbotham 1996, 2000; Koch

2014), the mechanisms that exposed the locals to the Egyptian culture were: (1) the policy initiated by Thutmose III that children of Canaanite rulers would be raised and educated in Egypt (e.g., EA 296); (2) service of Canaanites in the Egyptian administration; and (3) participation of Canaanite rulers in festivals held in the Egyptian court. There is no doubt that such a long stay in Egypt, or even the shortest visit, was a remarkable experience, remembered for many years—an experience that might have initiated a change in behavior, perhaps by objects that were taken from Egypt and thus served as containers of these memories.

Other sorts of agents probably brought to some bottom–up changes. Such as the Canaanite scribes who were active in the Amarna correspondence (Vita 2015) and in the hieratic-based administration (Sweeney 2004: 1615 with earlier literature), which produced the relatively large assemblage of early-Alphabetic inscriptions (Finkelstein and Sass 2013; Sass et al. 2015). Some, if not all, were trained in colonial hubs, such as the estate at Tel Aphek Stratum XII—where grain was stored, wine was produced, and scribes were educated. Each of the encounters exposed the agents to various ideas that could have been appropriated and transmitted by them to their social circles; a major transmitter of ideas of that period was the Mesopotamian scribal curriculum, which included repeated coping of mythic texts, god-lists and lexicons (Smith 2010: 45–48 with literature).

Recent years have seen the abandonment of terms related to acculturation, such as Hellenization, Romanization, and here—Egyptianization. The main problem being that center–periphery models presuppose "imperial" cultural superiority and "provincial" cultural inferiority in a macro-level picture that blurs particularities and disguises the importance of agency of the members of societies in what is called a periphery (Dietler 1997: 296–297 with earlier literature; 2005: 55–61; 2009: 27–28; Van Dommelen 1998: 20–24 with literature; Alcock 2005: 323–327; Smith 2013: 94–97).[15] They became passive receptors of others' interest, "while in reality the agency of members of peripheral societies should be regarded as decisive for the efficacy of relations between a so-called center and a periphery" (Maran 2011: 283). Moreover, and related to the concept of passive resistance, appropriation can sometimes be an act of usurpation, as it reflects the ways in which the dominated or colonized culture can use the tools of the dominant discourse to resist its political or cultural control (Ashcroft et al. 2004: 58–76).

---

15 See the papers in *Archaeological Dialogues* 21 (2014) on the attempt to resurrect the term Romanization (Versluys 2014) and its critics (Hingley 2014; Hodos 2014; Van Dommelen 2014a; Woolf 2014).

In addition, the locals interacted with agents from diverse background that held various functions. Major players were those acting under the direct auspice of the Egyptian court, who were based in the imperial hubs, primarily Tell el-Ajjul and Gaza: officials, soldiers, merchants, artisans, and priests. In the beginning of the period, the majority of these were most likely from Upper Egypt, the hub of the 18th Dynasty, and thus would have stood out in the southwest Canaanite landscape. Imperial agents with Canaanite names are known by the mid-18th Dynasty, indicating the integration of personnel from the Delta and, perhaps from the southern Levant.[16] They were able to communicate with the locals more easily and hence were valued as mediators, while at the same time functioned as channels through which Canaanite ideas spread to Egyptian audience.

Centuries of interaction and integration of southwest Canaan and Egypt created multiple meeting points located in the Egyptian heartland, in the Egyptian centers in southwest Canaan and in the neighboring local centers. These contact zones can be seen as "social spaces," where, in the words of Pratt (2008: 7), "disparate cultures meet, clash and grapple with each other, often in highly asymmetrical relations of dominance and subordination." The asymmetrical relations clearly led to the flow of Egyptian practices into the Canaanite milieu, yet these were carefully curated and adapted while simultaneously, some local customs spread into the Egyptian centers in Canaan. Such reciprocal influence can be described transculturalism, a term originally coined to denote the active appropriation of practices originating in the intrusive state by the colonized entity (Ashcroft et al. 2013: 213–214), nowadays used to emphasize multivocal cultural discourse.[17]

Many of these changes include the introduction of imported objects into the local context. Those objects—often well-executed and decorated with elaborate images—had a transformative capacity that sparked a process of translation according to existing social structures (Van Dommelen and Rowlands 2012). The appropriation thus involves the localization of something foreign

---

16 See also Bunimovitz (2019: 273–274) and see, for example, Papyrus Anastasi III (6:1–5), in which Gaza is mentioned as the place of residence of a number of officials with Canaanite names active along the "Ways of Horus" (Morris 2005: 478–486).

17 Alternative terms found in many publications dealing with cultural exchange are *hybridity* and *creolization*, describing the combination of two forms to create a third form. While useful, both borrowings have been criticized. Hybridity depends on the idea of purity of cultures or society, an ideological means embedded in racial categories of the past (Young 2005: 21–27; Silliman 2015). But see recent reservations by Liebmann (2015). Creolization is closely connected to language changes in a colonial situation, and more specifically under the historical peculiarities of the Caribbean archipelago (Palmié 2006).

that requires the agents to go beyond rules and structures and thus to modify their practices and eventually a portion of their own social identity (Hitchcock 2011: 273–276; Panagiotopoulos 2011: 36; 2013; Knapp 2012: 32–34; Hitchcock and Maeir 2013: 51–59). Such a process would include the intellectual appropriation of an object and its entanglement with existing objects according to local practice (Dietler 1997, 2010; Stockhammer 2013). If appropriation succeeds, the next-generation product would be a modified version of the imported artifact. In that case, one would talk about fusion or synergy, a description of the process of creating a new object that includes elements from all predecessors (Ashcroft et al. 2013: 210).

To sum-up, the interconnectedness of the colonial network, the participation of agents of Canaanite background in various roles in the network, and the constant exposure of Canaanites and Egyptians to each other all shaped the local society, its structure and its practices, in order to fit the colonial arena. These innovations were selectively picked and localized to fit local norms and needs. Their new owners used them in structuring their perception of the colonial setting, in locating their place in it, and in their acquisition of social status.

CHAPTER 5

Collapse

The reign of the last rulers of the 19th Dynasty was rife with internal problems (Dodson 2010), but Egypt's hold on Canaan apparently remained stable (Gilmour and Kitchen 2012; Kahn 2012: 263–266). Unknown circumstances led to the rise of Setnakhte, the founder of the 20th Dynasty, who reigned for three or four years. He was succeeded by Ramesses III (1195–1164 BCE), who restored Egypt's military might, strengthened the power of the central authority over the kingdom, and launched the construction of monumental projects (Cline and O'Connor 2012). Best known is his mortuary temple with its reliefs and inscriptions commemorating his wars against his enemies, including the "Sea Peoples,"[1] which has received much attention in scholarship (Kitchen 2012). Ramesses III ruled for 32 years before what may have been his assassination in a 'harem conspiracy' and the coronation of his son, who became known as Ramesses IV. Papyrus Harris I, a detailed description of Ramesses III's achievements, written during the reign of Ramesses IV (probably in order to legitimize it) (Peden 1994: 211), is the prime source for the history of the period. Ramesses IV was the first of a line of rulers, all sons and grandsons of Ramesses III who each ruled for a short period of time, left a few construction projects, and are known from a limited number of sources (Snape 2012: 410–416).

The last of Ramesses III's sons, Ramesses VIII, died in the second year of his reign (ca. 1137 BCE) and was succeeded by Ramesses IX. During his 18 years as a king, Ramesses IX conducted a military campaign against *shasu* in the Eastern Desert (Peden 1994: 73–76) and launched several construction projects, but it was apparently during those same years that Egyptian rule in Upper Nubia was terminated (Spencer et al. 2012). Following the brief reign of Ramesses X, Ramesses XI ascended to the throne and ruled for a relatively long period (ca. 1115–1086 BCE)[2] known for internal problems and competition among high officials who divided the kingdom into several sub-territories. Upon his death, the division of Egypt was cemented with the coronation of

---

1   For the term "Sea Peoples," see Killebrew and Lehmann (2013: 1 n. 1).
2   There is disagreement among Egyptologists regarding the chronology of Ramesses IX, Ramesses X and Ramesses XI. The majority follow the traditional "dynastic" order and other suggesting co-regencies or overlaps of rival rulers; for arguments favoring the former, see Schneider (2010b: 396–397).

two former officials (and possibly Ramesses XI's sons-in-law)—Smendes (Nesubanebjet) in Tanis and Harihor in Thebes (Snape 2012: 425–437). There are indications that the Egyptian court maintained its connections with Western Asia. Inscriptions by Tiglath-pileser I (ca. 1114–1076 BCE) and Ashur-bel-kala (ca. 1074/3–1056 BCE) documented gifts received from Egyptian kings, each including a crocodile and an ape (Grayson 2002: 99–105, A.o.89.7; Frahm 2009: 28–30). Synchronized with the Egyptian chronology, it seems that these texts refer to Ramesses XI and Smendes (Schneider 2010b: 400–401).

Despite these connections, the Egyptian court was unable to maintain its control over Canaan itself. It is currently agreed that the Egyptian presence in the southern Levant was stable during the days of Ramesses III and Ramesses IV, attested in written sources and the distribution of Egyptian-style objects (Brandl 2004; Finkelstein 2007: 517–518). Beyond that line, the situation becomes elusive. Egyptian sources from the days of the latter Ramesside rulers do not mention Canaan or any of its toponyms. The distribution of Egyptian royal names from the southern Levant greatly declines: Ramesses V is known from a bracelet found at Timna (Schulman 1988); Ramesses VI, the last ruler to be mentioned at Serabit el-Khadim (Gardiner et al. 1955: 192, nos. 290–293), is commemorated on a bronze pedestal of a statue found at Tel Megiddo (Breasted 1948) that should probably be attributed to Stratum VIIA (Singer 1988–1989: 106–107).[3] Beyond the royal name corpus, distribution of Egyptian-style objects declined greatly during the Levantine Iron Age I, and became limited to amulets (discussed in the following chapters) and imported containers (such as storage jars) found in harbor sites such as Tel Dor and Tel Qasile (Ben-Dor Evian 2011: 99–113; Waiman-Barak et al. 2014; Gilboa 2015).

It can be concluded that the collapse of the Egyptian colonial network in Canaan took place sometime during the second half of the 12th century BCE. Clearly, when troubles became more frequent, the ability of the Egyptian court to control its holdings weakened and Canaan would have been the first to be abandoned. The collapse could have been a single event or, more likely, a process. A plausible scenario would be that the weakness of the Egyptian court during the decades of the latter Ramessides might have prevented the maintenance of the Egyptian centers in Canaan and the renewal of centers that were destroyed while other Egyptian garrisons became autonomous; its local clients were left with no protection and were hit by internal clashes (compare the many violent episodes mentioned in the Amarna correspondence), such

---

3 The last royal name from the southern Levant is that of Ramesses IX, seen on a scaraboid found by Macalister at Tel Gezer in what appears to be an Iron Age II context (Keel 2013a: 214–215, no. 103).

as attacks by 'apiru bandits, shasu raiders, pirates along the coast, and intraregional rivalry among competing local groups (Millek 2017).

From the southwest Canaanite point of view, the twilight of the colonial network is characterized by reconfigurations of the settlement pattern, alternations in animal-based economy, and various innovations in production and practice, such as pottery forms and decoration, figurines and architectural elements—most of which originated in coastal regions of the eastern Mediterranean. The following chapters will deal with these transformations in light of the disintegration of the Egyptian network and its impact on the local society in these two centuries. But before that, a brief discussion regarding the common historical reconstruction of the same period is needed.

1 Questioning the Philistine Paradigm

Wedged between two periods of extensive record keeping—the Late Bronze Age with its myriad archives, inscriptions and associated pictorial depictions, and the Iron Age II, with similar types of records supplemented by assumed contemporaneous narratives embedded in the Hebrew Bible—the archaeology of the Levant bridged the Iron Age I gap by extrapolating information described in these early or later sources and by deducing the meaning of the changes observed in the material remains.

For more than a century (Macalister 1914), scholars entangled the picture that emerged from biblical narratives depicting the struggle between the Philistines and the Israelites with their understanding of Egyptian sources from the days of Ramesses III and Ramesses IV. They interpreted the commemorative inscriptions and reliefs from the mortuary temple of Ramesses III that describe his wars against the Philistines (among other Sea Peoples and additional enemies) as evidence of mass migration on land and sea that threatened Egypt's hegemony in Canaan and combined it with the description in Papyrus Harris I regarding the forced settlement of Sea Peoples by Ramesses III. They also read Egyptian literary texts (like the Tale of Wenamun) which depict the settlement of the Sea Peoples along the Levantine coast in the 11th century BCE. In this context, the discovery of Aegean-style pottery and other innovations from Iron Age I southwest Canaan was logically associated with Philistine settlement. The historical conclusion had been that the Sea Peoples colonized the southwestern coast of Canaan and were the destructive force that vanquished the Canaanite centers and brought about the collapse of the Egyptian network (Stager 2006; Ussishkin 2007: 603–604). Over the years this historical interpretation became a paradigm. And yet we must ask a methodological question: What evidence supports ascribing the innovations in Iron Age I southwest Canaan to the settlement of groups that have been clustered under the heading "Sea Peoples"?

The Gordian knot between the Philistines and the Aegean has been present ever since early scholarship on the Philistines. Based on the information from the Hebrew Bible about their connection to Crete—their origin from Caphtor (Amos 9:7) and their relation to the Cherethites (Ezekiel 25:16)—the Philistines and other groups mentioned in the Egyptian sources were long ago associated with groups known from the Homeric literature (Dothan and Dothan 1992: 8–9; Sharon 2001: 557–560 with literature). Consequently, it was further argued that the appearance of these groups in the Levant and Egypt should be understood as a side effect of the fall of Troy that led to migrations and displacement of peoples from one region to the other. The ultimate variant of this reconstruction was masterfully presented by Maspero (1875): domino-like migration waves of dislocated groups that started with the Illyrians in northern Europe and ended with the spread of the "Sea Peoples" from the Aegean and Western Anatolia across the eastern Mediterranean, their struggle with Egypt and eventually the settlement of the Philistines in southwest Canaan.

The impact of this approach on the formation of the archaeology of the Philistines was immediate. Back then, archaeologists shared a similar *Kulturgeschichte* mindset that understood changes in material records as attesting to population turnover (Silberman 1998; Trigger 2006: 211–313). Hence the appearance of pottery known from a specific region in a remote place was interpreted as evidence for the presence of people coming from the same specific region. It is best exemplified in the work of W.M. Flinders Petrie at the end of the 19th century, who attributed Aegean vessels unearthed in Egypt to "Graeco-Libyan" waves of immigration and conquest (Petrie 1890: 274), in the framework of his general conception of war of races, which also served him in his interpretation of the findings of his excavations in Palestine (Silberman 1999: 70–75). It is therefore understood why the definition of the Bichrome Ware of the Iron Age I as a local version of Aegean-style vessels was followed by its interpretation as reflecting the settlement of Philistines (Thiersch 1908) and how easily it was woven into the grand historical narrative that was established decades earlier (Macalister 1914).

Following this historical scenario, Dothan (1958, 1967, 1982) articulated a whole set of cultural and technological innovations as "Philistine material culture" to include a list of "foreign," mostly Aegean-style, imports and innovations that appeared in southwest Canaan during the Iron Age I (cf. Wright 1966).[4]

---

4 Prominent among the few scholars who doubted this reconstruction was Brug (1985), who claimed that the material remains in southwest Canaan during the Iron Age I was largely a

This assemblage was updated with the discovery of Monochrome Aegean-style vessels manufactured locally in Tel Ashdod (Asaro et al. 1971; Dothan 1971), and subsequently at Tel Miqne and Ashkelon as well. These assemblages were dated to the first half of the 12th century BCE and were associated with the earliest Philistine settlers while the Bichrome Ware was interpreted as the outcome of later interaction between those settlers and the Canaanite population among whom they settled (Iakovidis 1979: 460–461; Mazar 1985c; Stager 1985: 62*). Subsequently, the ethnic labeling of the Bichrome Ware was challenged by Bunimovitz (1990: 212–213), who suggested understanding it as a regional phenomenon of "luxury tableware for the entire heterogeneous population" of the region.

Two alternative approaches accepted the common assumption of Aegean migration to southwest Canaan in the 12th century BCE but proposed a different understanding of the Philistines. Both Drews (1998, 2000) and Sharon (2001) pointed to flaws in the accepted reconstruction of massive Philistine migration and suggested different scenarios: According to Drews (1998: 49–61; 2000: 178), the Philistines were not Aegean but of nomadic origin who settled in Canaan and its vicinity, putting Egyptian interests at risk. Drews suggested that these settlers rejected the name Canaan, which was associated with the Egyptians, and preferred a new autochthonous identity named Philistine. According to Sharon (2001: 600–601), the Sea People Philistines documented in the Egyptian sources were "a phenomenon only one generation long" with no connection to the inhabitants of southwest Canaan during the Iron Age I. These communities, both locals and descendants of Aegean settlers, adopted this group identity as part of the restructuring of the society following the end of the Egyptian hegemony and the collapse of the previous social structure.

Contrary to these approaches, other scholars (Bauer 1998; 2014; Sherratt 1998, 2003) have argued against the migratory explanation for the appearance the Iron I innovations altogether and suggest an economy-based reconstruction. They emphasize the continuity in local traditions, the diversity of the innovations (not monolithically Aegean or Cypriot), and the reorientation of interregional interactions following destruction of palatial centers and the rise of non-palatial agents. They point to the evidence from other areas of the Mediterranean coast (where similar Aegean-style vessels were found) that rule out migratory scenarios, and the difficulty of associating certain vessels with specific groups (the "Pots and People" problem). According to this approach,

---

continuation of the culture from the Late Bronze Age with limited Cypriot influence. Hence he proposed that the settlement of the Sea Peoples was a takeover by a military elite of the local population, like the "Vikings" who took over extensive areas of Europe in the Middle Ages.

Aegean-style vessels appeared in all the areas that were connected by a far-reaching commercial network based mainly on the metal trade, which emerged as a result of the adoption by the local population of original imported vessels. It was the compartmentalized nature of this network that threatened the great powers, which sought to maintain their control over the copper trade, and was the background to their struggles with members of this network that were condemned as "Sea Peoples."

The main flaw in this approach was that it overlooked the peculiarities in the region and the concentration of innovations, some with no parallels in other parts of the Levant (Yasur-Landau 2002: 314–315). Nonetheless it brought scholars' attention to the methodological problems in the traditional narrative, the need to contextualize southwest Canaan within the broader changes in the eastern Mediterranean, and the need to adopt a nuanced, theory-based approach in the interpretation of the material remains. Indeed, current mainstream Philistine scholarship applies more refined approaches of archaeology of migration and intercultural encounters (Yasur-Landau 2007, 2010a; 2012a; Hitchcock 2011; Hitchcock and Maeir 2013; Stockhammer 2013; Cline 2014; Mazow 2014; Faust 2015; Maeir and Hitchcock 2017a) and focuses more on the diverse origins, distribution, and development of the innovations (Maeir and Hitchcock 2011; 2017b; Hitchcock and Maeir 2013; 2016a; Maeir et al. 2013; Davis et al. 2015; Ben-Dor Evian 2017a) and the changes in the domestic sphere and behavioral patterns (Killebrew 2005; Yasur-Landau 2005; 2011; Ben-Shlomo et al. 2008).

While these studies sharpened debate over the complexities of the archaeological findings and the continuity of local culture (and see the next chapter), their explanation for the appearance of the foreign traits as the result of migration(s) has seen some critics (Middleton 2015). Moreover, they still continue to identify the immigrants as the "Sea Peoples" based on the "factual" foundation accepted since the dawn of the research—the same written sources from Egypt and the biblical narratives, despite the great leaps achieved in these two fields in the many years that have passed since the masterpieces of Maspero, Macalister, and Dothan.

2 In Search of the Early Philistines

The argument that the Philistines settled in southwest Canaan during the Iron Age I is based on sources known since the early stages of scholarship, yet it should be reconsidered in light of the following:

1) It has been commonly assumed that the inscriptions and reliefs from the mortuary temple at Medinet Habu depict the efforts of Ramesses III to block a great and coordinated Sea Peoples attack by mass population on land and battle ships at sea in the eastern Delta (Weinstein 2012: 161–164; Cline 2014: 6; Hoffmeier 2018). A recent study by Ben-Dor Evian (2016) refutes this scenario and argued that there were two battles and each should be treated individually: One was a land battle during the fifth year of Ramesses III, who fought against the Philistines and the Sikila somewhere in the northern Levant, and the other was a naval battle that took place circa three years later near the Nile Delta, in which several groups of warriors on battle ships tried to raid the Egyptian coast. It is noteworthy that in both scenarios, neither Canaan nor any of its locales are mentioned at all.

2) Papyrus Harris I (76: 7–9) has often been referred to as allegedly documenting the settlement of the "Sea Peoples" in Egyptian strongholds by Ramesses III following the battle described at Medinet Habu (following Alt 1944: 15–20). It goes as follows (trans. by Ben-Dor Evian 2017a: 270):

> I extended all the frontiers of Egypt. I felled the aggressors—they were in their lands. I slew the Danuna [that came] from their isles. The Sikila and the Philistines were made into ashes. Sherden and Weshesh of the sea they were made non-existent, captured at one time, brought as captives to Egypt like the sand of the shore. I settled them in strongholds bound in my name.

According to the text, the Danuna were slain, the Sikila and the Philistines were made into ashes, and the Sherden and Weshesh were brought as captives to Egypt and settled in strongholds. The sentence "I settled them in strongholds bound in my name" may not actually refer at all to the Philistines. But even if one considers the sentence as concluding the entire episode, there is no indication that the strongholds were in Canaan since (1) the text refers specifically to Egypt, and (2) the Egyptian practice was to settle such prisoners in Egypt itself (Finkelstein 1995: 227; Morris 2005: 731–735; Kahn 2011b: 2–3; Ben-Dor Evian 2017a: 270).[5]

3) The Onomasticon of Amenemope (Gardiner 1947) is a toponym list that mentions (no. 262) Ashkelon, (263) Ashdod and (264) Gaza, (265–267) three unclear toponyms, (268) Sherden, (269) SKL, and (270) Philistines.

---

5 Significantly, the inclusion of the Sherden in this text raises doubts regarding its historicity, because this group is referred to in the Medinet Habu records as operating in the service of Ramesses III and not among his enemies (Emanuel 2013: 16 with literature).

It is sometimes used in historical reconstructions of the 12th century BCE as evidence for Philistine presence in southwest Canaan, although the presence of several names between the southwest Canaanite coastal towns and the Philistines is telling and excludes any association between them.[6]

4) Biblical references to Philistines frequently locate them in southwest Canaan (e.g., Josh 13:3). Pre- and early monarchic narratives referring to their political system, warrior aspect, and even specific historical events were sometimes taken as reflecting Iron Age I reality (Stager 2006; Millard 2009; Zorn 2010; Singer 2013b). Yet these texts are the product of scribes who operated in much later periods. Some stories might preserve memories from the late 10th or 9th centuries BCE, but since they reflect centuries-long processes of transmission and redaction, to say nothing of creative supplements added by later scribes, it is difficult to sift the historical kernel from the stories in their final form.[7]

It is clear, therefore, that there is no indication of the settlement of the Philistines in southwest Canaan during the Iron Age I. The identification of the innovations in the region as the materialization of Philistine settlement derives from scholarly interpretation of Egyptian sources based on the biblical placement of the Philistines in the region. Yet there is a gap of some two centuries between these two clusters of sources and with no direct, contemporaneous evidence this remains an unreliable scholarly speculation.

In search of the early Philistines, the concrete information about their identity is telling, albeit rather limited:

1) The term "Philistine" has been associated with the Aegean ever since Étienne Fourmont suggested comparing the name with Homer's πελασγοί (Dothan and Dothan 1992: 9–10). A recent proposal by Schneider (2012: 570) suggests that the name derives from the Mycenaean πλώϝιστοι, "seafarers, sailors," suggesting a semantic evolution similar to Old West Norse vikinger, which began as "maritime expedition" and "maritime warrior" and eventually gained an ethnic meaning.

---

6 The SKL are localized at Dor as per the Tale of Wenamun that was dated, based on its language and embedded ideology, to the late 21st or the early 22nd Dynasty (Helck 1986; Sass 2002; Schipper 2005: 315–319).

7 There is an enormous amount of scholarship dealing with the Philistine narratives in the Hebrew Bible. For the Samson stories (Jud 13–16), see summaries in Guillaume (2004: 155–159 with earlier bibliography) and Römer (2005: 138 and further bibliography in n. 66). For the stories in the Book of Samuel see diverse opinions by Na'aman (1996, 2002a, 2010a), Finkelstein (2002b), Van Seters (2009), Sergi (2015a), and Koch (2020).

2) Another detail about the Philistines is found at Medinet Habu in the inscription dealing with the events of Ramesses III's fifth regnal year, where they are described as *ṯhr*, a Semitic loanword denoting well-trained, paid men in the service of the courts of Hatti and Egypt (Ben-Dor Evian 2015).
3) In terms of pictorial representations, the Medinet Habu reliefs depict "Philistine" warriors wearing feathered- or, better to say reed-cap (Ben-Dor Evian 2016: 159 n. 40). They are either manning boats decorated with zoomorphic head devices that resemble Late Helladic portrayals of vessels adorned with sea-monster heads (Yasur-Landau 2010b) or in land battles, equipped with Aegean- and Anatolian-style weaponry and means of transportation (Yasur-Landau 2012b).

The Philistine headgear as depicted at Medinet Habu might suggest a wider connection: warriors wearing such a headgear are shown fighting in his service in the depiction of Ramesses III's Nubian campaign, and other variants of similar headgear are found in several depictions from the southern Levant, Cyprus and the Aegean (Yasur-Landau 2013; Emanuel 2015). Assuming that all of these non-Egyptian representations do depict the same headgear and that all who possessed such headgear can be grouped under similar social contexts (and not, for example, according to their specific taste in choosing a headgear), they can be clustered into four groups according to their setting: (1) isolated figures; (2) maritime scenes, such as the naval battle at Medinet Habu and portrayals of figures on several pottery vessels from the Aegean; (3) terrestrial battles at Medinet Habu, against and in the service of Ramesses III; and (4) engraved in a conspicuous scene decorating a scarab embedded in a gold ring found in an affluent Late Bronze III tomb at Tell el-Farʿah (S), a figure wearing similar headgear is seen receiving a large ʿnḫ from Amun-Re (Figure 20:1) in a setting otherwise reserved for royal figures (Figure 20: 2–4) (Keel and Uehlinger 1998: 110).

To sum up, "Philistine" seems to have been a designation given to a group or groups that might have originated in the Aegean or western Anatolia and were well-trained warriors fighting against Egypt on sea and land during the early 12th century BCE. They were similar to other warrior bands with an Aegean and Anatolian background that were active throughout the eastern Mediterranean during the final centuries of the second millennium BCE and especially during and after the disintegration of Hatti (Gilan 2013). Some were pirates (Hitchcock and Maeir 2014, 2016b) and some were mercenaries, like other warrior bands that fought in the service of Late Bronze Age polities. Some of these individuals even became propertied and achieved high social status, such as the lord depicted on the scarab from Tell el-Farʿah. The collapse of the palatial system

FIGURE 20   Scarab, Tell el-Farʻah (S), Tomb 936 (after Keel 2010b: 317 no. 675); 2—Tel Lachish, Tomb 4004 (after Tufnell 1958: pl. 36:316); 3—Tell el-Farʻah (S), Tomb 934 (after Keel 2010b: 265 no. 551); 4—Tel Azekah, Local Level T2–3a (after Koch et al. 2017: Fig. 7.1)

during the late thirteenth–twelfth century BCE, the turmoil in some parts of the eastern Mediterranean, and the consequent political fragmentation could have been exploited by such bands and their leaders.

Hypothetically, the Philistines could have arrived in the region during the days of Egyptian hegemony or after its collapse. If we opt for the former possibility, they could have served in an Egyptian garrison at Gaza and remained after the demise of the empire to become the lords of the new, post-collapse society. A fascinating illumination of such a scenario might be seen decorating the scarab from Tell el-Farʻah (S). Alternatively, the Philistines might be associated with the destruction wave during the late Iron Age I, a chaotic period that concluded with the emergence of Gath as the regional hegemon during the Iron Age IIA. Any combination of these scenarios is possible as well, yet the absence of written sources makes it impossible to determine which of these reconstructions is more likely.

CHAPTER 6

Regeneration

The integration of local rulers and Egyptian centers underwent a crisis during the Late Bronze Age IIB following the destruction or abandonment of major centers such as Tel Gezer (Dever et al. 1970: 22–24; Dever et al. 1974: 48–50; Dever 1986: 46–51), Tell eṣ-Ṣafi/Gath (Maeir 2012a: 18), Tel Lachish (Ussishkin 2004: 60–62), and Tel Haror/Yurza (Oren 1993a: 582). Minor Egyptian installations were destroyed as well—Tel Aphek (Gadot and Yadin 2009: 55, 59–66, 582–586) and Tel Mor (Barako 2007: 20–26, 45, 151). Nonetheless, Egyptian activity in the region of Gaza remained intact throughout these years: greater quantities of Egyptian-style pottery were locally produced (Martin 2011: 248), additional sites exhibited affiliation with the Egyptian system, and further evidence of Egyptian-oriented administration became evident in the shape of the hieratic inscriptions found across the region (above, Chapter 2.2.1).

During the Late Bronze Age III, some of the destroyed sites were resettled. Prominent settlements were Tel Lachish Level VI and Tel Azekah, sites that feature public buildings, specialized production areas, and a varied range of intensive participation in the Egyptian-oriented network.[1] Many other sites, however, including all former centers, were settled to a much more limited extent, hosting rural communities with no evident accumulation of wealth.

This phase was short-lived, and another disruption occurred some decades after the first crisis. The colonial hubs at Jaffa (Burke et al. 2017: 113–117) and Tel Seraʿ (Oren 1993b: 1331) were destroyed, as well as a small estate at Qubur al-Walaydah (Lehmann et al. 2010: 142–148) and a fortress at Tel Mor were abandoned (Barako 2007: 32). It appears that settlement at Tel Lachish was disturbed during the period when a temple located on the summit of the mound was sacked and a public building along the western slope was colonized by

---

1 For Lachish Level VI see Ussishkin (2004: 62–64). For a preliminary publication of a fortified complex and a temple found in the northeastern corner of the mound that were associated with the same Level, see Garfinkel et al. (2019: 129–132). Recent publications (Kleiman et al. 2016; Lipschits et al. 2017; Webster et al. 2017; Lipschits et al. 2019) attest to the prosperity of the Late Bronze Age III settlement at Tel Azekah, which covered the mound and a terrace to the southwest. A large architectural compound, consisted of least three different rooms and a large roofed courtyard area with several grinding installations, was exposed on the mound itself. The wealth of unearthed remains indicates the centrality of the Azekahites in the regional and interregional interactions and their participation in the colonial network (Koch et al. 2017; Sweeney et al. 2018).

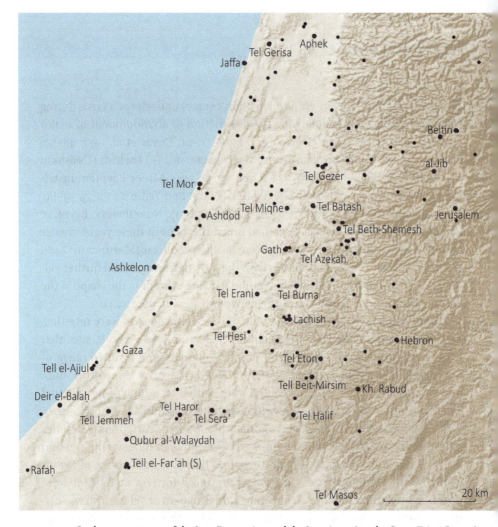

FIGURE 21   Settlement patterns of the Late Bronze Age and the Iron Age I (GIS by Omer Ze'evi-Berger)

squatters sometime prior to the town's destruction (Ussishkin 2004: 71).[2] Current evidence from Tel Azekah indicates sudden and violent destruction (Kleiman et al. 2016; Kleiman et al. 2019; Lipschits et al. 2019). Both Tel Azekah and Tel Lachish would remain abandoned for some 200 years, until the early Iron Age IIA.

The destruction of the old centers enabled the development of new ones (Figure 21). The most significant transformation, as shown below, occurred

---

2 A complex process of decline and destruction, rather than a single violent event, can be observed also at Tel Megiddo (Finkelstein et al. 2017: 275–276).

in the heart of the territory that was devastated at the end of the Late Bronze Age IIB, at Tel Miqne. The latter became the focus of the social processes from which the first significant urban center in centuries was established in the region.

1 The Yarkon Basin

The harbor town of Jaffa was set on fire during the second half of the 12th century BCE. Excavations at the gate area unearthed the remains of its destruction, rebuilding, and further damage and repair before its final destruction (Burke et al. 2017: 127). The scant remains of the next settlement, pits where Iron Age I pottery was retrieved (Herzog 2008: 1792), indicate meager activity.

It appears that the main harbor of this area moved a few kilometers northward to Tel Qasile, situated about 2 km east of the Yarkon estuary. Three developing phases of Iron I occupation were traced at this small site (Strata XII–X), featuring an expanding settlement, with a temple, storage facilities and specialized workshops, and various remains indicating the trade connections of the inhabitants with the northern Levantine littoral, Cyprus, and Egypt (Mazar 1980; 1985; 2009). A remarkable attestation to the wealth of the settlement is the group of four flasks stored at the temple's storeroom that contained remains of cinnamon, which traveled through the Arabian Sea trade routes (Gilboa and Namdar 2015). The settlement was destroyed in a major conflagration dated to the latter part of the Iron Age I (Mazar 1980: 33–46; 2009: 330). The settlement was renewed sometime thereafter (Stratum IX), albeit smaller and without the temple, and was apparently abandoned in the early Iron Age IIA (Mazar 2009: 327; Herzog and Singer-Avitz 2011: 167–168).

Other settlements along the Yarkon River were inhabited as well during that period. Located a few kilometers southeast of Tel Qasile, two farmhouses were built at Tel Gerisa sometime after the abandonment of the previous settlement (Herzog 1993a; Herzog and Singer-Avitz 2011: 161–164; Golan 2016)—Several phases were discerned in the settlement before it was destroyed in a major fire dated to the end of the Iron Age I. Settlement at the site was renewed during the late Iron Age IIA.[3] Further to the east, there was a rural settlement at Tel Aphek (Stratum X11) with a few dwellings that were abandoned after a few decades. This stratum was followed by a solitary structure surrounded by threshing floors and installations, probably a farm, which was dated to the Iron Age I (Strata X10–9) (Gadot and Yadin 2009: 88, 91–98, 586–587). New settlements were established east of Tel Aphek, on hills near the intermittent tributaries of the Yarkon River. One village, at the site of Izbeth Ṣarṭa, left remains of a row of peripheral rooms dated to the Iron Age I (Finkelstein 1986: 5–12; Finkelstein and Piasetzky 2006: 50) and material remains that, despite the site's location on the foothills, indicate close connections with the Yarkon Basin (Gadot 2006; 2008: 63–66). Another village was established at the site of Qurnat el-Haramiya (Torgë and Avner 2018), with similar evidence for its inhabitant's connections to the Yarkon Basin, and the Coastal Plain more generally. This general pattern of continuity is complemented by the data from the archaeological survey that points to intensification of human activity on the

---

3 I would like to thank Prof. Ze'ev Herzog for sharing details from his excavations at Tel Gerisa.

flood plain of the Yarkon and the surrounding hills (Kochavi and Beit-Arieh 1991; Beit-Arieh and Ayalon 2012; Gophna et al. 2015).

Farther to the south along the lower course of Naḥal Ayalon, two new settlements appeared: Occupation was renewed at Tel Azor, some 400 years after the fierce destruction of the previous settlement, with remains of brick structures dated to the Iron Age I and burials in the plain south and east of the mound (Ad et al. 2014). Burial at Azor continued in the Iron Age IIA (Buschennino and Yannai 2010; Ben-Shlomo 2012) but nothing is known about the nearby settlement at this time. Another settlement was apparently established at Beth-Dagan, whose remains were recorded in a brief salvage dig (Peilstöcker and Kapitaikin 2000).

Socio-politically speaking, it is generally believed that the framework that unified the entire area, which became well developed during the time of Egyptian hegemony, was preserved in some way even in the post-Egyptian period, with the regional center at Tel Qasile (Na'aman 2010b: 72–73). Tel Qasile has been described more than once as an extension of a larger center—Ashkelon (Finkelstein 1996b: 235; Gadot 2006) or Tel Miqne (Fantalkin and Tal 2008: 241–242 n. 66; Koch 2012: 57–58). Such reconstructions are largely based on the distribution of "Philistine" Bichrome Ware, which has been interpreted as a reflection of the Philistine origins of the settlement's founders. According to this theory, the Philistines spread beyond their initial region during the 11th century BCE, with these pottery vessels constituting physical evidence of their presence (Mazar 1980: 120; Singer 1985). However, it must be noted that the similarities in consumption between the two areas could have stemmed from a variety of economic and social factors, not necessarily one being an extension of another.

Another possibility is that the framework that unified the area fell apart after the destruction of Tel Aphek at the end of Late Bronze Age IIB, and especially after the destruction of Jaffa in the Late Bronze Age III. A new pattern then emerged that did not have a single clear center. The settlements in the eastern part of the area included villages and estates with no clear hierarchy. These locales traded their goods with the harbor at Tel Qasile (Gadot 2003: 249–253; 2008: 64), whose sphere of influence extended to the eastern part of the region. It may also be posited that what emerged from the rural area to the east was an elite that took advantage of the Egyptian withdrawal and established an anchorage to trade its goods with other settlements along the coast.

The attempt to establish a new center in the Yarkon basin—Tel Qasile—was unsuccessful, as can be seen from its destruction only a few decades later and from the fact that its status was never restored. No center came into being to replace Tel Qasile in the Yarkon basin and there is no evidence of the accumulation of wealth among settlements in the area during the Iron Age IIA (Herzog and Singer-Avitz 2011: 171–172).

2 The Shephelah and the Coastal Plain

The destruction of the local centers during the Late Bronze Age IIB led to the end of the political pattern that had developed under the Egyptians. The exceptions were Tel Lachish and Tel Azekah, although they were destroyed some time later. This is the context in which the rise of a power center at Tel Miqne should be understood.

It was only sometime during the latter part of the Late Bronze Age III, and more probably during the early Iron Age I, that Tel Miqne grew in size from the village located on the 4-ha mound (Stratum VIIIA) (Meehl et al. 2006: 28–29; Killebrew 2013: 83–84 and Fig. 2) to a large center—a city, in local terms, covering the entire 20-ha site (Stratum VIB). The large settlement at Tel Miqne evolved until the late Iron Age I (Strata VIB–IVA), with public buildings, workshops with specialized production reflecting nascent industries, and a varied material culture, all of which attest to social stratification (Bireling 1998; Meehl et al. 2006: 34–53; Killebrew 2013: 87, 89–95; Dothan et al. 2016).[4] Another change compared to the Late Bronze Age is the large area of Iron Age I Tel Miqne vis-à-vis the lack of rural hinterland, possibly indicating that a large population cultivated the surrounding area but lived within the settlement at Tel Miqne itself.[5] This large settlement was destroyed in the early 10th century BCE (Dothan and Gitin 1993: 1056) and rebuilt some time later (Stratum III) but its meager remains dated to the Iron Age IIA were restricted to the upper mound (Dothan and Gitin 2008: 1955).

In order to understand the change in the settlement pattern we must examine the other settlements around Tel Miqne, all featuring gradual

---

4 The excavators have also argued that a massive wall was built around the entire site in this phase, but see Ussishkin's (2005) reservations.

5 One scenario aimed at explaining this absence of rural hinterland argued, based on the assumption that the Philistines came from an urban culture and resided in the large cities of the "Pentapolis," that they initiated a policy of synoecism that forced the rural population to relocate and concentrate in a few sites (Bunimovitz 1998: 107–108; Shavit 2008: 160; Faust and Katz 2011: 235–236). Another scenario would be that the depopulation of the countryside reflects changes in land tenure, the extension of control over land by the elite located at Tel Miqne, and the subordination of the less powerful groups that were relocated close to their patrons. At the same time, the rise of the rulers of Tel Miqne could have actually been a pull-factor, as people were attracted by the security and opportunities powerful patrons could offer.

development but different trajectories across the era. The Iron Age I town of Tel Gezer developed gradually (HUC Strata XIII–XI), featuring large structures with several phases (and possibly several disruptions) and a fortification wall. Following the abandonment of the site, it was reoccupied (HUC Strata X–IX) until it was destroyed in the Late Iron Age I (Dever et al. 1970: 26–28; Dever et al. 1974: 53–61; Dever 1986: 60–124; Ortiz and Wolff 2012). The settlement at Tel Gezer was renewed during the Iron Age IIA (HUC Stratum VIII) and left behind remains of a casemate wall, a gate, a large structure adjacent to the gate and other structures (Dever et al. 1970: 62; Dever 1986: 126; Ortiz and Wolff 2017: 78–89).[6]

The data about sites on the Coastal Plain from the Late Bronze Age III attest to continuity of settlement at Tel Ashdod (Stratum XIII) and renewal of settlement at Ashkelon sometime after the abandonment of the Egyptian fortress (Phase 20 in Grid 38). Both remained settled much as they had been in the Late Bronze Age II—confined to their inner mounds (Yasur-Landau 2007: 615). Settlement at Ashkelon developed with no interruption into the Iron Age IIA (Stager et al. 2008: 262–274, 306) while settlement at Tel Ashdod (Stratum XI) was terminated before the late Iron Age I (Dothan 1971: 29–31; Dothan and Porath 1993: 86–88; Finkelstein and Singer-Avitz 2001: 239; Dothan and Ben-Shlomo 2005: 30–37). Resettled Ashdod seems to have reached its height during the early Iron Age IIA (Stratum X) however only for a few decades before its destruction (Finkelstein and Singer-Avitz 2001: 239–240; Dothan and Ben-Shlomo 2005: 7, 39–43, 170–180).[7]

Information about the Iron Age I settlement at Tell eṣ-Ṣafi is still vague (Maeir 2012a; 2012b: 352–354 and Table 1), though evidence suggests that the town grew in importance during the late Iron Age I–early Iron Age IIA.[8] Tel Batash (Stratum V), Tel Miqne's immediate neighbor to the east, enjoyed prosperity for a few decades until it was abandoned sometime in the late Iron Age I (Mazar 1997: 27–28, 76–81, 94, 177–180; Panitz-Cohen and Mazar 2006: 134–138). Settlement at the site was renewed some time thereafter (Stratum IV) for a short time before being abandoned in the early Iron Age IIA (Mazar 1997: 180–186; Mazar and Panitz-Cohen 2001: 154–156).

Up along the Sorek, Tel Beth-Shemesh featured gradual growth and accumulation of wealth during the Iron Age I (Stratum 6); this was interrupted and

---

6 On the relative chronology of Stratum VIII, see Herzog and Singer-Avitz (2006: 183).
7 North of there, along Naḥal Sorek, the settlement at Yavne-Yam was abandoned during the Late Bronze Age, and nothing is known about the few remaining settlements in the area (Fischer and Taxel 2006).
8 Aren M. Maeir, personal communication.

followed by renewed occupation that dates to the Late Iron Age I (Strata 5–4) (Bunimovitz and Lederman 2016: 173–187 and 677–694). The fate of this settlement is unknown; its remains were covered with the well-built structures of the Iron IIA settlement that followed (Stratum 3). Farther to the east, the Late Bronze Age village at Tel Yarmout experienced similar growth until it was abandoned in the Late Iron Age I (Strata Acr-6–3) (de Miroschedji 2008). At Kh. Qeiyafa, south of Tel Yarmout, a walled settlement was built at the end of the Iron Age I–early Iron Age IIA and was destroyed in a fire dated to the mid-10th century BCE (Garfinkel and Ganor 2009; Garfinkel et al. 2014). Farther southeast, a cluster of rural settlements include Tel Beit-Mirsim (Strata B_1–B_3) (Greenberg 1987), Tel Eton (Faust 2014: 588), and Tel Ḥalif (Stratum VII), where settlement continued with no interruption from the Late Bronze Age IIB through the Iron Age I (Seger 1983: 9–10; Jacobs and Seger 2007). Those inland clusters of sites in the Shephelah were located close to the topographic corridors that connect their valleys with the highland, where human activity at the few sites that existed during the Late Bronze Age intensified during the Iron Age I, part of a settlement process that reshaped the local landscape.[9]

It can be concluded that the data about the development of the city at Tel Miqne during the Iron Age I, the extensive evidence of the accumulation of wealth, the absence of similar data from its neighboring centers—all show that the social framework established at Tel Miqne was a nexus of power and influence that exceeded the sphere of their city (Finkelstein 2007: 520; Yasur-Landau 2007: 615; Fantalkin 2008: 31; Fantalkin and Tal 2008: 241–242; Koch 2012: 53–58). The regional politics has been understood (Bunimovitz and Lederman 2011; Lederman and Bunimovitz 2014: 63–66) as aggressive: the rulers of Tel Miqne fought their neighbors, giving rise to a new power center at

---

9 The long, narrow spurs of the moderate hills of the "Beth Horon Ascent" led to the al-Jib Plateau. The closest settlements during the Late Bronze Age were at Beitin (Finkelstein and Singer-Avitz 2009: 37) and Jerusalem (Finkelstein et al. 2011: 11; Maeir 2011: 179–182), and Late Bronze Age pottery was recorded at Deir el-'Azar (McKinny et al. 2018) and Qalunia (Kisilevitz et al. 2014). Late Bronze Age burials were found at al-Jib, the UN Headquarter (Baramki 1935), Mt. Olives (Saller 1964), and see also Amiran (1960). By the Iron Age I there were settlements at Beitin and Jerusalem and they were joined by dozens of sites around the previous settlements (Magen and Finkelstein 1993; Sergi 2015b). The upper intermittent streams of Naḥal Ha'Elah, Naḥal Shiqma and Naḥal Adorayim allow direct access from the Shephelah to the western slopes of the Hebron Hills. There, the same sites were occupied during both the Late Bronze Age II and the Iron Age I: a settlement Tell er-Rumeida/Hebron, the traditional center of the region (Eisenberg and Nagorski 2002; Eisenberg and Ben-Shlomo 2016), and two settlements on hills that dominate the ascents from the Shephelah: Kh. Tubeiqa (Sellers 1968; Funk 1993) to the northwest, and Kh. Rabud (Kochavi 1974) to the southwest. Late Bronze Age burials were found at Kh. Rabud and as-Sif (Ofer 1993). See Herzog and Singer-Avitz (2004: 220) on the problems in the survey of the highland around Hebron and Bethlehem by Ofer (1993).

Kh. Qeiyafa as the latter's last stronghold (Na'aman 2010b: 88–89). In that vein, it might be proposed that the walled settlement established at Kh. Qeiyafa replaced its neighbors (like Tel Beth-Shemesh and Tel Yarmout) and served as a local center until its destruction some time later. However, evidence from these sites indicates regional interaction rather than segregation. The settlement at Tel Beth-Shemesh flourished despite its proximity to Tel Miqne. Trade connections also existed between the two centers, as attested by the animal husbandry practiced at each site, which might be seen as complementary to that of its neighbor (Sapir-Hen et al. 2014: 715, and see below), and by the distribution pattern of the pottery typical to the coastal plain (Koch 2017b: 190–191). Similarly, the findings at Kh. Qeiyafa—including early alphabetic inscriptions, "Ashdod Ware" and hearths—show ties between the inhabitants of the site and neighboring settlements to the west (Na'aman 2017: 11, 17, 25).[10]

Nothing is known about the end of Tel Miqne and the reasons for the destruction of the settlement at the end of the Iron Age I or the early years of the early Iron Age IIA. The fall of this system made way for the growth of a new political constellation, which gradually developed during the Iron Age IIA, led by Tell eṣ-Ṣafi/Gath that became the main successor to Tel Miqne and grew within its settled area during the early Iron Age IIA, reaching its demographic zenith during the late Iron Age IIA.

3   The Besor Basin, or: The Problem with Gaza

The Egyptian holdings in the Besor region were islands of stability during the period after the destruction of the Canaanite centers one after the other at the end of the Late Bronze Age IIB. Two small sites (Tel Seraʿ and Qubur al-Walaydah) were destroyed during the Late Bronze Age III but renewed shortly thereafter. An examination of the settlement pattern from the Iron Age I gives the impression of continuity:[11] Remains of settlements from that period were documented at Tell Jemmeh (Ben-Shlomo and Van Beek 2014: 130–141, 337–398), and Tell el-Farʿah (S) (Yisraeli 1993: 442–443)—including continuous

---

10   It should be noted that the findings uncovered at Kh. Qeiyafa—especially the pottery assemblage, coroplastic art, and inscriptions—attest to the local character of the settlement and its wide interregional connections (Na'aman 2010b: 82–88; 2017:16–19; Koch 2012: 54–56; Lederman and Bunimovitz 2014: 66–70; Lehmann and Niemann 2014: 86; Niemann 2017: 251–253) and it is difficult to deduce from this a political affiliation of one kind or another (pace Garfinkel et al. 2011; Finkelstein and Fantalkin 2012; Garfinkel et al. 2012; Garfinkel et al. 2016; Garfinkel 2017: 42–44).

11   The meager finds from the mound of Gaza, Tall al-Kharuba, point to the existence of a settlement of unknown size.

occupation of public structures that were built during the Late Bronze Age III—as well as at Deir el-Balaḥ (Dothan and Brandl 2010), Netiv Ha'Asarah (Shavit and Yasur-Landau 2005), Tel Haror (Oren 1993a: 582; 1995), and Tel Maaravim (Oren and Mazar 1993; Shavit 2003: Site no. 208); Tel Seraʻ (Oren 1993b: 1331–1332; Ben-Shlomo et al. 2004: 15) and Qubur el-Walayda (Lehmann et al. 2010: 149–154) were resettled. This general pattern of continuity is complemented by the data from the archaeological survey that points to intensification of human activity on the alluvial plain northeast of Gaza and on the banks of Naḥal Shiqmah, as well as dozens of new encampments in the upper reaches of Naḥal HaBesor.[12]

Can we glean from the persistence of the settlement pattern that occupation was also continuous? Three considerations support this supposition, although it is impossible to prove without evidence from Gaza itself. First, it may be assumed, that the status of Gaza as a military and political hub for centuries, and its size and ties with regional trade networks made it easier for local institutions to survive the Egyptian withdrawal.[13] Another consideration involves the holdings around Gaza, which existed in the Late Bronze Age II–III, and may have drawn rural population to settle there. A third factor is the function of the Besor region settlements in the flourishing copper trade, which was produced in the Arabah and distributed westward.[14] One of the important centers in this network (but not the only one) was at Tel Masos, which grew during the Iron Age I and flourished until the Iron Age IIA (Herzog and Singer-Avitz 2004: 222–223 with earlier literature; Martin and Finkelstein 2013: 6–10). The connection between the Besor region and Tel Masos, no doubt through dozens of encampments in the area between them, also emerges from the results of petrographic examinations of pottery at sites in the Negev Highlands. These show that some of the pottery was made locally, some was brought from the Arabah, and some came from the Besor region (Martin et al. 2013; Martin and Finkelstein 2013).

---

12 See Herzog and Singer-Avitz (2004: 225–226) on the Iron Age I–early Iron Age IIA date of the Ḥeṣarim in the Besor basin.
13 Noteworthy in this regard is the continuity at Beth-Shean during the Iron Age I, both in settlement and in (re-)use of Egyptian monumental architecture, which might attest to the inhabitants' familiarity with the prominent role of the town during the Egyptian Period (Panitz-Cohen and Mazar 2009: 27–30).
14 For copper production in the Arabah in the Iron Age I–IIA, see Ben-Yosef et al. (2012).

4   Retrospective

In retrospect, the most prominent process in the entire region was the continuous founding and re-founding of local centers at the very same sites from the Middle Bronze Age II to the Iron Age II. The criteria for identifying these centers are the extent of the settled area and evidence of large-scale construction and the accumulation of wealth. Clearly not all the centers were established simultaneously or even existed at the same time, and the migration of a center of settlement gravity can be traced from one site to a neighboring site—for example the fluctuation in the status of Tel Miqne and its neighbors, Tel Gezer to the north, Tell eṣ-Ṣafi to the south, and Tel Beth-Shemesh to the east (Bunimovitz and Lederman 2006; 2017; Maeir and Uziel 2007; Na'aman 2010b: 501; Uziel et al. 2014).

Exceptions to this are the centers at Tel Qasile and Khirbet Qeiyafa, which were not established on mounds and whose regional status did not rejuvenate after they were destroyed. The fact that sites fulfilled the same role time and time again demonstrates their inherent settlement potential; the opposite is true for the few centers that were established at new sites, failed to thrive and subsequently left no imprint on the settlement pattern of the region. As illustrated above (Chapter 1), the driving factor behind the return to the large tells in southwest Canaan is not always clear, but might have been associated with familial connections to their hometown, traditions of governance and holiness that attracted would-be-rulers, or the sites' physical appearance.

But continuity in habitation site selection does not necessarily imply continuity in the political system. Changes in the region's settlement patterns reflect a concentration of power at different centers than those that had flourished in the days of Egyptian hegemony. These changes should be viewed against the backdrop of the breakdown of the previous social order: The destruction of Jaffa provided an opportunity for the local population in the Yarkon Basin to change land tenure in the hinterland and to develop an alternative center, while the rise of a new group (or groups) at Tel Miqne was the outcome of the demise of the previous elite of the region. Both cases thus reflect the demise of the colonial network, a process that led to the emergence of a new social structure unrelated to the previous centers of power. The growth of Tel Miqne into an urban center was a formative event in the region's history, since cities are centers of intensive economic and social activities; hence the impact on local society of Tel Miqne's development must be examined (see below in the next chapter).

CHAPTER 7

Reorientations

The social structure that emerged in post-collapse southwest Canaan during the Iron Age I was different from its predecessor. New centers, and hence possibly new social structures, replaced the traditional ones, a different settlement pattern developed, and perhaps most important of all, Egyptian hegemony was gone, preserved only as a shadow that reappeared from time to time in the shape of commercial interactions. In light of these transformations, many questions arise regarding the intention, ideology and identity of the new society. For example, was there a deliberate rejection of places identified with the collapsed Egyptian network? Was the creation of a new urban center at Tel Miqne a response to the existence of the preceding Middle Bronze Age city in the local collective memory? Was the ideology associated with the Egyptian network kept, modified or completely rejected?

The material remains from the Iron Age I attest to major changes in local practices. Various innovations were introduced, transforming aspects such as pottery production, domestic architecture, cult and consumption. As argued in Chapter 5, explanations for the appearance of such innovations have usually been based on historical preconceptions bound up from early stages of scholarship with the assumed arrival of the Philistines during the early 12th century BCE, which in fact could have happened at any point during the 12th–10th centuries BCE. Instead, the many changes in the Iron Age I in southwest Canaan should be treated without unfounded historical assumptions and labels which may be anachronistic.

1   Animal-based Economy and Accumulation of Wealth

The Iron Age I renewed settlements in southwest Canaan were characterized by economic development. Changes in animal exploitation in southwest Canaan during the 12th century have been traditionally summarized as a rise in the ratio of cattle and/or pig bones in local assemblages. These have sometimes been taken as innovations in local diet which reflect the migration of a new population with new dietary preferences (Killebrew 2005: 219; Killebrew and Lev-Tov 2008; Faust and Lev-Tov 2011: 15), while other studies (Yasur-Landau 2010a: 296; Lev-Tov et al. 2011; Maeir et al. 2013: 4–7; Sapir-Hen et al. 2014: 736; Sapir-Hen et al. 2015: 309–311) have emphasized non-food agriculture, social stratification, economic foci and specializations that suggest a more composite story that will be elaborated below.

From the Late Bronze Age IIB–III, equal sheep:goat ratios indicate a general tendency towards nonspecialized herding, with different methods of exploitation suggested by the mortality rates (Sapir-Hen et al. 2014: 714): low level sheep infant slaughter at Tel Lachish Levels VII–VI might suggest a concentration on wool production (Croft 2004: 2270), while higher infant slaughter levels at Tel Aphek Strata X12–X11 and Tel Miqne Stratum VIII suggest herding for meat supply (Horwitz 2009: 544; Lev-Tov 2010: 95). Another trend was a growing reliance on cattle. Pathological evidence from Tel Lachish suggests that cattle were used in agricultural cultivation and it appears that nearby fields were cultivated better than before, perhaps at the expense of herding (Croft 2004: 2270, 2283–2284). Similar, though more profound reliance on cattle is seen in a cluster of sites farther to the north, at Tel Batash (Panitz-Cohen and Mazar 2006: 311 table 81) and Tel Miqne Stratum VIII (Lev-Tov 2010: 95), and perhaps also at Tel Ḥarasim Stratum V (Horwitz 1996). Tel Aphek Strata X12–X11 exhibit even greater reliance on cattle (Horwitz 2009: 545 Tables 21.1, 21.7) perhaps connected to the exploitation of nearby fertile fields by the colonial estate and its successor.

Moving to the Iron Age I, several trends are evident. A possible focus on prime-aged herding at Tel Miqne Strata VII–IV (Lev-Tov 2010: 97–98) and to a lesser degree at Tel Aphek Strata X10–9 (Horwitz 2009: 544 and Table 21.5a) and Tell eṣ-Ṣafi (Lev-Tov 2012: 594) as well might indicate a shift in preference for wool production, as was previously common at Tel Lachish. At the same time, several textile-production workshops located at Tel Miqne, Tel Ashdod and Ashkelon feature innovative techniques shared by other communities in the littoral areas of the Mediterranean, such as new types of loomweights (Rahmstorf 2005; Yasur-Landau 2009: 509–510; Rahmstorf 2011) and new means for wool processing (Mazow 2006–2007, 2013). One might suggest, following Sherratt's (1998: 306) preliminary observation, that textiles became a prime product of the region during this era.

At the same time, the already prominent cattle exploitation was intensified at Tel Aphek, Tel Miqne and apparently at Tel Batash (Panitz-Cohen and Mazar 2006: 311 Table 81), expanding during the later phases of the Iron Age I to Tel Ashdod and Tell eṣ-Ṣafi. Pathological evidence for use of cattle in traction at Tel Miqne (Lev-Tov 2006: 211–212; 2010: 96–97), Tell eṣ-Ṣafi (Lev-Tov 2012: 595–596) and Tel Ashdod (Maher 2005: 284) gave rise to scholarly reconstructions of intensified cultivation of surrounding fields (Yasur-Landau 2010a: 297).

Both developments might have contributed to the increase in consumption of pork during the early stages of the Iron Age I, reflecting adjustments of the local diet in light of the more specialized livestock economy (already Sherratt 1998: 304) and the concentration of population in a large settlement. It forced a shift in meat production, focusing more on pigs, which could be raised inside the settlement, at the household level, and supply large and immediate sources of meat (cf. Sapir-Hen et al. 2013: 12–13; Sapir-Hen et al. 2015: 309; Sapir-Hen 2019: 56). Noteworthy in this context is the articulation of another case of "sudden" pork consumption during the Iron Age, at Iron IIB Tel Beth-Shean, Tel Megiddo, Tel Yoqneam and Tel Hamid (Sapir-Hen et al. 2013: 12). It has been suggested (cf. Sapir-Hen et al. 2013: 12–13; Sapir-Hen et al. 2015: 309) that this change was a response to population growth and reduction of open areas suitable for herding, leading some groups to focus more on pigs that could be raised inside the settlements, at the household level, and provide a large and immediate source of meat.[1]

Returning to Iron I southwest Canaan, as time passed the social reconfiguration might have made the consumption of pork a culinary tradition among the inhabitants of several communities. As exemplified in Chapter 4, culinary practices change in given social circumstances, as exposure to new commodities and/or technological advancements in cultivation or production might trigger innovations in existing traditions. Conversely, animal exploitation at other sites, such as Tel Beth-Shemesh, remained in its traditional track with neither intensification nor specialization (Sapir-Hen et al. 2014: 715). This might be one of the factors contributing to their inhabitants' conservatism regarding dietary preferences (Bunimovitz and Lederman 2011; Tamar et al. 2015).

This overview suggests that during the Iron Age I there was an intensification of the already prominent land use at Tel Miqne and Tel Aphek and a focus on secondary products. The demise of the local elite might have led to a change in land rights, with a greater portion of ownership of fields and herds by the newly formed groups. Historically speaking, once the Egyptians had withdrawn there were no overlords to demand and consume local commodities.

---

1 Contrary to Meiri et al. (2013: 6), the appearance of European pigs in the southern Levant during the Iron II does not necessarily imply that they were brought by "Sea People" immigrants in the Iron I. The discussed database includes only two samples from Iron I southwestern Canaan, from Tell eṣ-Ṣafi, both with Near Eastern DNA; European DNA is attested in three samples from late-Iron IIA Tel Reḥov, two samples from Iron IIB Tel Megiddo, and a single sample from the contemporaneous Tel Dor (cf. Sapir-Hen et al. 2015: 308–309). An alternative explanation would be to associate the importation of pigs with a contemporaneous instance of faunal translocation—the Anatolian bees exploited at Tel Reḥov, imported for their superiority over local bees in terms of their milder temper and improved honey yield (Mazar and Panitz-Cohen 2007; Mazar et al. 2008). While the reasons behind the importation of pigs are elusive, the spread of this group might be connected to the growth in the consumption of pork observed in the same region during the Iron IIB.

Taking all these factors into consideration, it is possible that the restructuring of local society and development in continuing trends of animal exploitation (such as a growing reliance on cattle) led to the accumulation of great wealth by some groups, especially those located at Tel Miqne.

2   Pottery Production and Communal Feasting

Alongside greater agricultural expertise, additional technological innovations occurred during the Late Bronze Age IIB, which brought about the development of a local industry of pottery production. Local pottery production during the Late Bronze Age I–II in the southern Levant is generally characterized as elementary specialization—small-scale, household level manufacturing and limited-range distribution (Killebrew 1998: 255–256; Panitz-Cohen 2006: 276–293). Nonetheless, recently studies have demonstrated the quality of the local potters.

First, potters producing painted pottery during the Late Bronze Age IIA used non-local pigments common in Cypriot pottery making, thus suggesting that both pigments and technology were transferred from Cyprus to Canaan (Shalvi et al. 2020). Second, through the Late Bronze Age IIB and more visibly during the Late Bronze Age III there were two innovations in local pottery production that may be seen to have developed under Egyptian influence:

(1) A growing tendency to add straw temper to clay recipes, an otherwise Egyptian technique for mass-produced pottery, used in the production of bowls and kraters in local style found at Tel Beth-Shean, Tel Mor, Tel Seraʿ, and most probably at Tel Lachish (Martin 2011: 98–108).

(2) Semi-industrial production, such as at the workshop located in Cave 4034 at Tel Lachish, that produced vessels on a large scale (Magrill and Middleton 2004), interpreted as part of a wider change in local production that reflects a clear departure from the former household-level manufacture and limited distribution (Panitz-Cohen 2006: 311–318; 2009: 191).

These developments reflect specialization in pottery production. These innovations can be understood in light of a copying process model, whereas specialized craft enables technological progress (Roux 2013). The evidence from southwest Canaan reflects the local ability to accept technological advantages alongside some sort of specialization in several workshops. The mechanisms behind such borrowing of technology could have been the exposure of an individual to more efficient production technology (cf. Roux 2013: 317) seen against the general collective ability of the locals to accept and appropriate Egyptian practices. Following Panitz-Cohen (2006: 320), the specialization in pottery production during these years of exposure to Egyptian practices might have been the social and technological setting that gave rise to the ability of other potters to adopt new production techniques, forms and decoration styles.

Following that, during the Late Bronze Age IIB–III, several workshops along the Levantine littoral and further inland began producing local versions of a limited range of forms and decoration styles that reflect Aegean and Cypriot background (Lehmann 2007; Mountjoy 2010, 2013; Rutter 2013; Sherratt 2013; Stockhammer 2019). Such workshops were located near Tel Beth-Shean and Tel Akko (Yasur-Landau 2006; Cohen-Weinberger 2009; Zukerman 2009; Sherratt 2013: 650–651) and further to the south at Tel Ashdod Stratum XIIIB (Sherratt 2006), spreading further eastward to Tel Miqne Stratum VIIA (Killebrew 1998, 2013).[2]

As time passed, this production enjoyed popularity in southwest Canaan, giving rise to the development of the Bichrome style that vividly reflects the bi-directional intercultural discourses of that era. It embedded further "foreign" influences (Ben-Shlomo 2010; Ben-Dor Evian 2012), thus attesting to inter-regional contacts alongside regional exchange patterns of technologies, styles, and concepts, as attested by the spread of such production from Tel Miqne and Tel Ashdod to workshops located at Tell Qasile (Yellin and Gunneweg 1985) and Tel Jemmeh (Ben-Shlomo and Van Beek 2014: 793), and as far as Tell en-Naṣbeh in the central hill country (Gunneweg et al. 1994) and in or around Tel Megiddo in the Jezreel Valley (Martin 2017).

It has been suggested that the emphasis placed on serving and eating/drinking vessels reflect their role in communal feasting (Killebrew and Lev-Tov 2008; Maeir 2008; Hitchcock and Maeir 2013; Mazow 2014: 146–147; Faust 2015). A common view holds that such vessels (especially in their first phase) are of Aegean style and hence, so too was the consumption of the food practiced in an Aegean way. Nonetheless, Stockhammer (2012; 2013: 18–23; 2019: 241–242) emphasized the absence of key vessel shapes of the Aegean (such as the kylix

---

2 Regarding Tel Miqne Stratum VII, it has been noted that "[t]his factory-style mode of manufacture most likely continued earlier Late Helladic Mycenaean pottery traditions" (Killebrew 2013: 118) yet no exact Aegean parallel of the kilns at Tel Miqne Stratum VII is known (Yasur-Landau 2010a: 265). Indeed, there are indications that some of the producers of the Aegean-inspired pottery were local: Sherratt (2013: 634–635) noted the different surface treatment (compared to Cyprus) and the localized production technique, for some vessels were possibly handmade, or at least made by potters not used to wheels. Regarding Tell eṣ-Ṣafi, Ben-Shlomo and colleagues (2009) showed that despite the introduction of Aegean-inspired forms, produced sometimes with a specific clay recipe, and despite the increase in fire temperature, the basic production rather reflects continuation from Late Bronze Age II to Iron Age I in regard to forming techniques (multiple- and single-coil shaping, wheel smoothing, medium-high firing and careless finishing).

and the stirrup jar) and interpreted it as a "translation of Canaanite practices into the stylistic vocabulary of Aegean-type pottery" (Stockhammer 2013: 22).

Communal feasting has been used to bind the various groups of a region together, to build a social hierarchy on the one hand and to create cohesion on the other. Consequently, the limited appearance of such vessels at inland sites has been interpreted as the remains of a local elite that possibly associated itself with coastal feasting practices (Faust 2015a: 180). Such an appealing hypothesis must, however, wait for a detailed study of a coherent ceramic assemblage from a secured archaeological context before it can be accepted. For the time being, the distribution pattern of the Bichrome pottery can be seen as reflecting interregional interaction networks whose focal points were prosperous settlements located on the Coastal Plain and in the Lower Shephelah.

It can be concluded, that the development of Tel Miqne and neighboring towns brought about an intense web of economic contacts, leading to a wide distribution of shared material remains among major sites in these regions. The patterns of consumption and production of the Bichrome pottery attests to this intense network alongside other modes of interaction with neighboring regions, among them the inland Shephelah sites. Along these routes of interaction, ideas and practices transferred through unknown mechanisms of knowledge transfer (relocation of potters from the "homeland" to the margins, exchange of ideas and know-how methods, or from a combination of other factors).

3   Religion

The potential in analyzing cult practices in search of societal changes was presented in Chapter 3, and the benefits of understanding the colonial past are also valid in the postcolonial present. The main source of information about public cult in the Iron Age I is the temple precinct at Tel Qasile (Strata XII–X) (Mazar 1980, 1985a, 2000).[3] The three phases of the precinct had central structures whose holiest space was consistently located at their back, their walls were lined with benches, and they were integrated with courtyards with additional structures. Their ground plans changed considerably over the years and

---

3 The large Building 350 in the lower mound of Tel Miqne Strata V–IV has been interpreted as a temple by the excavators (Dothan 2002). However, based on the ground plan and spatial analysis of the finds other scholars support the interpretation of the structure as an elite residence that might have hosted some sort of cultic activity (Mazow 2005: 295–301; Yasur-Landau 2010a: 308).

incorporated local traditions with features that are known from contemporaneous Cyprus and the Aegean (Mazar 1980: 68).

The transformations in the ground plan of the temples were explained by Mazar (2000: 222): "The inhabitants of Tell Qasile lacked a definite concept of temple architecture. Innovation and the lack of a well-defined architectural tradition are perhaps the most noticeable characteristics of the sacred complex at Tell Qasile." Another explanation is that the persistence of the three architectural elements—the location of the holy space, the benches used for votive placements, and the courtyard hosting the rituals themselves—suggest that the flexibility in the ground plan of the temple reflects the ability of the inhabitants of Tel Qasile to appropriate architectural concepts while keeping the essence of their cult.

Continuity is seen also in the paraphernalia of the Tel Qasile temples. Most of the many objects uncovered in the temple are associated with Canaanite traditions, or alternatively a site-specific version of that tradition (Mazar 1980: 119; 1985a: 126). A particularly important object found at the foot of the altar of Stratum X is a clay plaque in the form of a temple façade, with remains of two nude, standing female figures, the hands apparently grasping their breasts (Mazar 1980: 82–84 and fig. 20; 1985b). The plaque resembles shrine models from Canaan and the figures it bears may be associated with clay figurines from the Late Bronze Age, in which a female figure appears grasping her breasts in identical fashion (Keel and Uehlinger 1998: 100–103). It seems therefore that the items from the temple at Tel Qasile reveal a cult dedicated to a goddess, whose image and cultic objects were associated with a local tradition that had developed during the Late Bronze Age.

Another aspect of continuity is visible in the ritual placement of building deposits. As discussed in Chapter 4, lamp-and-bowl building deposits were a colonial practice, perhaps even a localization of an Egyptian practice of foundation deposits, that spread among the communities living in and around the Egyptian centers. This practice continued in southwest Canaan during the Iron Age I, at Tel Gezer, Ashkelon, Tel Beth-Shemesh, and Tel Miqne and further into the Iron Age IIA. In addition, the integration of other types of vessels, observed already in the Late Bronze Age III, was expanded and closed vessels, such as juglets and pilgrim flasks, were now deposited at Ashkelon (Aja 2009: 383 table 4.6) and Tel Qasile, although there, they were incorporated into a wall (Mazar 1980: 38).

An additional aspect of the local cult involves the clay figurines. The figurines that depict a goddess grasping branches mostly disappeared in the Late Bronze Age III. In their place, two types of figurines became common which are also mainly known from southwest Canaan. One type is an Aegean-style figurine of the type known as PSI—a standing figure with arms raised and small breasts in the form of circles, which first appeared during the Late Bronze Age IIB at Tel Ashdod, Tel Beth-Shemesh, and Tel Lachish (Leonard 1994: nos. 2183, 2190, 2201, 2213, 2254; Hankey et al. 2004: nos. 91–91). It next appeared in the Iron Age I, this time probably locally produced, at Tel Miqne, Tel Ashdod, Ashkelon and Tel Qasile (Ben-Shlomo and Press 2009: 47–48; Ben-Shlomo 2010: 37–38; Press 2012: 145–160). The dialogue between the local traditions and Aegean-style images led to the development of a new and unique type of figurine, depicting a seated female whose body is incorporated into her chair (Yasur-Landau 2001; Ben-Shlomo and Press 2009: 49–54; Russell 2009; Ben-Shlomo 2010: 45–51; Press 2012: 154–156, 160–165). Items of this type, commonly referred to as "Ashdoda," were found throughout southwest Canaan, including in the Yarkon Basin, the coastal plain, the Shephelah and perhaps in Jerusalem as well (Ben-Shlomo and Press 2009: 53).

The standing figure appears to have been common mainly among the coastal inhabitants in southwest Canaan, which may reflect their cultural association with Cyprus and the Aegean sphere, while the seated figure was more widely distributed and thus may represent a cult that was accepted among significant portions of the local population. Like previous cases of the appearance of "foreign" motifs in local imagery, it is difficult to know whether the image was of a Mediterranean goddess that became accepted in southwest Canaan or perhaps a local goddess presented in a new way. This is another example of the integration of local and foreign cult traditions that can be regarded as part of the longtime continuity in which local female deities added foreign elements and new meanings to their images, and in some cases even lost their place to new goddesses that became popular among the local people. This instance may belong to a broader phenomenon that might reflect similar phenomena along the coasts of the Mediterranean following encounters between Aegean goddesses and their local counterparts (Budin 2014).

Lastly, there was a marked change in the charm practices in the region during the Iron Age I. Glyptic assemblages of that period are characterized by a decline in the number of scarabs. Scarabs found in Iron Age I contexts are mostly restricted to a specific group, the "mass-produced early Iron Age series." These scarabs were used for sealing (and not only as amulets) and were widely consumed in the region of Gaza, in the Nile Delta, and in several north Canaanite sites—predominantly Tel Dor (Münger 2003, 2005; Ben-Shlomo 2006; Keel 2013b; Ben-Tor 2016; Ben-Dor Evian 2017b). They are quite rare in the inland regions of southwest Canaan, where New Kingdom scarabs were the most popular amulet during the Late Bronze Age, appearing in limited numbers during the Late Iron Age I and more commonly during the Early Iron Age IIA.

Other types of amulets common in the Iron Age I were locally produced conoids and oval, button-like artifacts, mostly made of limestone and decorated with simple and schematic scenes. The images chosen for these charms attest to a focus on local pictorial traditions, they are best exemplified by the popularity of the horned animal, commonly attested in the region as early as the Chalcolithic period (Schroer and Keel 2005: 109–111, 114ff). This image was popular in the Middle Bronze Age (Schroer 2008: 48 with literature, 194–203), becoming scarce in the Late Bronze Age, when it was mostly restricted to Mitannian-style cylinder seals and locally produced plaques. It became popular once again during the Iron Age I (Figure 22), depicted on dozens of artifacts within a variety of scenes with floral motifs, scorpions, anthropomorphic figures and sucklings (Shuval 1990: 105–111; Keel and Uehlinger 1998: 125; Staubli 2009: 611–616; Ornan 2016: 293–297).

The main reason for the decline in the popularity of scarabs at these sites in the Shephelah, the same region where large numbers of these artifacts were once found, was obviously the weakening of the interaction with Egypt itself. But additional factors might have been at work here. As the Iron Age I amulets were also found in burials, no change in function can be observed; there was, however, a selective preference for non-Egyptian artifacts and non-Egyptian imagery. The attention given to locally manufactured limestone artifacts decorated with local imagery that had been "underground" during the days of Egyptian hegemony can thus be explained as reflecting a broader local tendency to modify practices associated with the previous system, at times even replacing them with a more pronounced local flavor.

4   Interpreting Reorientations

The Iron Age I in southwest Canaan is characterized by the appearance of multiple innovations in various aspects and the rejection of traditional practices. The innovations include the aforementioned textile production means, Aegean-style pottery and figurines, alongside additional innovations such as:

(1) Construction of hearths: hearths reappear in the southern Levant after a long period of absence; they were small, varied in shape (circular, rectangular, square, or "keyhole"), and built inside and outside structures in various construction methods. They echo traditions previously common on Crete and Cyprus (Maeir and Hitchcock 2011).

(2) Introduction of new cooking practices: cooking in the southern Levant that traditionally utilized pots—wide handleless vessels—was supplemented with a new form, a type of jug that was popular in the Aegean

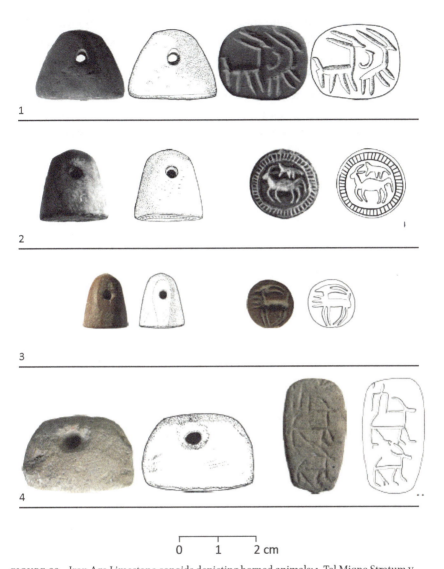

FIGURE 22 Iron Age Limestone conoids depicting horned animals: 1. Tel Miqne Stratum V (after Keel 2010a: 551 no. 72); 2. Tel Beth-Shemesh Stratum III (after Keel 2010a: 279 no. 144); 3. Tell eṣ-Ṣafi Area T (after Keel 2013a: 121 no. 56); 4. Tel Gezer, 'Fourth Semitic Period' (after Keel 2013a: 185 no. 44)

and on Cyprus; with the passage of time, the jug as a cooking vessel was accepted by a growing number of consumers across the southern Levant (Yasur-Landau 2005; Ben-Shlomo et al. 2008).

The traditional explanation for the appearance of these innovations as directly imported by Aegean immigrants has been modified in recent years, once the various elements constituting this "culture" were scrutinized (Yasur-Landau 2012a; Hitchcock and Maeir 2013; 2016a; Maeir et al. 2013; Stockhammer 2013; Mazow 2014; Maeir and Hitchcock 2017b). It has become clear that they exhibited a wide range of "homelands," including Egypt (Birney and Doak 2011; Ben-Dor Evian 2012); that the artifacts of this "culture" appeared gradually at various sites in the region and were produced in different sizes and shapes, occasionally appropriated in accordance with local practices, and were used, sometimes, in diverse ways.

How many of these innovations were imported by migrants? Can one know the number of these migrants? What role did local populations play in interactions with migrants? And, what was the local reaction to these new innovations? Clearly, migrations are a fundamental part of human interaction (Van Dommelen 2014b), but the notion of mass migration is, as discussed in Chapter 5, not flawless. Clearly, one should consider the possibility that the Philistines, whenever they arrived, brought with them some innovations. Yet other sorts of limited migrations occurred, including the movement of individuals and groups across the Levant since time immemorial. Along the Levantine littoral, migrations would more likey have taken the shape of sporadic movements and exchanges of individuals and groups, including skilled workers, sailors, and merchants seeking new markets alongside others looking for new opportunities (Gates 2011: 388 with literature). A fine example comes from the royal archive of Ugarit, documenting the presence of merchants from the southern Levant and Cilicia, some based there for an extended period and achieving high status in the local administration (Vidal 2006).

For centuries, multifocal trade networks connected the various ports in the eastern Mediterranean and contributed to transcultural discourses in these regions; now they reoriented following the collapse of the great polities and the decline in the quantity and quality of the traded commodities (Pedrazzi 2010; Gilboa et al. 2015; Knapp and Manning 2016). The most prominent player in the east Mediterranean interactions was Cyprus, where various communities transacted with coastal regions close and far, hosted a varied range of foreign traders, artisans, and other newcomers, and consequently appropriated a varied range of practices (Hitchcock 2008; 2011; Voskos and Knapp 2008; Knapp 2012). Current data suggest that Cypriot society did not collapse in the 12th century BCE. Rather, it was was transformed and continued to develop despite being surrounded by the upheaval that was happening all around the eastern Mediterranean basin (Georgiou 2015). While the consensus has been that the collapse of the Late Bronze Age trading networks severed connections between Cyprus and southwest Canaan (Barako 2000: 515–516), recent finds of

Late Cypriot IIIA imports at Ashkelon (Master et al. 2015)[4] indicate that this was not the case.

This may be an indication that a Cypriot merchant diaspora had settled in southwest Canaan, though it could likewise indicate that Levantine traders had been based abroad. Either option would have served as a conduit for transcultural innovation. The economic development of the region, especially at Tel Miqne, would have attracted newcomers and even migrants from other parts of the southern Levant. Possible evidence of such newcomers in southwest Canaan varies according to each scholar's perception of the archaeological data, although introduction of cooking vessels, burial practices and other deep changes at the household level have enjoyed the greatest popularity in recent discourse (Faust and Lev-Tov 2011; 2014; Yasur-Landau 2012a; Hitchcock and Maeir 2013; Maeir et al. 2013). Less persuasive are conclusions based on distribution patterns of these innovations, dealing with the origin(s) of settlers or their number in a given community. There are social mechanisms that are, currently, invisible in the archaeological record, yet were most likely in motion during these dynamic years, leading to various newcomer–local interactions, appropriations and rejections (Maeir and Hitchcock 2011: 58).

Certainly, the possibility that some of the innovations were championed by local agency should be considered in light of the discussion in the preceding chapters about the openness of the local population in southwest Canaan to appropriated innovations that affected its daily life. The innovations that appeared during the Late Bronze Age were part of a wider process of colonial encounters and discourses in the wake of the integration with the Egyptian state. The archaeological remains convey both the prime focus of the locals to interact with the Egyptians and the wide range of exposure and appropriation that included the transfer of concepts, vocabulary, and daily practices that led to the integration of Egypt within their social identity. They were exposed to a limited range of Egyptian practices and actively and passively appropriated those they perceived as strengthening their connections with the Egyptians and as status markers in the local setting.

But nothing lasts forever. The disappearance of Egyptian officials, soldiers and other groups, as well as the collapse of the Egyptian-oriented system, created a vacuum that was soon to be filled. The collapse of the Egyptian colonial network in southwest Canaan and the regeneration of the local society may be

---

4   A handful of similar imports were recently found at Tel Azekah (O. Lipschits and Y. Gadot, personal communication), thus increasing evidence of connections with Cyprus during the 12th century BCE beyond the immediate port of Ashkelon.

compared to other cases of political breakdown and its aftermath (Schwartz and Nichols 2006; McAnany and Yoffee 2009; Faulseit 2016; Middleton 2017). The collapse of political structure is frequently accompanied by social fragmentation that opens the way to social mobility. Ambitious non-elite individuals are able, with the breakdown of social limitations, to pursue power more successfully than before and to establish new focal points (Conlee 2006: 107–108; Schwartz 2006: 9, 12; Ristvet 2012). At the same time, remnants of the previous system might join with and contribute to the regeneration. These might include lower-level administrators, artisans, and specialized farmers who would provide foundations for the economic infrastructure of the reestablished social structure. Together, the various components of the emerging network would search for new paths to expand their capital, including intensification of production, access to new resources and interaction with neighboring networks (Conlee 2003).

Regenerated societies treat their past in various ways. A previous ideological framework can be adjusted to signal continuity and provide legitimacy, but the adjustment is selective and can involve the denunciation of previous values and concepts that are entangled with the memory of the collapsed society. The transformation of collective identity may include the appropriation of new practices, symbols and ideologies that are integrated into the existing indigenous substratum (Conlee 2006: 112; Kolata 2006: 219). They are used to promote the status of the new elite in search of new means to manifest its power. Other innovations can also be used in establishing new coalitions with other prominent groups and in mechanisms for building cohesion among the people (Sharratt 2016: 145).

It is within such a framework that (some of) the transformations in southwest Canaan should be understood. With greater wealth in their hands than ever before, the dominant groups in Iron Age I southwest Canaan were stronger than their predecessors and were able to reinforce their economic connections with other regions, in the southern Levant and beyond, and to enjoy economic prosperity. As is indicated by the specialization of animal-based economy (Sapir-Hen et al. 2014) and the rising importance of the olive and its products (Finkelstein and Langgut 2018: 161–163) which may reflect growing organization and development of intensive trade relations over time. The decline of Egyptian influence paved the way to further acceptance of other (Mediterranean) concepts and technologies. For indeed, the many innovations were never part of a monolithic culture but rather the result of a process in the making shared by several communities, which selectively adopted and adapted practices and concepts that were usable in the local context.

Thus, the regenerated society in Iron Age I southwest Canaan exhibits both continuity and transformation. While the location of power shifted, the economic developments achieved during the days of the Egyptian hegemony were kept, effectively attesting to continuity in knowledge and the existence of skilled workers. The new society contemplated the past and reflected upon, and used, collective memory in the creation of new identities. This was achieved via constant discourse centered around the appropriation and rejection of practices and concepts identified with the collapsed society. During the regeneration, existing modes of interaction were intensified, unknown numbers of newcomers of multiple origins arrived, and new practices were appropriated and integrated into the local context. Diversity dominated as various communities experimented with new production modes and new performances, some adopting the innovations and some rejecting them after a short period. As time passed, some of these innovations were further advanced, combining additional innovations from abroad together with local developments, producing a varied range of remains that are associated with the vivid material record of the Iron Age I in the region.

CHAPTER 8

In the Eye of the Beholder

Throughout the four centuries of widespread use of Egyptian seal-amulets, local workshops experimented with seal production.¹ Evidence of such experimentation is present in a number of cases. One such example is a workshop located at Tel Beth-Shean Stratum IX which produced scarabs of composite-material that were cast from molds in the shape of Egyptian scarabs (Ben-Tor and Keel 2012). Similarly, a Late Bronze Age IIA–IIB workshop specialized in bifacial plaques that exhibit Syrian influence (Keel 1994: 226–230; Brandl 2008).² Lastly, the mass-produced series of scarabs from the early Iron Age mentioned in the previous chapter are associated with workshops located either at Tanis (Münger 2003, 2005; Schipper 2005: 300–308; Ben-Dor Evian 2017b) or in Canaan (Keel 1994: 231–233; 2013b; Ben-Tor 2016).

Southwest Canaanite glyptic production of the Iron Age I is best exemplified by the multi-faceted decorated seal-amulet. A notable innovation dated to the late Iron Age I, this seal-amulet type was unknown in Egypt itself and thus may represent local production. The shape is an elaborated derivation of locally styled conoids (Keel-Leu 1990: 47–48; Keel 1995: 98), which deviates from this tradition by way of their multi-facet decoration. Seal-amulets of this type are known from Stratum 6 at Tel Gerisa (Figure 23), allegedly from Stratum X at Tel Qasile (Figure 24),³ Cemetery 800 at Tell el-Farʿah (S) (Figure 24), an unknown context from Ashkelon (Figure 25) and recently, a late Iron Age I context at Tell eṣ-Ṣafi.⁴ Decorated on the base and all four sides, altogether they depict 10 different scenes that thoroughly represent the pictorial assemblage of the period.

---

1 A previous version of this chapter was published as Koch 2018c.
2 A suggested south Levantine provenience of 19th Dynasty style scarabs (Brandl 2003; Lalkin 2008: 182–184) has recently been questioned (Ben-Tor 2017).
3 The amulet from Tel Qasile was found in the dump of the excavation directed by Dunayevski (Mazar 1967: 64), hence its exact provenance is questionable.
4 For the preliminary publication of the seal from Tell eṣ-Ṣafi see http//gath.wordpress.com/2014/08/13/a-neat-seal-from-this-season. According to A.M. Maeir (personal communication, June 2016), the seal was found in a Late Iron Age I context. Three more seals are known from private collections; one was published by Shuval (1990: 73, fig. 1), another by Keel-Leu (1990: no. 55), and the third by Cornelius (1994: no. BM56).

IN THE EYE OF THE BEHOLDER 107

FIGURE 23   Multi-faceted decorated seal-amulet from Tel Gerisa Stratum 6 (after Keel 2013a: 143 no. 7)

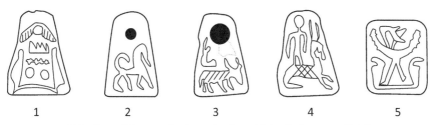

FIGURE 24   Multi-faceted decorated seal-amulet from Tel Qasile Stratum X(?) (after Mazar 1967: pl. 4–5; Shuval 1990: 73 fig. 2, 123 no. 1)

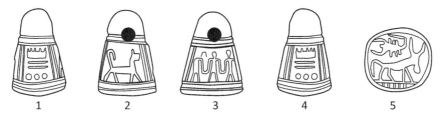

FIGURE 25   Multi-faceted decorated seal-amulet from Tell el-Farʿah (S), Cemetery 800 (after Keel 2010b: 117 no. 210)

FIGURE 26   Multi-faceted decorated seal-amulet from Ashkelon, unknown context (after Keel 1997: 721 no. 83)

1   The Egyptian Connection

Previous studies have emphasised the Egyptian origins reflected in the majority of motifs that decorate artifacts within this group. Decorating one or two faces on each seal-amulet, the name of Amun-Re is the most obvious connection between these artifacts and Egyptian iconography. The seal-amulet from Tel Qasile (Figure 27:1) depicts the full name of Amun-Re with the duplication of the reed sign, perhaps created for the sake of symmetry (Brandl 1999: 18), a double sun disk, and a winged disk hovering above it. A similar duplication of the reed sign is present on the seal-amulet from Tel Gerisa (Figure 27:2), though it is missing the winged disk and includes an unidentified engraving in the place usually occupied by the doubled sun disk. The seal-amulets from Tell el-Farʿah (Fig. Figure 27:3) and Ashkelon (Figure 27:4) are decorated with a different variant. In this instance, where the reed sign is missing, the n-sign is doubled, and three sun disks are depicted as dots or short lines. The name of Amun-Re was a popular theme during the 19th–20th Dynasties, with ca. 200 artifacts decorated with its variants; more than 150 such items were found in southwest Canaan (mainly in the region of Gaza and Tel Lachish) (Lalkin 2008: 151–159). The popularity of the theme was related to the widespread appearance of Amun iconography, and was a dominant feature within divine-related iconography in Egyptian glyptic imagery during the New Kingdom (Schroer 2011: 44, 144–158). Subsequently, the appearance of such iconography on the early Iron Age mass-produced scarabs has been explained as reflecting the prominence of Amun-Re in the Egyptian religion of the turn of the millennium (Schipper 2005: 300–308). But its appearance on seal-amulets that were apparently locally made in southwest Canaan during the early Iron Age is noteworthy and provokes questions regarding the importance of this deity or its symbolism in the region (see below).

Another scene depicted on all four seal-amulets is a marching lion (Figure 28:1–4). Other late Iron Age I–early Iron Age IIA artifacts depict a similar scene (Figure 28:5–8). Frequently, the depiction includes a vertical object to the right, and a long horizontal object (resembling a branch) above or below

1   2   3   4

FIGURE 27   Name of Amun-Re on multi-faceted seal-amulets

FIGURE 28 Late Iron Age I–Early Iron Age IIA Depictions of Marching Lion: No. 1. Tel Gerisa (Figure 23:1, above); 2. Tel Qasile Stratum X (Figure 24:2, above); 3. Tell el-Farʿah (S) Cemetery 800 (Figure 25:2, above); 4. Ashkelon (Figure 26:2, above); 5. Tell el-Farʿah (S), Tomb 135 (after Keel 2010b: 123 no. 223); 6. Tel Haror, Stratum B1/2 (after Brandl in Keel 2013a: 573 no. 1); 7. Tel Lachish, Tomb 191 (after Tufnell 1953: pl. 45:130); 8. Tel Beth-Shemesh, Tomb 1 (after Keel 2010a: 221 no. 6)

the lion. Similar scenes (though of differing styles) are known from the Late Bronze Age IIB–III (Figure 29) including a particular group of scarabs that were found mainly in southwest Canaan, predominantly at Tell el-Farʿah (S) (Figure 29:1–2).[5]

Both the name of Amun-Re and the lion are depicted on the base of the seal-amulet from Tel Gerisa (Figure 30:1). This composition stems from 19th-Dynasty iconography, which typically depicts the ram-headed sphinx (an attribute of Amun-Re), the name of Amun-Re above the sphinx, and an accompanying throne name of Ramesses II (Figure 30:2). A parallel of this depiction reflects a more schematic style with a feather-sign instead of the royal name (Figure 30:3). Another version of this scene (Figure 30:4) includes the name of Amun-Re alongside a royal sphinx, accompanied by a figure of Mȝʿt. These scenes continued to be reproduced well into the Iron Age I, together with the partial spelling of Amun's name. Reproductions also included both depictions of the sphinx, (1) the ram-headed sphinx accompanied by a

---

[5] For symbolism of the lion motif in the Ancient Near East see Strawn (2005: 131–228). Keel (1990b: 346–351; 1994: 37–40) interprets the Iron Age I–IIA scenes as cryptographic writing of the name of Amun (*jmn*), where the lion stands for the sound *m* (from *mȝj*).

FIGURE 29   Late Bronze Age IIB–III Depictions of Marching Lion: No. 1. Tell el-Farʿah (S), Tomb 984 (after Keel 2010b: 367 no. 800); 2. Tell el-Farʿah (S), Tomb 935 (after Keel 2010b: 311 no. 660); 3. Tell Jemmeh, unknown (after Keel 2013a: 59 no. 135); 4. Tel Azekah, Area S2–Late Bronze Age IIB level (courtesy of Oded Lipschits); 5. Tel Beth-Shemesh, Stratum IV–III (after Keel 2010a: 283 no. 153); 6. Tel Gezer, "2nd Semitic Period" (after Keel 2013a: 297 no. 293); 7. Tel Gezer, Area VI Stratum 6C/B (after Keel 2013a: 447 no. 650); 8. Tel Gerisa, unknown (after Keel 2013a: 153 no. 33)

reed-sign (Figure 30:5), and (2) the royal sphinx accompanied by a figure of Mꜣʿt (Figure 30:6). During the Iron Age I, a third variation of this scene also appears in which a crouching lion was the central motif, accompanied by a reed-sign (Figure 30:7) or even a caprid (Figure 30:8). Thus it appears as though the base of the seal-amulet from Tel Gerisa depicts a common two-motif scene that originated during the reign of Ramesses II, which was then modified and further developed in the 12th–11th centuries BCE.[6]

The base of the seal-amulet from Tel Qasile (Figure 31:1) depicts a winged anthropomorphic figure wearing a tall crown with a streamer, accompanied by two uraei. A similar motif appears on a scarab from Iron Age IB–IIA tomb at Tell el-Farʿah (S) (Figure 31:2), on additional items from Tel Akko, several sites in the Delta, and Byblos (Cornelius 1994: BM24–BM30). A variation of this motif, located on a scarab from a late Jerusalem context, depicts the winged

---

6   Keel (2013a: 142) suggests that the lion is used in this scene as part of the cryptographic writing of the name Amun-Re as well. In his opinion (already Keel 1990b: 348, 350), the base of the seal bears the name of Amun-Re twice, the reed-sign (j), the lion ($mꜣj$) and the nb-sign stand for the full name of Amun-Re (jmn), while the sun-disk (jtn) and the board-sign (mn) stand for a partial second version ($jm[n]$).

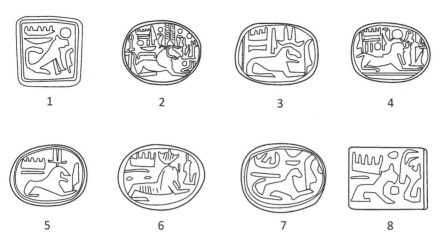

FIGURE 30 Late Bronze Age IIB–III and Iron Age I–Early Iron Age IIA Depictions of Amun-Re's Name Accompanied by Attributes: No. 1. Tel Gerisa, Level 6 (fig. 1, above); 2. Deir el-Balaḥ, unknown (after Keel 2010a: 455 no. 131); 3. Tell el-Farʿah (S), Tomb 981 (after Keel 2010b: 351 no. 758); 4. Deir el-Balaḥ, unknown (after Keel 2010a: 455 no. 132); 5. Tel Beth-Shemesh, Stratum III (after Keel 2010a: 265 no. 111); 6. Tel Akko, unknown (after Keel 1997: 609 no. 225); 7. Tell el-Farʿah (S), unknown (after Keel 2010b: 409 no. 909); 8. Lisht, 20th–21st Dynasty (after: http://www.metmuseum.org/collection/the-collection-online/search/565101?rpp=30&pg=1&ft=09.180.899&pos=1)

figure without the uraei, standing on a lion (Figure 31:3). A version of this also appears on a scarab from Iron Age IB–IIA context at Tell el-Farʿah (S) in a scene that combines it with an anthropomorphic figure standing on a long-eared or horned quadruped (Figure 39:4; below).

The Late Bronze Age predecessors of the motif include the winged figure (1) accompanied by a hippopotamus and a falcon, appearing on a scarab from a Late Bronze Age III tomb at Tell el-Farʿah (Fig. Figure 31:5) (See Keel 2010b: 334 for the symbolism of the scene), or (2) as a serpent slayer, portrayed on a scarab from a nearby contemporaneous tomb (Figure 31:6). A similar (though wingless) serpent slayer is depicted on a cylinder seal from Tell eṣ-Ṣafi, alongside a Seth figure subduing a lion (Figure 31:7). Another wingless figure with similar headgear and kilt is depicted holding a wꜣs scepter on a scarab from a Late Bronze Age IIB tomb at Deir el-Balaḥ (Figure 31:8). This group of figures has been interpreted as connected to Seth with his Levantine attributes (Keel 1990a: 309–320; Cornelius 1994: 161–167, 181–224; Schroer 2011: 54, 332–348), who enjoyed the zenith of his worship during the days of the Ramessides (see Chapter 4).

FIGURE 31　Late Iron Age I–Early Iron Age IIA Depictions of a Winged Deity: No. 1. Tel Qasile (Figure 24:5, above); 2. Tell el-Farʿah (S), Tomb 542 (after Keel 2010b: 93 no. 153); 3. Jerusalem, City of David Strata 9–8 (after Keel 2015: 432 no. 2); 4. Tell el-Farʿah (S), Stratum V/W (after Keel 2010b: 477 no. 919). Late Bronze Age IIB–III Associated Figures: 5. Tell el-Farʿah (S), Tomb 960c (after Keel 2010b: 335 no. 718); 6. Tell el-Farʿah (S), Tomb 902c (after Keel 2010b: 87 no. 138); 7. Tell eṣ-Ṣafi, unknown (after Keel 1990a: 311 fig. 82); 8. Deir el-Balaḥ, Tomb 118 (after Keel 2010a: 406 no. 17)

One face of the seal-amulet from Tel Gerisa depicts a winged, falcon-headed deity accompanied by a uraeus (Figure 32:1). A similar scene appears on a plate from Tel Miqne Stratum VIA (Figure 32:2), plates from a contemporaneous tomb at Tell el-Farʿah (S) (Figure 32:3; cf. Figure 32:4), and on a scarab from late Iron Age I–early Iron Age IIA Tomb 643 of the same site (Figure 32:5). A schematic variant of the same scene (where a reed-sign or a branch replaces the uraeus) is depicted on additional contemporaneous scarabs (Figure 32:6–8). This scene has its roots in a Late Bronze Age prototype, illustrated on a handful of artifacts from Canaan (Münger 2007a: 95) (Figure 32:9–10).

One face of the seal-amulet from Tel Gerisa depicts a winged uraeus (Figure 33:1). A similar motif appears on artifacts from Iron Age I tombs at Tell el-Farʿah (S) (Figure 33:2–3). This motif derives from Late Bronze Age depictions of a winged uraeus accompanied by a sun disk and an *nb*-sign

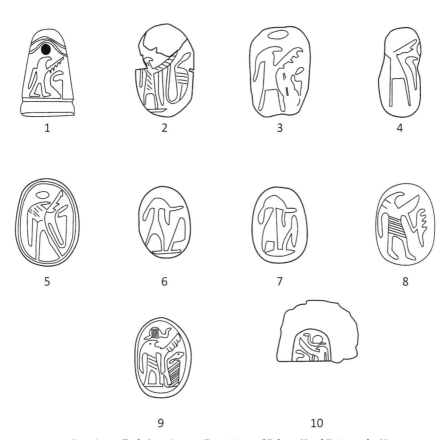

FIGURE 32   Iron Age I–Early Iron Age IIA Depictions of Falcon-Head Deity and a Uraeus: No. 1: Tel Gerisa, Level 6 (Figure 23:4, above); 2: Tel Miqne, Stratum VIA (after Keel 2010a: 549 no. 69); 3: Tell el-Farʿah (S), Tomb 222 (after Keel 2010b: 145 no. 271); 4: Tell el-Farʿah (S), unknown (after Keel 2010b: 421 no. 944); 5: Tell el-Farʿah (S), Tomb 643 (after Keel 2010b: 155 no. 293); 6: Tel Megiddo, Stratum VIA (after Münger 2003: 68 fig. 1:3); 7: Tel Kinrot, Local Stratum S2a (after Münger 2007a: 94 fig. 8); 8: Tel Dothan, unspecified (after Keel 2010a: 497 no. 20); Late Bronze Age IIB–III: 9: el-Ahwat, surface (after Brandl 2012: 249 fig. 14:8); 10: Tel Miqne, unstratified (after Keel 2010a: 547 no. 68)

(Figure 33:4), or a board-sign (Figure 33:5). Interestingly, the uraeus on the seal-amulet from Tel Gerisa has a long, curly tail that is reminiscent of 18th Dynasty depictions (e.g., Figure 33:6).

Last but not least, one face of the seal-amulet from Tell el-Farʿah (S) depicts a triad of anthropomorphic figures (Figure 34:1), while two anthropomorphic

FIGURE 33 Late Bronze Age IIB–III and Iron Age I–Early Iron Age IIA Depictions of Winged Uraeus as Main Motif: No. 1. Tel Gerisa, Level 6 (Figure 23, above); 2: Tell el-Farʿah (S), Tomb 562 (after Keel 2010b: 103 no. 171); 3: Tell el-Farʿah (S), Tomb 960 (after Keel 2010b: 345 no. 743); 4: Tel Beth-Shemesh, Stratum IVB (after Keel 2010a: 279 no. 145); 5: Tell el-Farʿah (S), Area South, Room EF, Stratum E (after Keel 2010b: 387 no. 852); 6: Tel Gezer, unknown (after Keel 2013a: 429 no. 609)

figures appear on a face of the seal-amulet from Ashkelon (Figure 34:2). Similar depictions of couples are identified on two contemporaneous artifacts from Tel Miqne (Figure 34:3–4), and on additional unstratified artifacts from southwest Canaan (Fig. Figure 34:5–7).

Keel suggested that the triad was a derivative of a common New Kingdom triad motif (Keel 1990b: 348), one that typically depicted the pharaoh and two deities (Figure 35:1–3) or three deities, usually Amun-Re accompanied by two falcon-headed figures (Figure 35:4–6) (see discussions by Keel 1995: 214–215; Brandl 2007: 193). Developing his proposal further, Keel suggested that the couplets are based on the Egyptian motif of a pair of deities or of a pharaoh and a deity. Such imagery is a common from the 19th–20th dynasties (Keel 1997: 720), where examples include the figure of Ramesses II holding the scepter of Amun-Re (Figure 35:7), the figure of a king holding hands with a deity

FIGURE 34   Late Iron Age I–Early Iron Age IIA Depictions of Anthropomorphic Figures as Main Motifs: No. 1: Tell el-Farʿah (S) (Figure 25:3, above); 2: Ashkelon (Figure 26:3, above); 3: Tel Miqne, Stratum VB (after Keel 2010a: 543 no. 59); 4: Tel Miqne, Stratum VA (after Keel 2010a: 545 no. 65); (after idem, 545 no. 65); 5: Tel Gerisa, Stratum 10(?) (after Keel 2013a: 158 no. 46); 6: Tell el-Farʿah (S), surface (after Keel 2010b: 77 no. 119); 7: Tell el-Ajjul, unknown (after Keel 1997: 443 no. 995)

(Figure 35:8), or alternatively, two deities holding hands (Figure 35:9). The triad or couplet depicted on the seal-amulets from Tell el-Farʿah (S), Ashkelon, and other artifacts from late Iron Age I–early Iron Age IIA Canaan, are therefore a local adoption and expression of an Egyptian tradition, typically associated with Amun-Re, which was primarily popular during the 19th and 20th dynasties.

Yet Keel (2010b: 116) shifted his position on the issue, and instead chose to interpret these (and other similar Iron Age I–IIA scenes) as a ritual dance (following Mazar 2003: 126–131; Ben-Shlomo 2006: 143). Dancing scenes, however, rarely appear on items from the southern Levant. There are only two known depictions of this motif from the Late Bronze Age, a bulla of a cylinder seal from Tel Halif and possibly a cylinder seal from Tel Lachish (Seger 1992: 124*; Mazar 2003: 126–127). If this is the case, one could argue for a continuation of a rarely depicted concept of ritual dance, or for an Iron Age I innovation in which the ritual-dancing scene was a novelty in local imagery. Consequently, this scene should be linked to the three scenes discussed in the following sections, scenes that feature local innovations.

FIGURE 35 Late Bronze Age IIB–III Depictions of Anthropomorphic Figures as Main Motifs: No. 1: Tel Lachish, Tomb 4004 (after Tufnell 1958: pl. 36:316); 2: Tel Lachish, Tomb 4002 (after Tufnell 1958: pl. 39:365); 3: Tell el-Farʿah (S), Tomb 934 (after Keel 2010b: 271 no. 567); 4: Tell el-Farʿah (S), Tomb 935 (after Keel 2010a: 305 no. 647); 5: Deir el-Balaḥ, Tomb 116 (after Keel 2010a: 405 no. 11); 6: Tel Miqne, LBA Tomb (after Keel 2010a: 519 no. 9); 7: Tell el-Farʿah (S), Tomb 934 (after Keel 2010b: 265 no. 551); 8: Tell el-Farʿah (S), Area South, Room EF, Stratum E (after Keel 2010b: 389 no. 855); 9: Ḥ. Eleq (after Keel 2010a: 555 no. 2)

2 Canaanite Innovations

It has been observed above that the two scenes depicted on the multi-faceted seal-amulets of the triads and couplets, which have in recent years been interpreted as ritual dances, might share no connection to Egyptian imagery. This joins three scenes depicted on the multi-faceted seal-amulets that feature little or no resemblance to New Kingdom Egyptian iconographic traditions and reflect a creative adaptation into local context:

1) A bull accompanied by a scorpion decorate the base of the seal-amulet from Tell el-Farʿah (Figure 25:5);
2) A chariot scene appears on the base of the seal-amulet from Ashkelon (Figure 26:5);
3) An anthropomorphic figure standing on a long-eared or horned animal depicted on one face of the seal-amulet from Tell Qasile (Figure 24:4).

The first scene, the bull accompanied by a scorpion that decorates the base of the seal-amulet from Tell el-Farʿah (Figure 36:1), can be compared to the somewhat damaged face of the seal-amulet from Tel Qasile (Figure 36:2),

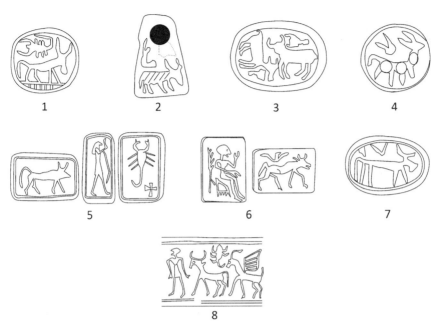

FIGURE 36 Depictions of a Bull and Accompanying Elements: Iron Age I–Early Iron Age IIA: 1: Tell el-Farʿah (S), Cemetery 800 (Figure 25:5, above); 2: Tel Qasile (fig. 2, above); 3: Tel Megiddo, Stratum VB (after Loud 1948: pl. 153:225); 4: Tell eṣ-Ṣafi/Gath, Stratum A3 (after Keel 2013a: 117 no. 47). Late Bronze Age IIB–III: No. 5. Tel Gezer, "2nd Semitic Period" (after Keel 2013a: 323 no. 356); 6: Tel Gerisa, unknown context (after Brandl 2008: 147* fig. 8b); 7: Tel Beth-Shemesh, Stratum IV (after Keel 2010a: 285 no. 156); 8: Tel Lachish, Tomb 4004 (after Eggler 2008: fig. 62)

which depicts an unclear object above a quadruped (Shuval 1990: 72).[7] Similar scenes appear on other items dated to the late Iron Age I–Iron Age IIA, such as a bull accompanied by a scorpion (e.g., Figure 36:3) or a bird (Figure 36:4).[8] A possible background to this scene can perhaps be found in Late Bronze Age Canaanite bifacial plaques. Artifacts from this group depict the bull and scorpion (Figure 36:5) or a bull with a bird above it (Figure 36:6). The later scene is possibly also depicted on a scarab from Tel Beth-Shemesh Stratum IV

---

7 Shuval (1990: 72 and n. 2) understood the figure as *Mȝʿt* above a bull, whereas Keel (1990a: 296) has stated his doubts about this interpretation due to the dissimilarities between the figure and the traditional image of *Mȝʿt*.

8 It has been suggested that a third type of scene depicts a leaping anthropomorphic figure above the bull. For further information regarding the debate on the meaning of the scene, and the interpretation of various elements, see Blockman and Guillaume (2005); Guillaume (2007, 2011) and Staubli (2009).

FIGURE 37 Late Iron Age I–Early Iron Age IIA Depictions of a Chariot Scene: 1: Ashkelon (Figure 26:5, above); 2: Tel Qasile, Stratum XII (after Mazar 1985a: 19 fig. 6:1); 3: Tell el-Farʿah (S), Tomb 533 609 (after Keel 2010b: 125 no. 224); 4: Tell el-Farʿah (S), Tomb 609 (after Keel 2010b: 131 no. 236); 5: Tell el-Farʿah (S), Tomb 503 (after Keel 2010b: 125 no. 226); 6: Tel Jemmeh, Room KB (after Keel 2013a: 37 no. 83); 7: Tel Gezer, "4th Semitic Period" (after Keel 2013a: 361 no. 448)

(Figure 36:7). This group of plaques was the product of the aforementioned Late Bronze Age IIA–B Levantine workshop, whose iconographic features had a marked influence on Mitannian "Common Style" cylinder seals (Keel 1994: 226–230; Brandl 2008), such as a seal depicting a scene with a scorpion above a bull from a Late Bronze Age II context at Tel Lachish (Figure 36:8).

The base of the seal-amulet from Ashkelon (Figure 37:1) is decorated with a chariot scene, in which an anthropomorphic rider wears a crown, holds a bow, and carries a sword or a dagger at its waist. A horse pulls the chariot, above which a horned animal hops, while another anthropomorphic figure appears to the right. A scarab from Tel Qasile Stratum XII (Figure 37:2) depicts a similar scene, as do additional artifacts from late Iron Age I–early Iron Age IIA tombs at Tell el-Farʿah (Figure 37:3–5) and a couple of artifacts from southwest Canaan (Figure 37:6–7).

The notion that the motif derives from Egyptian royal iconography is widely accepted (Keel 1990a: 285–292; Shuval 1990: 76–86; Keel and Uehlinger 1998: 120; Münger 2003: 67). Yet while Shuval has argued that the ambiguous animal above the chariot constitutes inclusion of a Syrian motif, a hare above a chariot, Keel argues against the identification of the animal as a hare and

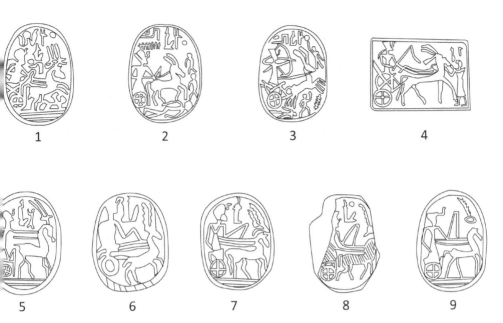

FIGURE 38 Late Bronze Age IIB–III Depictions of a Chariot Scene: 1: Tell el-Ajjul, Tomb 1116E (after Keel 1997: 205 no. 302); 2: Tell el-Far'ah (S), Tomb 960 (after Keel 2010b: 333 no. 712); 3: Jaffa, unknown (after Lalkin 2008: pl. 30:523); Deir el-Balaḥ, Tomb 116 (after Keel 2010a: 405 no. 11); 5: Tel Gezer, "3rd Semitic Period" (after Keel 2013a: 289 no. 275); 6: Tell el-Far'ah (S), Tomb 606 (after Keel 2010b: 133 no. 240); 7: Tell el-Far'ah (S), Tomb 934 (after Keel 2010b: 269 no. 563); 8: Beth-Zur, Locus 90 (after Keel 2010a: 321 no. 8); 9: Tel Dothan, Tomb 2 (after Keel 2010a: 489 no. 3)

suggests it be identified as a caprid. According to Keel a caprid would derive from a strictly Egyptian background, as seen on a handful of unprovenanced artifacts. I would like to suggest an alternative reconstruction for the history of the scene, following Keel's interpretation of the animal above the horse as a horned animal.

Chariot scenes appeared in Egyptian royal iconography beginning in the 18th Dynasty, depicting a battle or a hunt (Schneider 2003a: 159–160 with literature; Feldman and Sauvage 2010: 120–132), but their main appearance on seal-amulets dates from the 19th and 20th Dynasties. Starting in the days of Ramesses II, the chariot is depicted driven by the pharaoh, identified by his name (*Wsr-Mȝʿt-Rʿ Stp.n-Rʿ*) that is written in the upper register. In most cases, the horse, which tramples the enemy, is depicted wearing a feather crown (Figure 38:1), whereas in other variants the horse's headdress resembles two horns (Figure 38:2–3). This scene is a miniaturization of the complex chariot scenes known from monumental art decorating Egyptian temples such as the many depictions of the Battle of Kadesh (Spalinger 2003). In a third variant of this scene, on a plaque from Deir el-Balaḥ, the second figure in the scene is a groom (Figure 38:4), perhaps preparing for battle(Survey 1930: Plate 16). Common to the first and second variants is the preference to place only a few components above the pharaoh or his chariot, signifying his name and titles. A similar trend is seen in monumental art, which include additional elements such as the figure of the goddess Nekhbet, a winged disk, and at times there are also indications as to the location of the scene (e.g., Survey 1932: pls. 116–117; Survey 1996: pls. 2–6 and many others).

Additional chariot scenes appear in less detail on other artifacts (Figure 38:5–9). The primary difference between these chariot scenes and those previously described is the absence of the royal name (except for a schematic *Mꜣꜥt*-sign). Another notable difference is the further simplification of the horse's feather crown (Figure 38:5), occasionally presented as two horns (Figure 38:6), or as a hovering object above the horse's head (Figure 38:7–9).

Considering the above, I would cautiously suggest that the continued alteration of the feather crown would have led to the Iron Age I depiction of the horned animal above the horse. Whether due to "mechanical" reproduction, a deteriorated master copy in the course of mass production, a misunderstanding of the hovering feather crown, or for an unknown reason the feather-crown was replaced with a similar-looking figure—a horned animal. Bearing in mind the process of iconographic change in Canaan, the traditional scene showing the pharaoh riding his chariot and trampling an enemy was adapted, a horned animal was depicted accompanying the riding figure. The identity of the rider is thus questioned—is it still the figure of a ruler or was the scene meant to depict a deity, and in that case, was the horned animal its attribute?

The final scene to consider is depicted on one face of the seal-amulet from Tel Qasile (Figure 39:1): an anthropomorphic figure standing on a quadruped with long ears or horns. Other artifacts dating to late Iron Age I–early Iron Age IIA (Figure 39:2–8) depict similar scenes. Additional variants of the scene include another motif of either an anthropomorphic figure (sometimes winged, see above) standing above a lion (Figure 39:9–12), or a pair of lions (Figure 39:13).

According to Keel (1990a: 302–304) the scene depicts the figure of Resheph standing above a gazelle (followed by Cornelius 1994: 113; Münger 2003: 67; Ben-Shlomo 2006: 139; 2010: 82–83). Alternatively, Lipiński (1996: 258) has called for additional evidence to support such an identification. Indeed, the figure shown on the artifacts (Figure 39) does not conform to the characteristics of

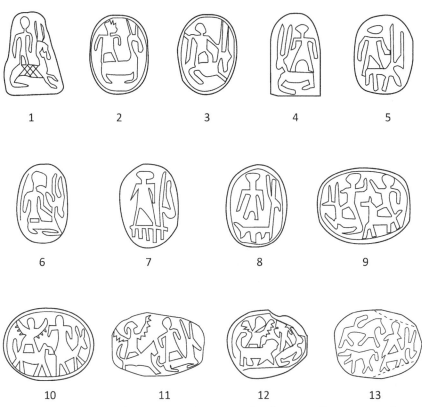

FIGURE 39 Iron Age I–Early Iron Age IIA Depictions of Anthropomorphic Figure Standing on an Animal with Long Ears or Horns: 1: Tel Qasile (Figure 24:4, above); 2: Badari, Tomb 5545 (after Brunton 1930: pl. 34:20); 3: Tell Keisan, Stratum 9a (after Shuval 1990: 142 no. 43); 4: Tell en-Naṣbeh, Tomb 32 (after Shuval 1990: 142 no. 44); 5: Tell el-Farʿah (S), Tomb 241 (after Keel 2010b: 183 no. 358); 6: Tel Akko, Surface (after Keel 1997: 561 no. 84); 7: Tel Akko, Surface (after Keel 1997: 571 no. 111); 8: Tell Abu Salima, unknown (after Petrie 1937: pl. 6:58); 9: Tel Miqne, Stratum V (after Keel 2010a: 549 no. 70); 10: Tell el-Farʿah (S), Tomb 225 934 (after Keel 2010b: 189 no. 374); 11: Tell el-Farʿah (S), Area North, Room VL, Niveau 376', Stratum V/W (after Keel 2010b: 411 no. 919); 12: Tel Lachish, Surface (after Shuval 1990: 144 no. 47); 13: Tell el-Farʿah (S), Tomb 229 (after Keel 2010b: 165 no. 314)

the figure of Resheph, as depicted on the few known artifacts from Late Bronze Age Canaan or Egypt (Figure 40) by posture or by the absence of accompanying weapons.[9] Furthermore, the connection between Resheph and the gazelle is known from the Egyptian variants of the deity—that was adopted in the

---

9 On the iconography of Resheph, see Schroer (2011: 54–55 with literature).

FIGURE 40
Late Bronze Age Depictions of Resheph: 1: Tel Gezer, Cave 10A (after Keel 2013a: 439 no. 630); 2: Tel Gezer, Fourth Semitic Period (after Keel 2013a: 352 no. 425); 3: Tel Lachish, Fosse Temple unknown (after Keel and Uehlinger 1998: 77 fig. 85a)

southern Levant[10]—represented as wearing a tiara decorated with a gazelle's head (Strandberg 2009: 140; Tazawa 2009: 126–127 with literature; Münnich 2013: 119).[11]

There are, therefore, core concerns associated with identifying the deity with Resheph. The figure depicted in these scenes might have been a modified image of Resheph, where he was stripped (for unknown reasons) of his weapons. It is this revised image that was positioned over the gazelle, which then became his pedestal, following Egyptian inspiration. Yet even the identification of the animal as a gazelle is problematic, as there is only a single depiction where the animal has gazelle horns, preserved on an unstratified artifact from Tel Akko (Figure 39:6). Thus the animal should be viewed as a horned animal and not specifically a gazelle.

In light of this, I would suggest an alternative interpretation of this scene. The Levantine topos of an anthropomorphic figure and a horned animal has traditionally been associated with goddesses (Keel and Uehlinger 1998: 19–20; Ben-Tor 2007: 175; Schroer 2008: 48, 194–203). During the Late Bronze Age the topos was primarily common in northern Levantine imagery (e.g., Schroer 2011: 302–303 no. 859). It was attested to in southwest Canaanite pictorial depictions, such as on various vessels from the Fosse Temple at Lachish which depict ibexes and a tree, or ibexes and an elaborated triangle (Tufnell et al. 1940: pl. 47A and 47B no. 229). The context for the innovation of placing the horned animal as the goddess's pedestal should be understood in light of the general rise in the importance of horned animals during the Iron Age I as discussed in the previous chapter.

The inspiration for this Iron Age I scene may have been a parallel, contemporaneous scene, which depicted an anthropomorphic figure standing on a

---

10   A yet unpublished cylinder seal from Late Bronze Age IIB Tel Gezer depicts a figure wearing the white crown adorned with a gazelle's head holding his bow and defeating his many enemies in a scene that resembles royal battle reliefs (see https://www.haaretz.com/archaeology/1.798934).

11   Münnich (2009) traced the change in the worship of Resheph in New Kingdom Egypt from a war deity, particularly during the 18th Dynasty, to a protective deity responsible for healing during the 19th and 20th Dynasties. In this light, see Strandberg (2009: 190) who interpreted the gazelle-tiara as associated with the animal's symbolic ability to heal.

FIGURE 41   Iron Age I–Early Iron Age IIA Depictions of an Anthropomorphic Figure Standing on the Back of a Horse: 1: Tel Eton, Tomb 1 (after Keel 2010a: 607 no. 5); 2: Tell el-Ajjul, Tomb 1074 (after Keel 1997: 185 no. 245); 3: Tell el-Farʿah (S), Tomb 509 (after Keel 2010b: 139 no. 356); 4: Taʾanach, unknown (after Keel and Uehlinger 1998: 142 fig. 164b); 5: Tel Beth-Shemesh, Tomb 1 (after Keel 2010a: 233 no. 35); 6: Giveon, Tomb 3 (after Keel 2013a: 469 no. 8); 7: Kadesh Barnea, Substratum 3c (after Münger 2007b: 240 fig. 14.4); 8: Tel Reḥov, Stratum IV (after Keel and Mazar 2009: 58* fig. 2:15)

horse (Keel and Uehlinger 1998: 141–143) (Figure 41), possibly a development of the preceding scene of a naked goddess standing on a horse known from Tel Lachish (see above, Chapter 4). Significantly, the horse from Tel Lachish is adorned with a feather-crown similar to contemporaneous and earlier Egyptian depictions of Astarte, sometimes styled as two long horns/ears (Figure 19). Considering both the development of the depiction of the feather-crown and the prominence of horned animals in Iron Age I local imagery, I suggest that the horse was replaced by a horned animal in at least one workshop, in order to serve as the goddess's pedestal.

3   Local Glyptic Production during the Iron Age I–IIA

The above overview of the imagery depicted on the multi-faceted seal-amulets leads towards the isolation of four aspects of local glyptic production in southwest Canaan during the Iron Age I–IIA. First, it is evident that the majority of the motifs are of Egyptian background. Some derive directly from imagery of the 19th–20th Dynasties, and thus reflect a high level of exposure to Egyptian motifs and their localization. Other scenes also find close parallels to artifacts unearthed in Egypt, and hence they might reflect the influence of the imagery of the late 21st–early 22nd Dynasties, as seen on the mass-produced scarabs from the early Iron Age. The overwhelming "Egyptian" and "Egyptian-derived" components in the multi-faceted corpus is indicative of the shared cultural milieu of local artisans with contemporaneous Egyptian workshops, and the similarity in the selection and stylization of the depicted scenes. Such images may therefore reflect a wider phenomenon of southwest Canaanite glyptic production that elaborated on Egyptian-inspired motifs and scenes, the remains of which have traditionally been interpreted in scholarship as Egyptian imports.

The second issue is the process of adoption of "foreign" motifs, and their appropriation by local artisans. This issue is exemplified by three scenes: (1) the bull and accompanying scorpion or bird is a development of local tradition that was created through fusion of north Levantine and local imagery during the Late Bronze Age; (2) the chariot scene and (3) the anthropomorphic figure standing above a horned animal reflect appropriation of Egyptian concepts of the 19th–20th Dynasties. All three exemplify how icons and scenes are extracted from their original context and adapted to suit local norms and cultural associations (Uehlinger 2000: xv–xvii; Suter and Uehlinger 2005: xx). In other words, they were not simply copied but rather selectively chosen and altered as befitted local concepts.

The third issue is the prominence of the Amun-Re iconography in the local glyptic production. Does it reflect trade connections with the late-20th–21st Dynasty Delta (Münger 2003; Schipper 2005; Ben-Dor Evian 2017b) and the consequent appropriation of Egyptian symbols by Canaanite artisans? Or does it suggest a continuation of Amun-Re worship in the southern Levant despite the withdrawal of the Egyptians (Keel and Uehlinger 1998: 113–114)? The latter option would support the suggested continued importance of Gaza as raised in Chapter 6.

Finally, this corpus reflects no "Mediterranean" pictorial influence. Generally speaking, Aegean- or Cypriot-inspired motifs or scenes are attested to on a handful of artifacts from Iron Age I southwest Canaan, accounting for a small minority, and overshadowed by local and Egyptian-inspired imagery (Ben-Shlomo 2006: 146–147; 2010: 72–73, 190). The disparity between pictorial influencers suggests that local glyptic production was shaped by different mechanisms than those of local pottery and textile production. Such processes were greatly affected by innovations that spread throughout the eastern Mediterranean basin, though it is difficult to trace the setting for this marked variation. It is anticipated that a future thorough study of the Iron Age I–IIA glyptics in the region would help in search of these aspects of production, distribution, and consumption.

SUMMARY

Colonial Encounters in Southwest Canaan in the Late Bronze Age and Early Iron Age

The goal of this book has been to scrutinize the networks of interactions that developed over time between the local population in southwest Canaan, the agents of the Egyptian state, and the various groups that came to the region over the course of the 16th through the 12th centuries BCE, and to explore how the Egyptian withdrawal from the Levant impacted these networks. The study's most salient conclusion has been that the local southwestern Canaanite population played an active part in shaping historical events of the Late Bronze Age through the Iron Age I. Local elites fulfilled an important role in the development and strengthening of Egyptian hegemony in Canaan, as well as in the molding of political and social systems in the post-Egyptian era.

An examination of the settlement patterns at the beginning of the period revealed two parallel processes. The first is that during Late Bronze Age I, local rulers established power centers at the same sites where sovereignty had been projected from during the Middle Bronze Age. In this light, it becomes clear that the local centers were repeatedly re-established in the same places, apparently due to traditions that became associated with these sites, and their visibility in the landscape as a tangible and symbolic manifestation of their owners' status. In contrast, the Egyptians initially established their bases along the coast, first at Tell el-Ajjul and later, in the 15th century BCE in Jaffa and Gaza. The archaeological information on Gaza is scant, but the data shows that the most clear-cut expression of Egyptian influence on the settlement pattern of southwest Canaan is the founding of a center at a site that had wielded less influence previously, but whose importance subsequently continued to hold sway (albeit with some gaps) throughout antiquity.

The Egyptian centers that were founded along the coast were initially intended as supply stations for the Egyptian army and fleet, when Egypt established its hold ahead of a confrontation with Mitanni. According to this suggestion, interaction between Egypt and the local population was accelerated in the decades following Thutmose III's campaigns, whether by way of intentional Egyptian policy (although such policy is known mainly with regard to cities on the north-Levantine coast, while conclusions are more difficult to draw regarding southwest Canaan), or whether due to unknown factors that motivated local groups to ally themselves with these power centers. A hint of such a process is the increase in the local use of Egyptian amulets, substituting locally produced amulets. The main outcome here of note is that this practice was shared by both Egyptians and locals for both the living and their dead.

Moreover, in this shared medium the image of the Egyptian king may have served as a guardian, and perhaps even as a mediator to the gods, but not as an aggressor to fear. It is thus suggested that the increasing demand of Egyptian centers for agricultural produce, and trade with local groups who provided this produce, was a central factor in these ties, which over the years grew closer and led to the further establishment of the local lords. The main evidence for this process is (1) the accumulation of wealth and power discerned at various sites in southwest Canaan, (2) the rise in the number of Egyptian sources that mention Canaanite locales, (3) the growing number of Canaanites that appear in Egyptian administrative documents, and (4) Canaanite involvement in the colonial network.

The extensive information in the el-Amarna letters reflects the nature of the relationship between the court and the local rulers about 100–150 years after the Egyptians established themselves along the coast. Discussion of the el-Amarna letters reveals the existence of rulers based at six or seven centers in the southwest part of the country during the Late Bronze Age IIA (from north to south): Maḥoz/Yavneh-Yam, Gezer, Tel Beth-Shemesh (?), Gath, Ashkelon, Lachish, and Yurza/Tel Haror. In addition, the content of the el-Amarna letters discloses the active part played by local rulers in expanding the Egyptian hegemony in Canaan. In their letters, local rulers repeatedly stressed their affinity to court, their service in the Egyptian administration, and their devotion to the king (usually in order to win Egyptian protection during local conflicts). The actions of the local rulers could be interpreted as surrender to colonial rule; however, the benefits they enjoyed as a result of their incorporation into the imperial system should also be emphasized. These included the buttressing of their rule, expansion of their ties with other rulers, and their participation in a broader economy.

A possible example of the active role that local rulers played in southwest Canaan in the consolidation of the Egyptian hegemonic framework during the 18th Dynasty is the appropriation of Egyptian cultic paraphernalia by inhabitants of Lachish. The analysis of the data from the Fosse Temple at Tel Lachish shows that cult there was devoted to a goddess called Elat, and it has been suggested that in the Late Bronze Age IIA she was associated with Hathor. The latter was in turn associated with the divine manifestation of Tiye, the wife of Amenhotep III. The worship of the goddess at Lachish might have been affiliated with the worship of the royal couple in the last decade of the reign of Amenhotep III. The dominance of the local component in the cult and the continued identification of the goddess by her local name, reveal the active involvement of the local population in this process, especially the desire of local rulers and their inner circles to incorporate Egypt into their culture. The persistence of the Fosse Temple cult into the Late Bronze Age IIB also reflects the close association between the Lachishites and Egypt during the 19th Dynasty, and the manner in which they identified themselves as part of the colonial network.

The ongoing contact between the local population and the Egyptians also manifested itself in areas other than cult. The main part of the process began during the Late Bronze Age IIB, at the same time that the colonial network was strengthening its presence in the Besor region, along the coast and east of Jaffa. In this context it is argued that the appearance of foreign motifs in local centers does not necessarily prove the *presence* of foreigners, but neither is it a sign of the dilution of local identity. On the contrary, it is primarily evidence of frequent contact between the locals and the agents of the court (and perhaps between local rulers and the court itself), and of the ways in which they integrated Egypt into their life when they became part of the colonial network. It constituted part of the ongoing process of "domesticating" foreign cultural motifs while keeping with accepted local social norms. Particularly outstanding is the adoption of an Egyptian foodway—the eating of goose meat—and conspicuous consumption at feasts, which symbolized the senior status of the participants and their associations with Egypt.

The rift in the relationship between Egypt and the local elites occurred at the end of the 13th century BCE with the destruction of the local centers in southwest Canaan. While the Egyptian army captured two of these, Gezer and Ashkelon (as far as we know), all the other centers, both large and small, were also destroyed or abandoned and the political array was completely transformed. For a brief time during the Late Bronze Age III, one local center existed, at Lachish, and smaller local centers were established in other places such as Tel Azekah. The inhabitants at Lachish in this period incorporated many practices that had originated in Egypt, such as the continued consumption of goose meat and innovations such as burials in clay coffins and the appropriation of iconography devoted to an Egyptian deity of Levantine origin—Astarte, which became increasingly popular in the Iron Age I. In this case too, it can be seen that the images of this deity included traditional Canaanite motifs, and thus this is yet another example of the entanglement of Egyptian and local ideas.

The sudden Egyptian withdrawal in the second half of the 12th century BCE created a political vacuum in southern Canaan that led to the emergence of two separate foci. The continuity of the settlement pattern in the Besor region and the pictorial motifs involving the cult of Amun led to speculation that the power center in Gaza remained in existence even after the Egyptian withdrawal from Canaan. Gaza therefore might belong to the limited group of historical phenomena—centers that persevered and preserved their regional influence even after they lost contact with the nexus of colonial power. Particularly prominent is the continuity of Amun's iconography during the post-Egyptian period. It was absorbed by the locals in Canaan through a complex process that included "translating" them into the local iconography, in a manner that conformed to local ways, sometimes disconnecting them from the Egyptian traditions, and occasionally with the addition of genuine Canaanite iconography.

As for the region north of Gaza, collapse of the political sphere there led to the growth of a new social structure. The important center of this network was at Tel Miqne; other centers developed over the years at Tel Ashdod and Tell eṣ-Ṣafi/Gath. This is also the region in which Cypriot, Aegean, Anatolian, and north-Levantine practices appeared, possibly via mediation of newcomers. As opposed to the accepted reconstruction in scholarly discourse, these settlers were not superior in power, numbers, or culture over the local population. On the contrary, they were a small number of migrants who integrated into the local culture. Analysis of the available evidence suggests that a rising elite located at Tel Miqne integrated various practices as part of a broader process in which they sought new means through which they could express their power and status, and perhaps their lack of affinity with the Egyptian cultural sphere.

In this assessment, it should be made clear that the Philistines were a group whose size, origin, and time of arrival to the region are not known, and that the establishment of their rule was limited to a few of the centers in southwest Canaan during the Iron Age I. Interpretive frameworks which analyze archaeological data based on unfounded historical assumptions that conflate the Philistines with Cypriot or Aegean settlers from the 12th century BCE should be rejected. Although the Philistines may have arrived at the same time as these other settlers, they may have otherwise arrived later, during the 11th century BCE, and become 'Lords' of the land under circumstances that remain unclear.

Throughout that time, the population in the rural hinterland to the east, such as at Tel Beth-Shemesh, retained their traditional practices. Nonetheless, ongoing dialogue with the emerging society can be seen at and around Tel Miqne, as well as in the trade ties among the various groups. In the Yarkon basin, the continuity of the local practices is pronounced, while remains of the new center established at Tel Qasile reveal connections with Tel Miqne and its surroundings (such as Bichrome Ware and cult figurines), as well as with the Levantine littoral, Cyprus, and Egypt.

In conclusion, discussion in this book underscores the active role played by the local population in the events that shaped the colonial situation. Local groups (especially their rulers) to some extent influenced the formulation of the colonizers' policy, and the latter's choice of hegemonic rule over the other alternatives, such as direct annexation. They incorporated the colonizer into their world, adopted practices and made them local. In the post-colonial period, they shaped their social spheres with an emphasis on imperial heritage on the one hand, and on a new identity *disconnected* from that heritage, on the other. In the process, they embraced new practices and, in all cases, tailored these innovations to the accepted social norms. These conclusions do not obviate the importance of "external" factors in shaping historical events, but rather they accentuate the continuous dialogue between the customs of the local population and its fundamental role in intercultural encounters.

APPENDIX

Chronology of Egyptian Kings

Absolute chronology of Egyptian kings has been debated for the last several decades, with factors such as radiocarbon dating providing new insights to be integrated into the scholarly discourse (Aston 2012–2013). The following table presents the result of such an integrative study (Schneider 2010b):

King	Chronology (all dates BCE)
18th Dynasty	1548–1301
Ahmose	1548–1523
Amenhotep I	1523–1502
Thutmose I	1502–1489
Thutmose II	1489–1476
Hatshepsut / Thutmose III	1476–1422
Amenhotep II	1422–1396
Thutmose IV	1396–1386
Amenhotep III	1386–1348
Amenhotep IV/Akhenaten	1348–1331
Transition period to Tutankhamun	1331–1327
Tutankhamun	1327–1318
Aya	1318–1315
Horemheb	1315–1301
19th Dynasty	1301–1198
Ramesses I	1301–1300
Seti I	1300–1290
Ramesses II	1290–1224
Merneptah	1224–1214
Seti II	1214–1208
Amenmesse	1208–1206
Siptah and Tewosre	1206–1198
20th Dynasty	1198–1086
Setnakhte	1198–1195
Ramesses III	1195–1164
Ramesses IV	1164–1156

(cont.)

King	Chronology (all dates BCE)
Ramesses V	1156–1152
Ramesses VI	1152–1144
Ramesses VII	1144–1137
Ramesses VIII	1137
Ramesses IX	1137–1118
Ramesses X	1118–1115
Ramesses XI	1115–1086
21st Dynasty	**1086–962**
Smendes	1086–1060
Amenemnesu	1060–1056
Psusennes I	1056–1010
Amenemope	1010–1001
Osochor	1001–995
Siamun	995–976
Psusennes II	976–962
22nd Dynasty	**962–733**
Shoshenq I	962–941

Bibliography

Ad, Uzi, Golani, Amir, and Segal, Orit (2014), 'Tel Azor', *Hadashot Arkheologiyot: Excavations and Surveys in Israel*, 126.

Aḥituv, Shmuel (1984), *Canaanite Toponyms in Ancient Egyptian Documents* (Jerusalem: Magnes Press, Hebrew University).

Ahrens, Alexander (2011a), 'A "Hyksos Connection"? Thoughts on the Date of Dispatch of Some of the Middle Kingdom Objects found in the Northern Levant', in Jana Mynářová (ed.), *Egypt and the Near East—the Crossroads: Proceedings of an International Conference on the Relations of Egypt and the Near East in the Bronze Age, Prague, September 1–3, 2010* (Prague: Charles University in Prague, Czech Institute of Egyptology), 21–40.

Ahrens, Alexander (2011b), 'Strangers in a Strange Land? The Function and Social Significance of Egyptian Imports in the Northern Levant during the 2nd Millennium BC', in Kim Duistermaat and Ilona Regulski (eds.), *Proceedings of the International Conference "Intercultural Contacts in the Ancient Mediterranean," held in Cairo, 26–29 October 2008, Netherlands-Flemish Institute in Cairo* (Orientalia Lovaniensia Analecta 202; Leuven: Peeters), 289–311.

Ahrens, Alexander (2015), 'The Early 18th Dynasty in the Northern Levant: New Finds and a Reassessment of the Sources', in Jana Mynářová, Pavel Onderka, and Peter Pavuk (eds.), *There and Back Again—Crossroads II: Proceedings of an International Conference held in Prague, September 15–18, 2014* (Prague: Czech Institute of Egyptology), 353–371.

Äikäs, Tiina and Salmi, Anna-Kaisa (2013), '"The Sieidi is a Better Altar/The Noaidi Drum's a Purer Church Bell": Long-Term Changes and Syncretism at Sámi Offering Sites', *World Archaeology*, 45 (1), 64–82.

Aja, Adam J. (2009), 'Philistine Domestic Architecture in the Iron Age I', Ph.D. dissertation (Harvard University).

Albarella, Umberto (2005), 'Alternate Fortunes? The Role of Domestic Ducks and Geese from Roman to Medieval Times in Britain', *Documenta archaeobiologiae*, 3 (4), 249–258.

Albright, William F. (1932), 'The Excavations of Tell Beit-Mirsim, 1: The Pottery of the First Three Campaigns', *Annual of the American Schools of Oriental Research*, 12, 1–165.

Albright, William F. (1938a), 'The Chronology of a South Palestinian City, Tell el-'Ajjûl', *American Journal of Semitic Languages and Literatures*, 55, 337–359.

Albright, William F. (1938b), 'The Excavation of Tell Beit Mirsim II: The Bronze Age', *Annual of the American Schools of Oriental Research*, 17, 1–141.

Albright, William F. (1939), 'The Israelite Conquest of Canaan in the Light of Srchaeology', *Bulletin of the American Schools of Oriental Research*, 74, 11–23.

Albright, William F. (1940), *From the Stone Age to Christianity* (Baltimore: Johns Hopkins University Press).

Albright, William F. (1949), *The Archaeology of Palestine* (London: Penguin Books).

Alcock, Susan E. (2005), 'Roman Colonies in the Eastern Empire: A Tale of Four Cities', in Gil Stein (ed.), *The Archaeology of Colonial Encounters* (Santa Fe: School of American Research Press), 297–329.

Allon, Niv (2007), 'Seth is Baal-Evidence from the Egyptian Script', *Egypt and the Levant*, 17, 15–22.

Alt, Albrecht (1944), 'Ägyptische Tempel in Palästina und die Landnahme der Philister', *Zeitschrift des Deutschen Palästina-Vereins*, 67, 1–20.

Amiran, Ruth (1960), 'A Late Bronze Age II Pottery Group from a Tomb in Jerusalem', *Eretz Israel*, 6, 25–37. (Hebrew).

Amiran, Ruth (1969), *Ancient Pottery of the Holy Land: From Its Beginnings in the Neolithic Period to the End of the Iron Age* (Jerusalem: Massada Press).

Anthony, Flora Brooke (2017), *Foreigners in Ancient Egypt: Theban Tomb Paintings from the Early Eighteenth Dynasty* (London: Bloomsbury Publishing).

Areshian, Gregory E. (2013), 'Variability and Complexity in Multidisciplinary and Interdisciplinary Studies of Empires', in Gregory E. Areshian (ed.), *Empires and Diversity: On the Crossroads of Archaeology, Anthropology, and History* (Ideas, Debates, and Perspectives; Los Angeles: Cotsen Institute of Archaeology University of California), 1–20.

Asaro, Frank, Perlman, Isadore, and Dothan, Moshe (1971), 'An Introductory Study of Mycenaean IIIC1 Ware from Tel Ashdod', *Archaeometry*, 13 (2), 169–175.

Ashcroft, Bill, Griffiths, Gareth, and Tiffin, Helen (2004), *The Empire Writes Back: Theory and Practice in Post-colonial Literatures* (Second edn.; London and New York: Routledge).

Ashcroft, Bill, Griffiths, Gareth, and Tiffin, Helen (2013), *Post-Colonial Studies: The Key Concepts* (Second edn.; London and New York: Routledge).

Aston, David (2012–2013), 'Radiocarbon, Wine Jars and New Kingdom Chronology', *Egypt and the Levant*, 22, 289–315.

Ayalon, Etan (ed.), (2009), *The Hidden History of Tel Aviv* (Tel Aviv: Eretz Israel Museum).

Bader, Bettina (2011), 'Contacts between Egypt and Syria–Palestine as seen in a Grown Settlement of the late Middle Kingdom at Tell el-Dab'a/Egypt', in Jana Mynářová (ed.), *Egypt and the Near East-the Crossroads. Proceedings of an International Conference on the Relations of Egypt and the Near East in the Bronze Age, Prague, September 1–3, 2010* (Prague: Charles University in Prague, Czech Institute of Egyptology, Faculty of Arts), 41–72.

Bader, Bettina (2013), 'Cultural Mixing in Egyptian Archaeology: The "Hyksos" as a Case Study', *Archaeological Review from Cambridge*, 28 (1), 257–286.

Bailleul-LeSuer, Rozenn (ed.), (2012), *Between Heaven and Earth: Birds in Ancient Egypt* (Oriental Institute Museum Publications 35; Chicago: Oriental Institute of the University of Chicago).

Baines, John (2003), 'On the Genre and Purpose of the "Large Commemorative Scarabs" of Amenhotep III', in Nicolas Grimal, Amr Kamel, and Cynthia May-Sheikholeslami (eds.), *Hommages à Fayza Haikal* (Cairo: Institut Franais d'archologie orientale), 29–43.

Barako, Tristan J. (2000), 'The Philistine Settlement as Mercantile Phenomenon?', *American Journal of Archaeology*, 104 (3), 513–530.

Barako, Tristan J. (2007), *Tel Mor: The Moshe Dothan Excavations, 1959–1960* (Israel Antiquities Authority Reports 32; Jerusalem: Israel Antiquities Authority).

Baramki, D.C. (1935), 'An Ancient Cistern in the Grounds of Government House, Jerusalem', *QDAP*, 4, 165–167.

Barker, Francis, Hulme, Peter, and Iversen, Margaret (eds.) (1994), *Colonial Discourse/Postcolonial Theory* (The Essex Symposia: Literature/Politics/Theory; Manchester: Manchester University Press).

Barnett, Richard D. (1982), *Ancient Ivories in the Middle East and Adjacent Countries* (Qedem; Jerusalem: Institute of Archaeology, Hebrew University of Jerusalem).

Bauer, Alexander A. (1998), 'Cities of the Sea: Maritime Trade and the Origin of Philistine Settlement in the Early Iron Age Southern Levant', *Oxford Journal of Archaeology*, 17 (2), 149–168.

Bauer, Alexander A. (2014), 'The Sea Peoples as an Emergent Phenomenon', in Yannis Galanakis, Toby Wilkinson, and John Bennet (eds.), *ΑΘΥΡΜΑΤΑ: Critical Essays on the Archaeology of the Eastern Mediterranean in Honour of E. Susan Sherratt* (Oxford: Archaeopress), 31–39.

Beit-Arieh, Itzhaq and Ayalon, Etan (2012), *Archaeological Survey of Israel: Map of Kefar Sava—77* [online text], Israel Antiquities Authority <http://www.antiquities.org.il/survey/new/default_en.aspx>.

Ben-Arieh, Sara and Edelstein, Gershon (1977), 'The Tombs and Their Contents', *'Atiqot*, 12, 1–44.

Ben-Dor Evian, Shirly (2011), 'Egypt and the Levant in the Iron Age I–IIA: The Ceramic Evidence', *Tel Aviv*, 38 (1), 94–119.

Ben-Dor Evian, Shirly (2012), 'Egypt and Philistia in the Iron Age I: The Case of the Philistine Lotus Flower', *Tel Aviv*, 39 (1), 20–37.

Ben-Dor Evian, Shirly (2015), '"They were ṯhr on Land, Others at Sea …" The Etymology of the Egyptian Term for "Sea-Peoples"', *Semitica*, 57, 57–75.

Ben-Dor Evian, Shirly (2016), 'The Battles between Ramesses III and the Sea-Peoples. When, Where and Who? An Iconic Analysis of the Egyptian Reliefs', *Zeitschrift für Ägyptische Sprache und Altertumskunde*, 143 (2), 151–168.

Ben-Dor Evian, Shirly (2017a), 'Ramesses III and the "Sea-Peoples": Towards a New Philistine Paradigm', *Oxford Journal of Archaeology*, 36 (3), 267–285.

Ben-Dor Evian, Shirly (2017b), 'Amun-of-the-Road: Trade and Religious Mobility between Egypt and the Levant at the Turn of the First Millennium BCE', *Die Welt des Orients*, 47 (1), 52–65.

Ben-Shlomo, David (2006), 'New Evidence of Seals and Sealings from Philistia', *Tel Aviv*, 33 (2), 134–162.

Ben-Shlomo, David (2010), *Philistine Iconography: A Wealth of Style and Symbolism* (Orbis Biblicus et Orientalis 241; Fribourg and Göttingen: Academic Press, Vandenhoeck and Ruprecht).

Ben-Shlomo, David (2012), *The Azor Cemetery: Moshe Dothan's Excavations, 1958 and 1960* (Israel Antiquities Authority Reports 50; Jerusalem: Israel Antiquities Authority).

Ben-Shlomo, David and Press, Michael D. (2009), 'A Reexamination of Aegean-Style Figurines in Light of New Evidence from Ashdod, Ashkelon, and Ekron', *Bulletin of the American Schools of Oriental Research*, 353, 39–74.

Ben-Shlomo, David and Van Beek, Gus (2014), *The Smithsonian Institution Excavation at Tell Jemmeh, Israel, 1970–1990* (Smithsonian Contributions to Anthropology 50; Washington, D.C.: Smithsonian Institution Scholarly Press).

Ben-Shlomo, David, Shai, Itzhaq, and Maeir, Aren M. (2004), 'Late Philistine Decorated Ware ("Ashdod Ware"): Typology, Chronology, and Production Centers', *Bulletin of the American Schools of Oriental Research*, 335, 1–35.

Ben-Shlomo, David, Uziel, Josef, and Maeir, Aren M. (2009), 'Pottery production at Tell es-Safi/Gath: a Longue Duree Perspective', *Journal of Archaeological Science*, 36 (10), 2258–2273.

Ben-Shlomo, David, et al. (2008), 'Cooking Identities: Aegean-style Cooking jugs and Cultural Interaction in Iron Age Philistia and Neighboring Regions', *American Journal of Archaeology*, 112 (2), 225–246.

Ben-Tor, Daphna (2007), *Scarabs, Chronology and Interconnections. Egypt and Palestine in the Second Intermediate Period* (Orbis Biblicus et Orientalis Series Archaeologica 27; Fribourg and Göttingen: Academic Press and Vandenhoeck & Ruprecht).

Ben-Tor, Daphna (2011a), 'Egyptian-Canaanite Relations in the Middle and Late Bronze Age as Reflected by Scarabs', in Shai Bar, Dan'el Kahn, and J.J. Shirley (eds.), *Egypt, Canaan and Israel: History, Imperialism, Ideology and Literature: Proceedings of a Conference at the University of Haifa, 3–7 May 2009* (Culture and History of the Ancient Near East 52; Leiden and Boston: Brill), 23–43.

Ben-Tor, Daphna (2011b), 'Political Implications of New Kingdom Scarabs in Palestine during the Reigns of Tuthmosis III and Ramesses II', in David Aston, et al. (eds.), *Under the Potter's Tree: Studies on Ancient Egypt Presented to Janine Bourriau on the Occasion of her 70th Birthday* (Orientalia Lovaniesia Analecta 204; Leuven, Paris and Walpole MA: Uitgeverij Peeters), 201–214.

Ben-Tor, Daphna (2016), 'A Scarab of the Mass-Production Groups: The Origin and Date of Early Iron Age Scarabs in the Southern Levant', in Anabel Zarzecki-Peleg (ed.), *Yadin's Expedition to Megiddo: Final Report of the Archaeological Excavations (1960, 1966, 1967, and 1971/2 Seasons)* (Qedem 56; Jerusalem: Institute of Archaeology, the Hebrew University of Jerusalem), 319–321.

Ben-Tor, Daphna (2017), 'Ramesside Scarabs Simulating Middle Bronze Age Canaanite Prototypes: Canaanite or Egyptian?', *Ägypten und Levante*, 27, 195–218.

Ben-Tor, Daphna (2018), 'Evidence for Middle Bronze Age Chronology and Synchronisms in the Levant: A Response to Höflmayer et al. 2016', *Bulletin of the American Schools of Oriental Research*, 379, 43–54.

Ben-Tor, Daphna and Keel, Othmar (2012), 'The Beth-Shean Level IX-Group: A Local Scarab Workshop of the Late Bronze Age I', in Mayer Gruber, et al. (eds.), *All the Wisdom of the East. Studies in Near Eastern Archaeology and History in Honor of Eliezer D. Oren* (Orbis Biblicus et Orientalis 255; Fribourg and Göttingen: Academic Press, Vandenhoeck and Ruprecht), 87–104.

Ben-Yosef, Erez, et al. (2012), 'A New Chronological Framework for Iron Age Copper Production at Timna (Israel)', *Bulletin of the American Schools of Oriental Research*, 367, 31–71.

Bender, Courtney and Cadge, Wendy (2006), 'Constructing Buddhism(s): Interreligious Dialogue and Religious Hybridity', *Sociology of Religion*, 67 (3), 229–247.

Berman, Ariel and Barda, Leticia (2005), *Archaeological Survey of Israel: Map of Nizzanim—87, 88* (Jerusalem: Israel Antiquities Authority).

Bhabha, Homi K. (1994), *The Location of Culture* (London and New York: Routledge).

Bietak, Manfred (2002), 'The Function and Some Archaeological Roots of the Fosse Temple at Lachish', in Eliezer D. Oren and Shmuel Aḥituv (eds.), *Aaron Kempinski Memorial Volume* (Beer-Sheva 15; Beer-Sheva: Ben Gurion University Press), 56–85.

Bietak, Manfred (2015), 'Recent Discussions about the Chronology of the Middle and the Late Bronze Ages in the Eastern Mediterranean: Part I', *Bibliotheca Orientalis*, 72 (3–ß4), 317–335.

Bietak, Manfred and Forstner-Müller, Irene (2011), 'The Topography of New Kingdom Avaris and per-Ramesses', in Mark Collier and Steven Snape (eds.), *Ramesside Studies in Honour of K.A. Kitchen* (Bolton: Rutherford), 11–50.

Bietak, Manfred, et al. (2008), 'Synchronisation of Stratigraphies: Ashkelon and Tell el-Dabʿa', *Ägypten und Levante/Egypt and the Levant*, 18, 49–60.

Bille, Mikkel and Sørensen, Tim Flohr (2007), 'An Anthropology of Luminosity: The Agency of Light', *Journal of Material Culture*, 12 (3), 263–284.

Bireling, Neal (1998), *Tel Miqne-Ekron Excavations 1995–1996, Field XNW, Areas 77, 78, 79, 89, 90, 101, 102: Iron Age I* (Jerusalem: Albright Institute of Archaeological Research).

Birney, Kathleen and Doak, Brian R. (2011), 'Funerary Iconography on an Infant Burial Jar from Ashkelon', *Israel Exploration Journal*, 61 (1), 32–53.
Blakely, Jeffrey A. (2018), 'Tell el-Hesi: A Type Site for Reevaluating so-called "Egyptian Governors' Residencies" of the South', *Palestine Exploration Quarterly*, 150 (4), 271–295.
Blockman, Noga and Guillaume, Philippe (2005), 'Bull-leaping in Ancient Israel', *Ugarit-Forschungen*, 37, 5–8.
Boessneck, Joachim (1986), 'Vogelknochenfunde aus dem alten Ägypten', *Annalen des Naturhistorischen Museums in Wien*, 88/89, 323–344.
Boessneck, Joachim (1995), 'Birds, Reptiles and Amphibians', in Øystein S. LaBianca and Angela Von den Driesch (eds.), *Faunal Remains: Taphonomical and Zooarchaeological Studies of the Animal Remains from Tell Hesban and Vicinity* (Hesban 15; Berrien Springs, MI: Andrews University Press in cooperation with the Institute of Archaeology).
Boessneck, Joachim and von den Driesch, Angela (1992), *Tell el-Dabʿa VII: Tiere und Historische Umwelt im Nordost-Delta im 2. Jahrtausend v. Chr. anhand der Knochenfunde der Ausgrabungen 1975–1986* (Österreichische Akademie der Wissenschaften Denkschriften der Gesamtakademie 11; Vienna: Verlag der Osterreichischen Akademie der Wissenschaften).
Booth, Charlotte (2005), *The Role of Foreigners in Ancient Egypt: A Study of Non-stereotypical Artistic Representations* (British Archaeological Reports 1426; Oxford: Archaeopress).
Bourke, Stephen (2012), 'The Six Canaanite Temples of Ṭabaqat Faḥil. Excavating Pella's 'Fortress' Temple (1994–2009)', in Jens Kamlah (ed.), *Temple Building and Temple Cult: Architecture and Cultic Paraphernalia of Temples in the Levant (2.–1. Mill. B.C.E.)* (Abhandlungen des Deutschen Palästina-Vereins 41; Wiesbaden: Harrassowitz), 159–201.
Brandl, Baruch (1999), 'Two Ramesside Scarabs from Jatt', *ʿAtiqot*, 37, 17*–22*.
Brandl, Baruch (2003), 'The Cape Gelidonya Shipwreck Scarabs Reconsidered', in Manfred Bietak (ed.), *The Synchronisation of Civilisations in the Eastern Mediterranean in the Second Millennium B.C. II* (Contributions to the Chronology of the Eastern Mediterranean 4; Vienna: Verlag der Osterreichischen Akademie der Wissenschaften), 249–261.
Brandl, Baruch (2004), 'Scarabs and Plaques Bearing Royal Names of the Early XXth Egyptian Dynasty Excavated in Canaan. From Sethnakht to Ramesses IV', in Manfred Bietak (ed.), *Scarabs of the Second Millennium BC from Egypt, Nubia, Crete and the Levant* (Contributions to the Chronology of the Eastern Mediterranean 8; Vienna: Verlag der Österreichischen Akademie der Wissenschaften), 57–71.
Brandl, Baruch (2006), 'Canaanite and Egyptian Seals and Sealings', in Nava Panitz-Cohen and Amihai Mazar (eds.), *Timnah (Tel Batash) 3: The Finds from the Second*

Millennium BCE (Qedem 45; Jerusalem: Institute of Archaeology, Hebrew University of Jerusalem), 213–233.

Brandl, Baruch (2007), 'Glyptics', in Tristan J. Barako (ed.), *Tel Mor: The Moshe Dothan Excavations, 1959–1960* (Israel Antiquities Authority Reports 32; Jerusalem: Israel Antiquities Authority), 191–210.

Brandl, Baruch (2008), 'From Milos-Phylakopi to Khirbet ed-Dēr: Additional Observations on A Canaanite Group of Bifacial Rectangular Plaques', in Shai Bar (ed.), *In the Hill-Country, and in the Shephelah, and in the Arabah (Joshua 12, 8): Studies and Researches presented to Adam Zertal in the Thirtieth Anniversary of the Manasseh Hill-Country Survey* (Jerusalem: Ariel), 134*–150*.

Brandl, Baruch (2012), 'Nine Scarabs, a Scaraboid, a Cylinder Seal, and a Bifacial Rectangular Plaque From El-Ahwat', in Adam Zertal (ed.), *El-Ahwat, A Fortified Site from the Early Iron Age Near Nahal 'Iron, Israel: Excavations 1993–2000* (Culture and History of the Ancient Near East 24; Leiden and Boston: Brill), 233–263.

Brandl, Baruch, Bunimovitz, Shlomo, and Lederman, Zvi (2013), 'Beth-Shemesh and Sellopoulo: Two Commemorative Scarabs of Amenhotep III and Their Contribution to Aegean Chronology', *Annual of the British School at Athens*, 108, 67–95.

Brandl, Baruch, Oren, Eliezer D., and Nahshoni, Pirhiya (2015), 'A Clay Door-lock Sealing from the Middle Bronze Age III Temple at Tel Haror, Israel', *Origini*, 36, 157–180.

Bräunlein, Peter J. (2016), 'Thinking Religion Through Things', *Method & Theory in the Study of Religion*, 28 (4–5), 365–399. (English)

Braunstein, Susan L. (2011), 'The Meaning of Egyptian-Style Objects in the Late Bronze Cemeteries of Tell el-Farʻah (South)', *Bulletin of the American Schools of Oriental Research*, 364, 1–36.

Breasted, James H. (1948), 'Bronze Base of a Statue of Ramses VI Discovered at Megiddo', in Gordon Loud (ed.), *Megiddo II: Seasons of 1935–39* (Oriental Institute Publications 62; Chicago: University of Chicago Press), 135–138.

Brisch, Nicole (2013), 'Of Gods and Kings: Divine Kingship in Ancient Mesopotamia', *Religion Compass*, 7 (2), 37–46.

Brisch, Nicole (ed.), (2008), *Religion and Power: Divine Kingship in the Ancient World and Beyond* (Oriental Institute Seminars; Chicago: The Oriental Institute).

Brody, Aaron J. (2016), 'New Perspectives on Levantine Mortuary Ritual', in Thomas E. Levy (ed.), *Historical Biblical Archaeology and the Future* (Oakville: David Brown Book Company), 123–141.

Brug, John F. (1985), *A Literary and Archaeological Study of the Philistines* (BAR International Series; Oxford: BAR).

Bruins, Hendrik J. and van der Plicht, Johannes (2017), 'The Minoan Santorini Eruption and its 14 C Position in Archaeological Strata: Preliminary Comparison Between Ashkelon and Tell el-Dabaʻ', *Radiocarbon*, 59 (5), 1295–1307.

Brunton, Guy (1930), *Qau and Badari III* (London: British School of Archaeology in Egypt).

Bryan, Betsy M. (1996), 'Art, Empire, and the End of the Late Bronze Age', in Jerrold S. Cooper and Glenn M. Schwartz (eds.), *The Study of the Ancient Near East in the Twenty-First Century* (Winona Lake: Eisenbrauns), 33–79.

Bryan, Betsy M. (1997), 'The Statue Program for the Mortuary Temple of Amenhotep III', in Stephen Quirke (ed.), *The Temple in Ancient Egypt: New Discoveries and Recent Research* (London: Published for the Trustees of the British Museum by British Museum Press), 57–81.

Bryce, Trevor R. (2005), *The Kingdom of the Hittites, New Edition* (Oxford: Oxford University Press).

Budin, Stephanie L. (2014), 'Before Kypris was Aphrodite', in David T. Sugimoto (ed.), *Transformation of a Goddess: Ishtar—Astarte—Aphrodite* (Orbis Biblicus et Orientalis 263; Fribourg and Göttingen: Academic Press, Vandenhoeck and Ruprecht), 195–215.

Budin, Stephanie L. (2015), 'The Nude Female in the Southern Levant: a mixing of Syro-Mesopotamian and Egyptian Iconographies', *Baal Hors-Série*, 10, 315–335.

Bunimovitz, Shlomo (1983), 'Glacis 10014 and Gezer's Late Bronze Age Fortifications', *Tel Aviv*, 10 (1), 61–70.

Bunimovitz, Shlomo (1988), 'An Egyptian "Governor's Residency" at Gezer?—Another Suggestion', *Tel Aviv*, 15 (1), 68–76.

Bunimovitz, Shlomo (1989), 'The Land of Israel in the Late Bronze Age: A Case Study of Socio-cultural Change in a Complex Society', Ph.D. dissertation (Tel Aviv University).

Bunimovitz, Shlomo (1990), 'Problems in the "Ethnic" Identification of the Philistine Material Culture', *Tel Aviv*, 17 (2), 210–222.

Bunimovitz, Shlomo (1995), 'On the Edge of Empires—Late Bronze Age (1500–1200 BCE)', in Thomas E. Levy (ed.), *The Archaeology of Society in the Holy Land* (London: Leicester University), 320–331.

Bunimovitz, Shlomo (1998), 'Sea Peoples in Cyprus and Israel: A Comparative Study of Immigration Processes', in Seymour Gitin, Amihai Mazar, and Ephraim Stern (eds.), *Mediterranean Peoples in Transition: Thirteenth to Early Tenth Centuries BCE, In Honor of Trude Dothan* (Jerusalem: Israel Exploration Society), 103–113.

Bunimovitz, Shlomo (2019), '"Canaan is Your Land and its Kings are Your Servants": Conceptualizing the Late Bronze Age Egyptian Government in the Southern Levant', in Assaf Yasur-Landau, Eric H. Cline, and Rowan M. Yorke (eds.), *The Social Archaeology of the Levant: From Prehistory to the Present* (Cambridge: Cambridge University Press), 265–279.

Bunimovitz, Shlomo and Lederman, Zvi (1993), 'Beth-Shemesh', in Ephraim Stern (ed.), *New Encyclopedia of Archaeological Excavations in the Holy Land* (1; Jerusalem: Israel Exploration Society), 249–253.

Bunimovitz, Shlomo and Lederman, Zvi (2006), 'The Early Israelite Monarchy in the Sorek Valley: Tel Beth-Shemesh and Tel Batash (Timnah) in the 10th and 9th Centuries BCE', in Aren M. Maeir and Pierre de Miroschedji (eds.), *"I will Speak the Riddles of Ancient Times": Archaeological and Historical Studies in Honor of Amihai Mazar on the Occasion of His Sixtieth Birthday* (Winona Lake: Eisenbrauns), 407–427.

Bunimovitz, Shlomo and Lederman, Zvi (2008), 'Beth-Shemesh', in Ephraim Stern (ed.), *New Encyclopedia of Archaeological Excavations in the Holy Land* (5; Jerusalem and Washington, DC: Israel Exploration Society and Biblical Archaeological Society), 1644–1648.

Bunimovitz, Shlomo and Lederman, Zvi (2011), 'Canaanite Resistance: The Philistines and Beth-Shemesh—A Case Study from Iron Age I', *Bulletin of the American Schools of Oriental Research*, 364, 37–51.

Bunimovitz, Shlomo and Lederman, Zvi (2013), 'Solving a Century-Old Puzzle: New Discoveries at the Middle Bronze Gate of Tel Beth-Shemesh', *Palestine Exploration Quarterly*, 145 (1), 6–24.

Bunimovitz, Shlomo and Lederman, Zvi (2016), *Tel Beth-Shemesh: A Border Community in Judah—Renewed Excavations 1990-2000: The Iron Age* (Monograph Series of the Institute of Archaeology of Tel Aviv University 34; Winona Lake, Indiana: Eisenbrauns).

Bunimovitz, Shlomo and Lederman, Zvi (2017), 'Swinging on the "Sorek Seesaw": Tel Beth-Shemesh and the Sorek Valley in the Iron Age', in Oded Lipschits and Aren M. Maeir (eds.), *The Shephelah during the Iron Age: Recent Archaeological Studies* (Winona Lake: Eisenbrauns), 27–43.

Bunimovitz, Shlomo, Lederman, Zvi, and Hatzaki, Eleni (2013), 'Knossian Gifts? Two late Minoan IIIA1 Cups from Tel Beth-Shemesh, Israel', *Annual of the British School at Athens*, 108, 51–66.

Bunimovitz, Shlomo and Zimhoni, Orna (1993), '"Lamp-and-Bowl" Foundation Deposits in Canaan', *Israel Exploration Journal*, 43, 99–125.

Bunimovitz, Shlomo and Zimhoni, Orna (2004), 'Appendix: Lamp-and-Bowl Foundation Deposits in Areas P and S', in David Ussishkin (ed.), *The Renewed Archaeological Excavations at Tel Lachish (1973–1994)* (Monograph Series of the Institute of Archaeology of Tel Aviv University 22; Tel Aviv: Emery and Claire Yass Publications in Archaeology), 1147–1154.

Burke, Aaron A. (2008), *"Walled up to Heaven": The Evolution of Middle Bronze Age Fortification Strategies in the Levant* (Studies in the Archaeology and History of the Levant 4; Winona Lake: Eisenbrauns).

Burke, Aaron A. (2010), 'Canaan under Siege: Canaan and Archaeology of Egypt's War in Canaan during the Early Eighteenth Dynasty', in Jordi Vidal (ed.), *Studies on War in the Ancient Near East: Collected Essays on Military History* (Alter Orient und Altes Testament 372; Münster: Ugarit-Verlag), 43–66.

Burke, Aaron A. and Lords, Krystal V. (2010), 'Egyptians in Jaffa: A Portrait of Egyptian Presence in Jaffa during the Late Bronze Age', *Near Eastern Archaeology*, 73 (1), 2–30.

Burke, Aaron A., et al. (2017), 'Excavations of the New Kingdom Fortress in Jaffa, 2011–2014: Traces of Resistance to Egyptian Rule in Canaan', *American Journal of Archaeology*, 121 (1), 85–133.

Buschennino, Aviva and Yannai, Eli (2010), 'Iron Age I Tombs in the Azor Cemetery (with a contribution by Anat Cohen-Weinberger)', *'Atiqot*, 63, 17*–40*. (Hebrew)

Campbell, Roderick B. (2009), 'Toward a Networks and Boundaries approach to Early Complex Polities: The Late Shang Case', *Current Anthropology*, 50 (6), 821–848.

Carbillet, Aurélie (2011), *La figure hathorique à Chypre (IIe–Ier mill. av. J.-C.)* (Alter Orient und Altes Testament 388; Münster: Ugarit-Verlag).

Carney, Elizabeth D. (2001), 'Women and Military Leadership in Pharaonic Egypt', *Greek, Roman, and Byzantine Studies*, 42, 25–41.

Cassuto, Deborah R., Koch, Ido, and Shai, Itzhaq (2015), 'A Note on an Amenhotep III Plaque from Tel Burna', *Journal of Ancient Egyptian Interconnections*, 7 (4), 21–26.

Clack, Timothy (2011), 'Syncretism and Religious Fusion', in Timoty Insoll (ed.), *Oxford Handbook of the Archaeology of Ritual and Religion* (Oxford: Oxford University Press), 226–242.

Clamer, Christa (2004), 'The Pottery and Artefacts from the Level VI Temple in Area P', in David Ussishkin (ed.), *The Renewed Archaeological Excavations at Tel Lachish (1973–1994)* (Monograph Series of the Institute of Archaeology of Tel Aviv University, 22; Tel Aviv: Emery and Claire Yass Publications in Archaeology), 1288–1368.

Clarke, Joanne T., Steel, Louise, and Sadeq, Moain (2004), 'Gaza Research Project: 1998 Survey of the Old City', *Levant*, 132 (36), 31–36.

Cline, Eric H (2014), *1177 BC: The Year Civilization Collapsed* (Princeton and Oxford: Princeton University Press).

Cline, Eric H. and Yasur-Landau, Assaf (2009), 'Domination and (In)visibility: Reading Power Relations at Tel Mor', *American Journal of Archaeology*, 113 (1). <www.aja online.org/online-review-article/589>.

Cline, Eric H. and O'Connor, David (eds.) (2012), *Ramesses III: The Life and Times of Egypt's Last Hero* (Ann Arbor: University of Michigan Press) 1–26.

Cohen, Raymond and Westbrook, Raymond (eds.) (2000), *Amarna Diplomacy: The Beginnings of International Relations* (Baltimore: John Hopkins University Press).

Cohen, Susan L. (2017), 'Reevaluation of Connections between Egypt and the Southern Levant in the Middle Bronze Age in Light of the New Higher Chronology', *Journal of Ancient Egyptian Interconnections*, 13, 34–42.

Cohen-Weinberger, Anat (1997), 'Typology and Technology of the Egyptian Pottery from the Days of the Twentieth Dynasty at Beth-Shean (In Light of the Renewed Excavations)', M.A. Thesis (Hebrew University of Jerusalem).

Cohen-Weinberger, Anat (2009), 'Petrographic Studies', in Nava Panitz-Cohen and Amihai Mazar (eds.), *Excavations at Tel Beth-Shean, 1989–1996 Vol. 3: The 13th–11th Centuries BCE Strata in Areas N and S* (Jerusalem: Israel Exploration Society and the Institute of Archaeology, Hebrew University of Jerusalem), 519–529.

Conlee, Christina A. (2003), 'Local Elites and the Reformation of late Intermediate Period Sociopolitical and Economic Organization in Nasca, Peru', *Latin American Antiquity*, 14 (1), 47–65.

Conlee, Christina A. (2006), 'Regeneration as Transformation: Postcollapse Society in Nasca, Peru', in Glenn M. Schwartz and John J. Nichols (eds.), *After Collapse: the Regeneration of Complex Societies* (First paperback printing edn.; Tucson: University of Arizona press), 99–113.

Cooney, Kathlyn M. and Tyrrell, Johnna (2005), 'Scarabs in the Los Angeles County Museum of Art', *PalArch's Journal of Archaeology of Egypt/Egyptology*, 4, 1–98.

Cordani, Violetta (2011), 'One-year or Five-year War? A Reappraisal of Suppiluliuma's First Syrian Campaign', *Altorientalische Forschungen*, 38 (2), 240–253.

Cornelius, Izak (1994), *The Iconography of the Canaanite Gods Resheph and Ba'al* (Orbis Biblicus et Orientalis 140; Fribourg and Göttingen: Academic Press; Vandenhoeck and Ruprect).

Cornelius, Izak (2004), *The Many Faces of the Goddess: The Iconography of the Syro-Palestinian Goddesses Anat, Astarte, Qedeshet, and Ashera c.1500–1000 BCE* (Orbis Biblicus et Orientalis 204; Fribourg and Göttingen: Academic Press, Vandenhoeck and Ruprecht).

Cortebeeck, Kylie (2016), 'Stamp Seals in ancient Egyptian Tombs: A Revision of the Usages in Quest of the Sex of Their Owners', *Studien zur Altägyptischen Kultur*, 45, 105–123.

Croft, Paul (2004), 'The Osteological Remains (Mammalian and Avian)', in David Ussishkin (ed.), *The Renewed Archaeological Excavations at Tel Lachish (1973–1994)* (Monograph Series of the Institute of Archaeology of Tel Aviv University 22; Tel Aviv: Emery and Claire Yass Publications in Archaeology), 2254–2345.

Dan, Yoel (1988), 'The Soils of the Southern Shefelah', in Eliahu Stern and Dan Urman (eds.), *Man and Environment in the Southern Shefelah: Studies in Regional Geography and History* (Givatayim: Masada), 50–58. (Hebrew)

Dan, Yoel, Yaalon, Dan H., and Fine, Pinchas (2002), 'The Origin and Distribution of Soils and Landscapes in Pleshet Plain', in Avi Sasson, Zeev Safrai, and Nahum Sagiv (eds.), *Ashkelon: Bride of the South* (Ashkelon: Ashkelon Academic College), 289–318. (Hebrew)

Darnell, John Coleman and Manassa, Colleen (2007), *Tutankhamun's Armies: Battle and Conquest during Ancient Egypt's Late Eighteenth Dynasty* (Hoboken: John Wiley & Sons).

Davis, Brent, Maeir, Aren M., and Hitchcock, Louise A. (2015), 'Disentangling Entangled Objects: Iron Age Inscriptions from Philistia as a Reflection of Cultural Processes', *Israel Exploration Journal*, 65 (2), 140–166.

Day, Abby (2011), *Believing in Belonging: Belief and Social Identity in the Modern World* (Oxford: Oxford University Press).

De Maret, Pierre (2011), 'Divine Kings', in Timoty Insoll (ed.), *Oxford Handbook of the Archaeology of Ritual and Religion* (Oxford: Oxford University press), 1059–1067.

de Miroschedji, Pierre (2008), 'Jarmuth', in Ephraim Stern (ed.), *New Encyclopedia of Archaeological Excavations in the Holy Land* (5; Jerusalem and Washington, DC: Israel Exploration Society and Biblical Archaeological Society), 1792–1797.

De Vaux, Roland (1978), *The Early History of Israel* (Philadelphia: Westminster Press).

DeFrance, Susan D. (2009), 'Zooarchaeology in Complex Societies: Political Economy, Status, and Ideology', *Journal of Archaeological Research*, 17, 105–168.

DePietro, Dana Douglas (2012), 'Piety, Practice, and Politics: Agency and Ritual in the Late Bronze Age Southern Levant', (UC Berkeley).

Dever, William G. (1986), *Gezer IV: The 1969–71 Seasons in Field VI, the "Acropolis"* (Annual of the Nelson Glueck School of Biblical Archaeology 4; Jerusalem: Nelson Glueck School of Biblical Archaeology).

Dever, William G. (1990), '"Hyksos", Egyptian Destructions, and the End of the Palestinian Middle Bronze Age', *Levant*, 22 (1), 75–81.

Dever, William G. (1992), 'The Late Bronze Age–Early Iron I Horizon in Syria-Palestine: Egyptians, Canaanites, "Sea Peoples," and Proto-Israelites', in William A. Ward and Martha S. Joukowsky (eds.), *The Crisis Years: The 12th Century BC: From beyond the Danube to the Tigris* (Dubuque: Kendall Hunt), 99–110.

Dever, William G. (1993), 'Further Evidence on the Date of the Outer Wall at Gezer', *Bulletin of the American Schools of Oriental Research*, 289, 35–54.

Dever, William G., Lance, Hubert D., and Wright, George E. (1970), *Gezer I: Preliminary Report of the 1964–1966 Seasons* (Annual of the Nelson Glueck School of Biblical Archaeology 1; Jerusalem: Nelson Glueck School of Biblical Archaeology).

Dever, William G., et al. (1974), *Gezer II: Report of the 1967–70 Seasons in Fields I and II* (Annual of the Nelson Glueck School of Biblical Archaeology 2; Jerusalem: Nelson Glueck School of Biblical Archaeology).

Di Biase-Dyson, Camilla (2013), *Foreigners and Egyptians in the Late Egyptian Stories: Linguistic, Literary and Historical Perspectives* (Probleme der Ägyptologie 32; Leiden and Boston: Brill).

Di Segni, Leah (2004), 'The Territory of Gaza: Notes of Historical Geography', in Brouria Bitton-Ashkelony and Aryeh Kofsly (eds.), *Christian Gaza in Late Antiquity* (Jerusalem Studies in Religion and Culture; Leiden: Brill), 41–61.

Diener, Alexander C. and Hagen, Joshua (eds.) (2010), *Borderlines and Borderlands: Political Oddities at the Edge of the Nation-state* (London: Rowman & Littlefield Publishers).

Dietler, Michael (1995), 'The Cup of Gyptis: Rethinking the Colonial Encounter in Early-Iron-Age Western Europe and the Relevance of World-Systems Models', *Journal of European Archaeology*, 3 (2), 89–111.

Dietler, Michael (1997), 'The Iron Age in Mediterranean France: Colonial Encounters, Entanglement, and Transformations', *Journal of World Prehistory*, 11 (3), 269–358.

Dietler, Michael (2005), 'The Archaeology of Colonization and the Colonization of Archaeology: Theoretical Challenges from an Ancient Mediterranean Colonial Encounter', in Gil Stein (ed.), *The Archaeology of Colonial Encounters* (Santa Fe: School of American Research Press), 33–68.

Dietler, Michael (2007), 'Culinary Encounters: Food, Identity and Colonialism', in Katheryn C. Twiss (ed.), *The Archaeology of Food and Identity* (Center for Archaeological Investigations, Southern Illinois University Carbondale Occasional Paper 34; Carbondale: Center for Archaeological Investigations, Southern Illinois University), 218–242.

Dietler, Michael (2009), 'Colonial Encounters in Iberia and the Western Mediterranean: An Exploratory Framework', in Michael Dietler and Carolina López-Ruiz (eds.), *Colonial Encounters in Ancient Iberia: Phoenician, Greek, and Indigenous Relations* (Chicago and London: The University of Chicago Press), 3–48.

Dietler, Michael (2010), *Archaeologies of Colonialism: Consumption, Entanglement, and Violence in Ancient Mediterranean France* (Berkeley: University of California Press).

Dietler, Michael (2011), 'Feasting and Fasting', in Timoty Insoll (ed.), *Oxford Handbook of the Archaeology of Ritual and Religion* (Oxford: Oxford University press), 179–194.

Dietler, Michael and Hayden, Brian (2001), *Feasts: Archaeological and Ethnographic Perspectives on Food, Politics, and Power* (Washington: Smithsonian Institution Press).

Dietler, Michael and López-Ruiz, Carolina (eds.) (2009), *Colonial Encounters in Ancient Iberia: Phoenician, Greek, and Indigenous Relations* (Chicago and London: The University of Chicago Press).

Dijkstra, Meindert (2015), 'A Seated Queen Hathor Statue from Amenhotep III's 33rd Regnal Year at Serabit el-Khadim', *Tel Aviv*, 42 (2), 165–176.

Dodson, Aidan (2009), *Amarna Sunset: Nefertiti, Tutankhamun, Ay, Horemheb, and the Egyptian Counter-Reformation* (Oxford: Oxford University Press).

Dodson, Aidan (2010), *Poisoned Legacy: The Fall of the 19th Egyptian Dynasty* (Cairo and New York: The American University in Cairo Press).

Dodson, Aidan (2014), *Amarna Sunrise: Egypt from Golden Age to Age of Heresy* (Cairo and New York: The American University in Cairo Press).

Dothan, Moshe (1971), *Ashdod II–III: The Second and Third Seasons of Excavations* ('Atiqot 9–10; Jerusalem: Israel Antiquities Authority).

Dothan, Moshe and Ben-Shlomo, David (2005), *Ashdod VI: The Excavations of Areas H and K (1968–1969)* (Israel Antiquities Authority Reports 24; Jerusalem: Israel Antiquities Authority).

Dothan, Moshe and Porath, Yehoshua (1993), *Ashdod V: Excavation of Area G: The Fourth–Sixth Seasons of Excavations 1968–1970* ('Atiqot 23; Jerusalem: Israel Antiquities Authority).

Dothan, Trude (1958), 'Philistine Civilization in the Light of Archaeological Finds in Palestine and Egypt', *Eretz-Israel*, 5, 55–66. (Hebrew).

Dothan, Trude (1967), *The Philistines and Their Material Culture* (Jerusalem: Bialik Institute and the Israel Exploration Society). (Hebrew with summary).

Dothan, Trude (1979), *Excavations at The Cemetery of Deir el-Balaḥ* (Qedem; Jerusalem: Institute of Archaeology, Hebrew University of Jerusalem).

Dothan, Trude (1982), *The Philistines and Their Material Culture* (New Haven: Yale University Press).

Dothan, Trude (2002), 'Bronze and Iron Objects with Cultic Connotations from Philistine Temple Building 350 at Ekron', *Israel Exploration Journal*, 52 (1), 1–27.

Dothan, Trude and Dothan, Moshe (1992), *People of the Sea: The Search for the Philistines* (New York: Macmillan Pub Co).

Dothan, Trude and Gitin, Seymour (1993), 'Miqne, Tel', in Ephraim Stern (ed.), *New Encyclopedia of Archaeological Excavations in the Holy Land* (3; Jerusalem: Israel Exploration Society), 1051–1059.

Dothan, Trude and Gitin, Seymour (2008), 'Miqne, Tel (Ekron)', in Ephraim Stern (ed.), *New Encyclopedia of Archaeological Excavations in the Holy Land* (5; Jerusalem and Washington, DC: Israel Exploration Society and Biblical Archaeological Society), 1952–1958.

Dothan, Trude and Brandl, Baruch (2010), *Deir el-Balaḥ: Excavations in 1977–1982 in the Cemetery and Settlement, Vol. 1: Stratigraphy and Architecture* (Qedem 49; Jerusalem: Institute of Archaeology, Hebrew University of Jerusalem).

Dothan, Trude and Nahmias-Lotan, Tamar (2010), 'A Lamp and Bowl Deposit', in Trude Dothan and Baruch Brandl (eds.), *Deir el-Balaḥ: Excavations in 1977–1982 in the Cemetery and Settlement, Vol. 2: The Finds* (Qedem 50; Jerusalem: Institute of Archaeology, Hebrew University of Jerusalem), 111–113.

Dothan, Trude and Zukerman, Alexander (2015), 'Iron Age I: Philistia', in Seymour Gitin (ed.), *The Ancient Pottery of Israel and Its Neighbors: From the Iron Age through the Hellenistic Period* (1; Jerusalem: Israel Exploration Society), 71–96.

Dothan, Trude, Garfinkel, Yosef, and Gitin, Seymour (2016), *Tel Miqne-Ekron Excavations 1985–1988, 1990, 1992–1995: Field IV Lower—The Elite Zone Part 1 The Iron Age I Early Philistine City* (Final Reports of the Tel Miqne-Ekron Excavations; Winona Lake: Eisenbrauns).

Drews, Robert (1998), 'Canaanites and Philistines', *Journal for the Study of the Old Testament*, 81, 39–61.

Drews, Robert (2000), 'Medinet Habu: Oxcarts, Ships, and Migration Theories', *Journal of Near Eastern Studies*, 59, 161–190.

Dubiel, Ulrike (2012), 'Protection, Control and Prestige—Seals Among the Rural Population of Qau-Matmar', in Ilona Regulski, Kim Duistermaat, and Peter Verkinderen (eds.), *Seals and Sealing Practices in the Near East* (Orientalia Lovaniensia Analecta 219; Leuven, Paris and Walpole MA: Uitgeverij Peeters), 51–80.

Eggler, Jurg (2008), S*corpion. Iconography of Deities and Demons: Electronic Pre Publication.* http://www.religionswissenschaft.uzh.ch/idd/prepublications/e_idd_scorpion.pdf>.

Eisenberg, Emanuel and Nagorski, Alla (2002), 'Tel Ḥevron (Er-Rumeidi)', *Hadashot Arkheologiyot: Excavations and Surveys in Israel*, 114, 91*–92*.

Eisenberg, Emanuel and Ben-Shlomo, David (2016), 'Tel Hevron', *Hadashot Arkheologiyot: Excavations and Surveys in Israel*, 128. Accessed 16 March 2016.

Emanuel, Jeffrey P. (2013), '"Sherden from the Sea": The Arrival, Integration, and Acculturation of a "Sea People"', *Journal of Ancient Egyptian Interconnections*, 5 (1), 14–27.

Emanuel, Jeffrey P. (2015), '"Sea Peoples" in Egyptian Garrisons in Light of Beth-Shean, (Re-)Considered', *Mediterranean Archaeology*, 28, 1–22.

Ertman, Earl, Wilson, Roxanne, and Schaden, Otto (2006), 'Unravelling the Mysteries of KV 63: Challenging Clearance of the Newest Tomb in the Valley of the Kings', *KMT: A Modern Journal of Ancient Egypt*, 17 (3), 18–27.

Espinel, Andrés D. (2002), 'The Role of the Temple of Ba'alat Gebal as Intermediary between Egypt and Byblos during the Old Kingdom', *Studien zur Altägyptischen Kultur*, 30, 103–119.

Fanon, Frantz (1966), *The Wretched of the Earth*, trans. Constance Farrington (New York: Grove Press).

Fantalkin, Alexander (2008), 'The Appearance of Rock-Cut Bench Tombs in Iron Age Judah as a Reflection of State Formation', in Alexander Fantalkin and Assaf Yasur-Landau (eds.), *Bene Israel: Studies in the Archaeology of Israel and the Levant during the Bronze and Iron Ages in Honour of Israel Finkelstein* (Culture and History of the Ancient Near East 31; Leiden and Boston: Brill), 17–44.

Fantalkin, Alexander and Tal, Oren (2008), 'Navigating Between the Powers: Joppa and Its Vicinity in the 1st Millennium B.C.E.', *Ugarit-Forschungen*, 40, 229–276.

Fargo, Valerie M. (1993), 'Ḥesi, Tel', in Ephraim Stern (ed.), *New Encyclopedia of Archaeological Excavations in the Holy Land* (2; Jerusalem: Israel Exploration Society), 630–634.

Faulseit, Ronald K. (ed.), (2016), *Beyond Collapse: Archaeological Perspectives on Resilience, Revitalization, and Transformation in Complex Societies* (Center for Archaeological Investigations, Southern Illinois University Carbondale Occasional Paper 42; Carbondale: Southern Illinois University Press).

Faust, Avraham (2014), 'The history of Tel 'Eton following the results of the first seven seasons of excavations (2006–2012)', in Piotr Bieliński, Michał Gawlikowski, and

Rafał Koliński (eds.), *Proceedings of the 8th International Congress on the Archaeology of the Ancient Near East (ICAANE)* (Wiesbaden: Harrassowitz), 585–604.

Faust, Avraham (2015), 'Pottery and Society in Iron Age Philistia: Feasting, Identity, Economy, and Gender', *Bulletin of the American Schools of Oriental Research*, (373), 167–198.

Faust, Avraham and Katz, Hayah (2011), 'Philistines, Israelites and Canaanites in the Southern Trough Valley during the Iron Age I', *Egypt and the Levant*, 21, 231–247.

Faust, Avraham and Lev-Tov, Justin (2011), 'The Constitution of Philistine Identity: Ethnic Dynamics in Twelfth to Tenth Century Philistia', *Oxford Journal of Archaeology*, 30 (1), 13–31.

Faust, Avraham and Lev-Tov, Justin (2014), 'Philistia and the Philistines in the Iron Age I: Interaction, Ethnic Dynamics and Boundary Maintenance', *Hiphil Novum*, 1.

Feldman, Marian H. (2009), 'Hoarded Treasures: The Megiddo Ivories and the End of the Bronze Age', *Levant*, 41 (2), 175–194.

Feldman, Marian H. and Sauvage, Caroline (2010), 'Objects of Prestige? Chariots in the Late Bronze Age Eastern Mediterranean and Near East', *Ägypten und Levante/Egypt and the Levant*, 20, 67–181.

Finkelstein, Israel (1986), *Izbet Ṣarṭah: An Early Iron Age Site Near Rosh Ha'ayin, Israel* (BAR International Series 229; Oxford: BAR).

Finkelstein, Israel (1994), 'Penelope's Shroud Unravelled: Iron II Date of Gezer's Outer Wall Established', *Tel Aviv*, 21 (2), 276–282.

Finkelstein, Israel (1995), 'The Date of the Settlement of the Philistines in Canaan', *Tel Aviv*, 22 (2), 213–239.

Finkelstein, Israel (1996a), 'The Territorial-Political System of Canaan in the Late Bronze Age', *Ugarit-Forschungen*, 28, 221–255.

Finkelstein, Israel (1996b), 'The Philistine Countryside', *Israel Exploration Journal*, 46 (3–4), 225–242.

Finkelstein, Israel (2002a), 'Gezer Revisited and Revised', *Tel Aviv*, 29 (2), 262–296.

Finkelstein, Israel (2002b), 'The Philistines in the Bible: A Late-monarchic Perspective', *Journal for the Study of the Old Testament*, 27 (2), 131–167.

Finkelstein, Israel (2007), 'Is the Philistine Paradigm Still Viable?', in Manfred Bietak and Ernst Czerńy (eds.), *The Synchronization of Civilisations in the Eastern Mediterranean in the Second Millennium B.C. III* (Contributions to the Chronology of the Eastern Mediterranean 9; Vienna: Verlag der Osterreichischen Akademie der Wissenschaften), 517–523.

Finkelstein, Israel (2014), 'The Shephelah and Jerusalem's Western Border in the Amarna Period', *Egypt and the Levant*, 24, 267–276.

Finkelstein, Israel and Singer-Avitz, Lily (2001), 'Ashdod Revisited', *Tel Aviv*, 28 (2), 231–259.

Finkelstein, Israel and Na'aman, Nadav (2005), 'Shechem of the Amarna period and the rise of the Northern Kingdom of Israel', *Israel Exploration Journal*, 55 (2), 172–193.

Finkelstein, Israel and Piasetzky, Eli (2006), 'The Iron I–II in the Highlands and Beyond 14C Anchors, Pottery Phases and The Shoshenq I Campaign', *Levant*, 38, 45–61.

Finkelstein, Israel and Singer-Avitz, Lily (2009), 'Reevaluating Bethel', *Zeitschrift des Deutschen Palästina-Vereins*, 125 (1), 33–48.

Finkelstein, Israel and Fantalkin, Alexander (2012), 'Khirbet Qeiyafa: An Unsensational Archaeological and Historical Interpretation', *Tel Aviv*, 39 (1), 38–63.

Finkelstein, Israel and Sass, Benjamin (2013), 'The West Semitic Alphabetic Inscriptions, Late Bronze II to Iron IIA: Archeological Context, Distribution and Chronology', *Hebrew Bible and Ancient Israel*, 2, 149–220.

Finkelstein, Israel and Langgut, Dafna (2018), 'Climate, Settlement History, and Olive Cultivation in the Iron Age Southern Levant', *Bulletin of the American Schools of Oriental Research*, 379, 153–169.

Finkelstein, Israel, Koch, Ido, and Lipschits, Oded (2011), 'The Mound on the Mount: A Possible Solution to the "Problem with Jerusalem"', *Journal of Hebrew Scriptures*, 11 (Article 12), 2–24.

Finkelstein, Israel, et al. (2017), 'New Evidence on the Late Bronze/Iron I Transition at Megiddo: Implications for the End of the Egyptian Rule and the Appearance of Philistine Pottery', *Ägypten und Levante*, 27, 261–280.

Fischer, Erika (2011), *Tell el-Far'ah (Süd): Ägyptisch-levantinische Beziehungen im späten 2. Jahrtausend v. Chr.* (Orbis Biblicus et Orientalis 247; Fribourg and Göttingen: Academic Press, Vandenhoeck and Ruprecht).

Fischer, Moshe (2008), 'Yavneh-Yam', in Ephraim Stern (ed.), *New Encyclopedia of Archaeological Excavations in the Holy Land* (5; Jerusalem and Washington, DC: Israel Exploration Society and Biblical Archaeological Society), 2073–2075.

Fischer, Moshe and Taxel, Tamar (2006), 'Yavne, Survey Map', *Hadashot Arkheologiyot: Excavations and Surveys in Israel*, 118. <http://www.hadashot-esi.org.il/Report_Detail_Eng.aspx?id=437&mag_id=111>, accessed 16 March 2016.

Fischer, Peter M. and Sadeq, Moain (2002), 'Tell el-'Ajjul 2000: Second Season Preliminary Report', *Egypt and the Levant*, 12, 109–153.

Fischer-Elfert, Hans-Werner (1986), *Die satirische Streitschrift des Papyrus Anastasi I* (Ägyptologische Abhandlungen 44; Wiesbaden: Harrassowitz).

Flammini, Roxana (2010), 'Elite Emulation and Patronage Relationships in the Middle Bronze: The Egyptianized Dynasty of Byblos', *Tel Aviv*, 37 (2), 154–168.

Flammini, Roxana (2011), 'Northeast Africa and the Levant in Connection: A World-System Perspective on Interregional Relationship in the Early Second Millennium BCE', in Toby C. Wilkinson, Susan E. Sherratt, and John Bennet (eds.), *Interweaving Worlds: Systemic Interactions in Eurasia, 7th to 1st Millennia BC* (Oxford: Oxbow Books), 205–217.

Fleming, Daniel E. (2012), 'People without Town: The 'apiru in the Amarna Evidence', in Rebecca Hasselbach and Na'ama Pat-El (eds.), *Language and Nature: Papers Presented to John Huehnergard on the Occasion of His 60th Birthday* (Studies in Ancient Oriental Civilization 67; Chicago: The Oriental Institute of the University of Chicago).

Frahm, Eckart (2009), *Historische und historisch-literarische Texte, Ausgrabungen der Deutschen Orient-Gesellschaft in Assur, E. Inschriften* (Keilschrifttexte aus Assur literarischen Inhalts 3; Wiesbaden: Harrassowitz).

Frevel, Christian (2008), 'Gifts to the Gods? Votives as Communication Markers in Sanctuaries and other Places in the Bronze and Iron Ages in Palestine/Israel', in Izak Cornelius and Louis Jonker (eds.), *"From Ebla to Stellenbosch": Syro-Palestinian Religions and the Hebrew Bible* (Abhandlungen des Deutschen Palästina-Vereins 37; Wiesbaden: Harrassowitz), 25–48.

Funk, Robert W. (1993), 'Beth-Zur', in Ephraim Stern (ed.), *New Encyclopedia of Archaeological Excavations in the Holy Land* (1; Jerusalem: Israel Exploration Society), 259–261.

Gadot, Yuval (2003), 'Continuity and Change: Cultural Processes in the Late Bronze and Early Iron Ages in Israel's Central Coastal Plain', Ph.D. dissertation (Tel Aviv University).

Gadot, Yuval (2006), 'Aphek in the Sharon and the Philistine Northern Frontier', *Bulletin of the American Schools of Oriental Research*, 341, 21–36.

Gadot, Yuval (2008), 'Continuity and Change in the Late Bronze to Iron Age Transition in Israel's Coastal Plain: A Long Term Perspective', in Alexander Fantalkin and Assaf Yasur-Landau (eds.), *Bene Israel: Studies in the Archaeology of Israel and the Levant during the Bronze and Iron Ages in Honour of Israel Finkelstein* (Culture and History of the Ancient Near East 31; Leiden and Boston: Brill), 55–73.

Gadot, Yuval (2010), 'The Late Bronze Egyptian Estate at Aphek', *Tel Aviv*, 37 (1), 48–66.

Gadot, Yuval and Yadin, Esther (2009), *Aphek-Antipatris II: The Remains on the Acropolis—The Moshe Kochavi and Pirhiya Beck Excavations* (Monograph Series of the Institute of Archaeology of Tel Aviv University 27; Tel Aviv: Emery and Claire Yass Publications in Archaeology).

García, Margarita Díaz-Andreu (2007), *A World History of Nineteenth-century Archaeology: Nationalism, Colonialism, and the Past* (Oxford Studies in the History of Archaeology; Oxford: Oxford University Press).

Gardiner, Alan H. (1947), *Ancient Egyptian Onomastica* (London: Oxford University Press).

Gardiner, Alan H., Peet, T. Eric, and Černy, Jaroslav (1955), *The Inscriptions of Sinai II* (Memoirs of the Egypt Exploration Society 45; London: Egypt Exploration Society).

Garfinkel, Yosef (2017), 'Khirbet Qeiyafa in the Shephelah: Data and Interpretations', in Stefan Münger and Silvia Schroer (eds.), *Khirbet Qeiyafa in the Shephelah* (Orbis

Biblicus et Orientalis 282; Fribourg and Göttingen: Academic Press; Vandenhoeck & Ruprecht), 5–59.

Garfinkel, Yosef and Ganor, Saar (2009), *Khirbet Qeiyafa Vol. 1: Excavation report 2007–2008 Seasons* (Jerusalem: Israel Exploration Society).

Garfinkel, Yosef, Ganor, Saar, and Hasel, Michael G. (2011), 'Khirbet Qeiyafa and the Rise of the Kingdom of Judah', *Eretz-Israel*, 30, 174–194.

Garfinkel, Yosef, Ganor, Saar, and Hasel, Michael G. (2014), *Khirbet Qeiyafa Vol. 2: Excavation Report 2009–2013: Stratigraphy and Architecture (Areas B, C, D, E)* (Jerusalem: Israel Exploration Society).

Garfinkel, Yosef, Kreimerman, Igor, and Zilberg, Peter (2016), *Debating Khirbet Qeiyafa: A Fortified City in Judah from the Time of King David* (Jerusalem: Israel Exploration Society).

Garfinkel, Yosef, et al. (2012), 'State Formation in Judah: Biblical Tradition, Modern Historical Theories, and Radiometric Dates at Khirbet Qeiyafa', *Radiocarbon*, 54 (3–4).

Garfinkel, Yosef, et al. (2019), 'First Impression on the Urban Layout of the last Canaanite City of Lachish: A View from the Northeast Corner of the Site', in Aren M. Maeir, Itzhaq Shai, and Chris McKinny (eds.), *The Late Bronze and Early Iron Ages of Southern Canaan* (Archaeology of the Biblical World 2; Berlin: De Gruyter), 122–135.

Gates, Marie-Henriette (2011), 'Maritime Business in the Bronze Age Eastern Mediterranean: The View from its Ports', in Kim Duistermaat and Ilona Regulski (eds.), *Intercultural Contacts in the Ancient Mediterranean: Proceedings of the International Conference at the Netherlands-Flemish Institute in Cairo, 25th to 29th October 2008* (Orientalia Lovaniensia Analecta 202; Leuven, Paris and Walpole MA: Uitgeverij Peeters and Departement Oosterse Studies), 381–394.

Georgiou, Artemis (2015), 'Cyprus during the »Crisis Years« Revisited', in Andrea Babbi, et al. (eds.), *The Mediterranean Mirror: Cultural Contacts in the Mediterranean Sea between 1200 and 750 B.C.: International Post-doc and Young Researcher Conference, Heidelberg, 6th–9th October 2012* (Mainz: Verlag des Römisch-Germanischen Zentralmuseums), 129–145.

Gilan, Amir (2013), 'Pirates in the Mediterranean—A View from the Bronze Age', *Mittelmeerstudien* 3, 49–66.

Gilbert, M. Thomas P. and Shapiro, Michael D. (2014), 'Pigeons: Domestication', in Claire Smith (ed.), *Encyclopedia of Global Archaeology* (New York, NY: Springer), 5944–5948.

Gilboa, Ayelet (2015), 'Dor and Egypt in the Early Iron Age: an Archaeological Perspective of (Part of) the Wenamun Report', *Ägypten und Levante*, 25, 247–274.

Gilboa, Ayelet and Namdar, Dvory (2015), 'The Beginnings of South Asian Spice Trade with the Mediterranean Region: A Review', *Radiocarbon*, 57 (2), 265–283.

Gilboa, Ayelet, Waiman-Barak, Paula, and Sharon, Ilan (2015), 'Dor, the Carmer Coast and Early Iron Age Mediterranean Exchanges', in Andrea Babbi, et al. (eds.), *The Mediterranean Mirror: Cultural Contacts in the Mediterranean Sea between 1200 and 750 B.C.: International Post-doc and Young Researcher Conference, Heidelberg, 6th–9th October 2012* (Mainz: Verlag des Römisch-Germanischen Zentralmuseums), 85–109.

Gilmour, Garth and Kitchen, Kenneth A. (2012), 'Pharaoh Sety II and Egyptian Political Relations with Canaan at the End of the Late Bronze Age', *Israel Exploration Journal*, 62 (1), 1–21.

Given, Michael (2004), *The Archaeology of the Colonized* (London: Routledge).

Giveon, Raphael (1989), 'Egyptian Artifacts', in Zeev Herzog, George Robert Rapp, and Ora Negbi (eds.), *Excavations at Tel Michal, Israel* (Publications of the Institute of Archaeology 8; Minneapolis and Tel Aviv: University of Minnesota and the Institute of Archaeology of Tel Aviv University), 341–344.

Givon, Shmuel (2008), 'Ḥarasim, Tel', in Ephraim Stern (ed.), *New Encyclopedia of Archaeological Excavations in the Holy Land* (5; Jerusalem and Washington, DC: Israel Exploration Society and Biblical Archaeological Society), 1766–1767.

Glatz, Claudia (2009), 'Empire as Network: Spheres of Material Interaction in Late Bronze Age Anatolia', *Journal of Anthropological Archaeology*, 28, 127–141.

Glatz, Claudia (2013), 'Negotiating Empire: A Comparative Investigation into the Responses to Hittite Imperialism by the Vassal State of Ugarit and the Kaska Peoples of Pontic Anatolia', in Gregory E. Areshian (ed.), *Empires and Diversity: On the Crossroads of Archaeology, Anthropology, and History* (Ideas, Debates, and Perspectives; Los Angeles: Cotsen Institute of Archaeology University of California), 21–55.

Golan, Dor (2016), 'Tel Gerisa (B)', *Hadashot Arkheologiyot: Excavations and Surveys in Israel*, 128.

Goldstone, Jack A. and Haldon, John F. (2009), 'Ancient States, Empires, and Exploitation: Problems and Perspectives', in Ian Morris and Walter Scheidel (eds.), *The Dynamics of Ancient Empires: State Power from Assyria to Byzantium* (Oxford: Oxford University Press), 3–29.

Goldwasser, O. and Oren, E.D. (2015), 'Marine Units on the "Ways of Horus" in the Days of Seti I', *Journal of Ancient Egyptian Interconnections*, 7 (1), 25–38.

Goldwasser, Orly (2006), 'Canaanites Reading Hieroglyphs: Horus is Hathor?—The Invention of the Alphabet in Sinai', *Egypt and the Levant*, 16, 121–160.

Gonen, Rivka (1979), 'Burial in Canaan of the Late Bronze Age as a basis for the Study of Population and Settlements', Ph.D. Dissertation (Hebrew University of Jerusalem).

Gonen, Rivka (1981), 'Tell el-'Ajjul in the Late Bronze Age: City or Cemetery?', *Eretz-Israel*, 15, 69–78. (Hebrew)

Gonen, Rivka (1984), 'Urban Canaan in the Late Bronze Period', *Bulletin of the American Schools of Oriental Research*, 253, 61–73.

Gonen, Rivka (1992), *Burial Patterns and Cultural Diversity in Late Bronze Age Canaan* (American Schools of Oriental Research Dissertation Series; Winona Lake: Eisenbrauns).

González-Ruibal, Alfredo (2014), *An Archaeology of Resistance: Materiality and Time in an African Borderland* (Lanham, MD: Rowman & Littlefield).

Gophna, Ram, Ayalon, Etan, and Ben-Melech, Nitzan (2015), *Archaeological Survey of Israel: Map of Petah Tiqkva—71* [online text], Israel Antiquities Authority <http://www.antiquities.org.il/survey/new/default_en.aspx>.

Goren, Yuval, Finkelstein, Israel, and Na'aman, Nadav (2004), *Inscribed in Clay: Provenance Study of the Amarna Letters and Other Near Eastern Texts* (Monograph Series of the Institute of Archaeology of Tel Aviv University 23; Tel Aviv: Emery and Claire Yass Publications in Archaeology).

Gosden, Chris (1999), *Anthropology and Archaeology: A Changing Relationship* (London and New York: Routledge).

Gosden, Chris (2004), *Archaeology and Colonialism: Cultural Contact from 5000 BC to the Present* (Cambridge: Cambridge University Press).

Grayson, Kirk A. (2002), *Assyrian Rulers of the Early First Millennium BC I (1114–859 BC)* (The Royal Inscriptions of Mesopotamia Assyrian Periods 2; Toronto: University of Toronto Press).

Greenberg, Raphael (1987), 'New Light on the Early Iron Age at Tell Beit Mirsim', *Bulletin of the American Schools of Oriental Research*, 265, 55–80.

Greenberg, Raphael (2019), *The Archaeology of the Bronze Age Levant: From Urban Origins to the Demise of City-States, 3700–1000 BCE* (Cambridge: Cambridge University Press).

Grover, Rachel A. (2008), 'Queenship and Eternal Life: Tije Offering Palm Ribs at the Sed-Festival Thrones of Amenhotep III', *Studia Antiqua*, 6, 1–14.

Guillaume, Philippe (2004), *Waiting for Josiah: The Judges* (Journal for the Study of the Old Testament Supplement Series; London: T&T Clark).

Guillaume, Philippe (2007), 'More Bull-leapers, some bouncing Kids and less Scorpions', *Ugarit-Forschungen*, 39, 311–319.

Guillaume, Philippe (2011), 'Scorpiomania and how to Avoid It', *Ugarit-Forschungen*, 43, 223–227.

Gunneweg, Jan, et al. (1994), 'Interregional Contacts between Tell en-Nasbeh and Littoral Philistine Centres in Canaan during Early Iron Age I', *Archaeometry*, 36 (2), 227–239.

Guy, Philip L.O. (1938), *Megiddo Tombs* (Oriental Institutes Publications 33; Chicago: The Oriental Institute).

Hankey, Vronwy, et al. (2004), 'The Aegean Pottery Section A: Catalogue and Description', in David Ussishkin (ed.), *The Renewed Archaeological Excavations at Tel Lachish (1973–1994)* (Monograph Series of the Institute of Archaeology of Tel Aviv University 22; Tel Aviv: Emery and Claire Yass Publications in Archaeology), 1373–1425.

Hasel, Michael G. (1994), 'Israel in the Merneptah Stela', *Bulletin of the American Schools of Oriental Research*, 296, 45–61.

Hasel, Michael G. (1998), *Domination and Resistance: Egyptian Military Activity in the Southern Levant, ca. 1300–1185 B.C.* (Probleme der Ägyptologie 11; Leiden: Brill).

Hasel, Michael G. (2009), 'Pa-Canaan in the Egyptian New Kingdom: Canaan or Gaza?', *Journal of Ancient Egyptian Interconnections*, 1 (1), 8–17.

Hayden, Brian (2014), *The Power of Feasts: From Prehistory to the Present* (New York: Cambridge University Press).

Hazard, Sonia (2013), 'The Material Turn in the Study of Religion', *Religion and Society. Advances in Research*, 4, 58–78.

Helck, Wolfgang (1971), *Die Beziehungen Ägyptens zu Vorderasien im 3. und 2. Jahrtausend v. Chr.: Ägyptologische Abhandlungen* (Wiesbaden: Harrassowitz).

Helck, Wolfgang (1986), 'Wenamun', in Wolfgang Helck and Eberhard Otto (eds.), *Lexicon der Ägyptologie* (VI; Wiesbaden: Otto Harrassowitz), 1215–1217.

Hellwing, Salo and Feig, Nurit (1989), 'Animal Bones', in Zeev Herzog, George Rapp, and Ora Negbi (eds.), *Excavations at Tel Michal, Israel* (Publications of the Institute of Archaeology of Tel Aviv University; Tel Aviv: Institute of Archaeology of Tel Aviv University), 236–247.

Hellwing, Salo, Sadeh, Moshe, and Kishon, Vered (1993), 'Faunal Remains', in Israel Finkelstein (ed.), *Shiloh: The Archaeology of a Biblical Site* (Monograph Series of the Institute of Archaeology of Tel Aviv University; Tel Aviv: Emery and Claire Yass Publications in Archaeology), 309–350.

Herva, Vesa-Pekka (2005), 'The Life of Buildings: Minoan Building Deposits in an Ecological Perspective', *Oxford Journal of Archaeology*, 24 (3), 215–227.

Herzog, Ze'ev (1993a), 'Gerisa, Tel', in Ephraim Stern (ed.), *New Encyclopedia of Archaeological Excavations in the Holy Land* (2; Jerusalem: Israel Exploration Society), 480–484.

Herzog, Ze'ev (1993b), 'Michal, Tel', in Ephraim Stern (ed.), *New Encyclopedia of Archaeological Excavations in the Holy Land* (3; Jerusalem: Israel Exploration Society), 1036–1041.

Herzog, Ze'ev (2008), 'Jaffa', in Ephraim Stern (ed.), *New Encyclopedia of Archaeological Excavations in the Holy Land* (5; Jerusalem and Washington, DC: Israel Exploration Society and Biblical Archaeological Society), 1791–1792.

Herzog, Ze'ev and Singer-Avitz, Lily (2004), 'Redefining the Centre: The Emergence of State in Judah', *Tel Aviv*, 31 (2), 209–244.

Herzog, Ze'ev and Singer-Avitz, Lily (2006), 'Sub-Dividing the Iron Age IIA in Northern Israel: A Suggested Solution to the Chronological Debate', *Tel Aviv*, 33 (2), 163–195.

Herzog, Ze'ev and Singer-Avitz, Lily (2011), 'Iron Age IIA Occupational Phases in the Coastal Plain of Israel', in Israel Finkelstein and Nadav Na' aman (eds.), *The Fire Signals of Lachish* (Winona Lake: Eisenbrauns), 159–174.

Higginbotham, Carolyn R. (1996), 'Elite Emulation and Egyptian Governance in Ramesside Canaan', *Tel Aviv*, 23 (2), 154–169.

Higginbotham, Carolyn R. (2000), *Egyptianization and Élite Emulation in Ramesside Palestine: Governance and Accommodation on the Imperial Periphery* (Culture and History of the Ancient Near East 2; Leiden: Brill).

Hingley, Richard (2014), 'Struggling with a Roman Inheritance. A Response to Versluys', *Archaeological Dialogues*, 21 (1), 20–24.

Hitchcock, Louise A. (2008), '"Do You See a Man Skillful in His Work? He will stand before Kings": Interpreting Architectural Influences in the Bronze Age Mediterranean', *Ancient West and East* 7, 17–48.

Hitchcock, Louise A. (2011), '"Transculturalism" as a Model for Examining Migration to Cyprus and Philistia at the End of the Bronze Age', *Ancient West and East*, 10, 267–280.

Hitchcock, Louise A. and Maeir, Aren M. (2013), 'Beyond Creolization and Hybridity: Entangled and Transcultural Identities in Philistia', *Archaeological Review from Cambridge*, 28, 43–65.

Hitchcock, Louise A. and Maeir, Aren M. (2014), 'Yo-ho, Yo-ho, a Seren's Life for Me!', *World Archaeology*, 46 (4), 624–640.

Hitchcock, Louise A. and Maeir, Aren M. (2016a), 'Pulp Fiction: The Sea Peoples and the Study of "Mycenaean" Archaeology in Philistia', in Jan Driessen (ed.), *RA-PI-NE-U. Studies on the Mycenaean World Offered to Robert Laffineur for His 70th Birthday* (AEGIS 10; Louvain: Presses Univesitaires de Louvain), 145–155.

Hitchcock, Louise A. and Maeir, Aren M. (2016b), 'A Pirate's Life for Me: The Maritime Culture of the Sea Peoples', *Palestine Exploration Quarterly*, 148 (4), 245–264.

Hodos, Tamar (2006), *Local Responses to Colonization in the Iron Age Mediterranean* (London and New York: Routledge).

Hodos, Tamar (2014), 'Stage Settings for a Connected Scene. Globalization and Material-Culture Studies in the early First-Millennium B.C.E. Mediterranean', *Archaeological Dialogues*, 21 (1), 24–30.

Hoffmeier, James K. (1989), 'Reconsidering Egypt's Part in the Termination of the Middle Bronze Age in Palestine', *Levant*, 21, 181–193.

Hoffmeier, James K. (1991), 'James Weinstein's "Egypt and the Middle Bronze IIC/Late Bronze IA Transition": A Rejoinder', *Levant*, 23 (1), 117–124.

Hoffmeier, James K. (2004), 'Aspects of Egyptian Foreign Policy in the 18th Dynasty in Western Asia and Nubia', in Garry N. Knoppers and Antoine Hirsch (eds.), *Egypt,*

Israel, and the Ancient Mediterranean World: Studies in Honor of Donald B. Redford (Probleme der Ägyptologie 20; Leiden and Boston: Brill), 121–141.

Hoffmeier, James K. (2018), 'A Possible Location in Northwest Sinai for the Sea and Land Battles between the Sea Peoples and Ramesses III', *Bulletin of the American Schools of Oriental Research*, 380 (1), 1–25.

Hoffmeier, James K. and Kitchen, Kenneth A. (2007), 'Reshep and Astarte in North Sinai: A Recently Discovered Stela from Tell el-Borg', *Egypt and the Levant*, 18, 127–136.

Hoffmeier, James K. and Moshier, Stephen O. (2013), '"A Highway out of Egypt": The Main Road from Egypt to Canaan', in Frank Förster and Heiko Riemer (eds.), *Desert Road Archaeology in Ancient Egypt and Beyond* (Africa Prehistorica: Monographs on African Archaeology and Environment 27; Köln: Heinrich-Barth-Institut), 485–510.

Höflmayer, Felix (2015), 'Egypt's "Empire" in the Southern Levant during the Early 18th Dynasty', in Birgitta Eder and Regine Pruzsinszky (eds.), *Policies of Exchange: Political Systems and Modes of Interaction in the Aegean and the Near East in the 2nd Millennium B.C.E.* (Oriental and European Archaeology; Vienna: Austrian Academy of Sciences Press), 191–206.

Höflmayer, Felix (2017), 'A Radiocarbon Chronology for the Middle Bronze Age Southern Levant', *Journal of Ancient Egyptian Interconnections*, 13, 20–33.

Höflmayer, Felix, et al. (2016a), 'New Radiocarbon Dates from Tel Kabri Support a High Middle Bronze Age Chronology', *Radiocarbon*, 2016, 1–15.

Höflmayer, Felix, et al. (2016b), 'New Evidence for Middle Bronze Age Chronology and Synchronisms in the Levant: Radiocarbon Dates from Tell el-Burak, Tell el-Dabʿa, and Tel Ifshar Compared', *Bulletin of the American Schools of Oriental Research*, 375, 53–76.

Höflmayer, Felix and Eichmann, Ricardo (eds.) (2014), *Egypt and the Southern Levant in the Early Bronze Age* (Orient-Archäologie 31; Rahden: Verlag Marie Leidorf).

Horowitz, Wayne and Oshima, Takayoshi (2006), *Cuneiform in Canaan: Cuneiform Sources from the Land of Israel in Ancient Times* (Jerusalem: Israel Exploration Society).

Horwitz, Liora Kolska (1996), 'Late Bronze Age Fauna from the 1994 Season at Tel Harassim', in Shmuel Givon (ed.), *The Sixth Season of Excavation at Tel Harassim (Nahal Barkai) 1995* (Tel Aviv), 6*–13*.

Horwitz, Liora Kolska (2002), 'Appendix E: The Animal Remains', in Avraham Biran and Rachel Ben-Dov (eds.), *Dan II: Chronicle of the Excavations and the Late Bronze Age "Mycenaean" Tomb* (Jerusalem: Hebrew Union College), 219–221.

Horwitz, Liora Kolska (2003), 'Fauna from Tel Qashish', in Amnon Ben-Tor, Ruhama Bonfil, and Sharon Zuckerman (eds.), *Tel Qashish: A Village in the Jezreel Valley, Final Report of the Archaeological Excavations (1978–1987)* (Qedem Reports 5; Jerusalem: Institute of Archaeology of the Hebrew University of Jerusalem), 427–443.

Horwitz, Liora Kolska (2009), 'Terrestrial Fauna', in Yuval Gadot and Esther Yadin (eds.), *Aphek-Antipatris II: The Remains on the Acropolis—The Moshe Kochavi and Pirhiya Beck Excavations* (Monograph Series of the Institute of Archaeology of Tel Aviv University 27; Tel Aviv: Emery and Claire Yass Publications in Archaeology), 526–561.

Horwitz, Liora Kolska, et al. (2005), 'Faunal and Malacological Remains from the Middle Bronze, Late Bronze and Iron Age Levels at Tel Yoqneʿam', in Amnon Ben-Tor, Doron Ben-Ami, and Ariella Livneh (eds.), *Yoqneʿam III: The Middle and Late Bronze Ages, Final Report of the Archaeological Excavations (1977–1988)* (Qedem Reports 7; Jerusalem: Institute of Archaeology of the Hebrew University of Jerusalem), 395–435.

Houlihan, Patrick F. (1986), *The Birds of Ancient Egypt* (The Natural History of Egypt 1; Warminster: Aris & Phillips).

Houlihan, Patrick F. (2001), 'Birds', in Donald B. Redford (ed.), *The Oxford Encyclopedia of Ancient Egypt* (1; Oxford and New York: Oxford University Press), 189–191.

Humbert, Jean-Baptiste, Bauzou, Thomas, and Abu-Hassuneh, Yasser Mattar (2000), *Gaza Méditerranéenne* (Paris: Errance).

Hundley, Michael B. (2013), *Gods in Dwellings: Temples and Divine Presence in the Ancient Near East* (Writings from the Ancient World Supplement Series 3; Atlanta: Society of Biblical Literature).

Iakovidis, Spyros (1979), 'The Chronology of LH IIIC', *American Journal of Archaeology*, 83 (4), 454–462.

Jacobs, Paul F. and Seger, Joe D. (2007), 'Glimpses of the Iron Age I at Tel Halif', in Shelly White Crawford (ed.), *"Up to the Gates of Ekron": Essays on the Archaeology and History of the eastern Mediterranean in Honor of Seymour Gitin* (Jerusalem: Albright Institute of Archaeological research), 146–165.

Jaffe, Yitzchak Y. (2015), 'Questioning Religious Essentialism—Ritual Change and Religious Instability in Ancient China', *Journal of Social Archaeology*, 15 (1), 3–23.

Jasmin, Michaël (2006), 'The Political Organization of the City-States in Southwestern Palestine in the Late Bronze Age IIB (13th Century BC)', in Aren M. Maeir and P. de Miroschedji (eds.), *"I will Speak the Riddles of Ancient Times": Archaeological and Historical Studies in Honor of Amihai Mazar on the Occasion of His Sixtieth Birthday* (Winona Lake: Eisenbrauns), 161–191.

Jeske, Ann-Kathrin (2019), 'Mid-To-Late 18th Dynasty Egyptian Functionaries Serving in the Southern Levant: Can We Trace the Individuals?', *Journal of Ancient Egyptian Interconnections*, 21, 31–47.

Johnson, W. Raymond (1996), 'Amenhotep III and Amarna: Some New Considerations', *Journal of Egyptian Archaeology*, 82, 65–82.

Johnson, W. Raymond (1998), 'Monuments and Monumental Art under Amenhotep III: Evolution and Meaning', in David O'Connor and Eric H. Cline (eds.), *Amenhotep III: Perspectives on His Reign* (Ann Arbor: University of Michigan Press), 63–94.

Jordan, Kurt A. (2009), 'Colonies, Colonialism, and Cultural Entanglement: The Archaeology of Postcolumbian Intercultural Relations', in Teresita Majewski and David Gaimster (eds.), *International Handbook of Historical Archaeology* (New York: Springer), 31–49.

Kahn, Dan'el (2011a), 'One Step Forward, Two Steps Backward: The Relations between Amenhotep III, King of Egypt and Tushratta, King of Mitanni', in Shai Bar, Dan'el Kahn, and J.J. Shirley (eds.), *Egypt, Canaan and Israel: History, Imperialism, Ideology and Literature: Proceedings of a Conference at the University of Haifa, 3–7 May 2009* (Culture and History of the Ancient Near East 52; Leiden and Boston: Brill), 136–154.

Kahn, Dan'el (2011b), 'The Campaign of Ramesses III against Philistia', *Journal of Ancient Egyptian Interconnections*, 3 (4), 1–11.

Kahn, Dan'el (2012), 'Merneptah's Policy in Canaan in a Geo-Political Perspective', in Gershon Galil, et al. (eds.), *The Ancient Near East in the 12th–10th Centuries BCE Culture and History: Proceedings of the International Conference held at the University of Haifa, 2–5 May, 2010* (Alter Orient und Altes Testament 392; Münster: Ugarit-Verlag), 255–268.

Kamlah, Jens (2012), 'Temples of the Levant—Comparative Aspects', in Jens Kamlah (ed.), *Temple Building and Temple Cult: Architecture and Cultic Paraphernalia of Temples in the Levant (2.–1. Mill. B.C.E.)* (Abhandlugen des Deutschen Palästina-Vereins 41; Wiesbaden: Harrassowitz), 507–534.

Kaplan, Jacob and Ritter-Kaplan, Haya (1993), 'Jaffa', in Ephraim Stern (ed.), *New Encyclopedia of Archaeological Excavations in the Holy Land* (2; Jerusalem: Israel Exploration Society), 655–659.

Keel, Othmar (1972), *Die Welt der altorientalischen Bildsymbolik und das Alte Testament: Am Beispiel der Psalmen* (Zürich, Köln, and Neukirchen: Benziger Verlag, Einsiedeln, and Neukirchener Verlag).

Keel, Othmar (1990a), 'Berichtigungen und Nachträge zu den Beiträgen II–IV', in Othmar Keel, Menakhem Shuval, and Christoph Uehlinger (eds.), *Studien zu den Stempelsiegeln aus Palästina/Israel III* (Orbis Biblicus et Orientalis 100; Fribourg and Göttingen: Academic Press, Vandenhoeck and Ruprecht), 261–330.

Keel, Othmar (1990b), 'Früheisenzeitliche Glyptik in Palästina/Israel, mit einem Beitrag von H. Keel-Leu', in Othmar Keel, Menakhem Shuval, and Christoph Uehlinger (eds.), *Studien zu den Stempelsiegeln aus Palästina/Israel III* (Orbis Biblicus et Orientalis 100; Fribourg and Göttingen: Academic Press, Vandenhoeck and Ruprecht), 331–421.

Keel, Othmar (1994), *Studies zu den Stempelsiegeln aus Palästina/Israel IV* (Orbis Biblicus et Orientalis 135; Freiburg and Göttingen: Universitätverlag and Vandenhoeck & Ruprecht).

Keel, Othmar (1995), *Corpus der Stempelsiegel-Amulette aus Palästina/Israel. Von den Anfängen bis zur Perserzeit: Einleitung* (Orbis Biblicus et Orientalis Series

Archaeologica 10; Fribourg and Göttingen: Academic Press and Vandenhoeck & Ruprecht).

Keel, Othmar (1997), *Corpus der Stempelsiegel-Amulette aus Palästina/Israel. Von den Anfängen bis zur Perserzeit—Band I: Von Tell Abu Farağ bis ʿAtlit* (Orbis Biblicus et Orientalis Series Archaeologica 13; Fribourg and Göttingen: Academic Press and Vandenhoeck & Ruprecht).

Keel, Othmar (2010a), *Corpus der Stempelsiegel-Amulette aus Palästina/Israel. Von den Anfängen bis zur Perserzeit—Band II: Von Bahan bis Tel Eton* (Orbis Biblicus et Orientalis Series Archaeologica 29; Fribourg and Göttingen: Academic Press and Vandenhoeck & Ruprecht).

Keel, Othmar (2010b), *Corpus der Stempelsiegel-Amulette aus Palästina/Israel. Von den Anfängen bis zur Perserzeit—Band III: Von Tell el-Farʿa-Nord bis Tell el-Fir* (Orbis Biblicus et Orientalis Series Archaeologica 31; Fribourg and Göttingen: Academic Press and Vandenhoeck & Ruprecht).

Keel, Othmar (2013a), *Corpus der Stempelsiegel-Amulette aus Palästina/Israel. Von den Anfängen bis zur Perserzeit—Band IV: Von Tel Gamma bis Chirbet Husche* (Orbis Biblicus et Orientalis Series Archaeologica 33; Fribourg and Göttingen: Academic Press and Vandenhoeck & Ruprecht).

Keel, Othmar (2013b), 'Chapter 5: Glyptics', *NGSBA Archaeology* 2, 30–35.

Keel, Othmar (2015), 'Egyptian Glyptic Material', in Eilat Mazar (ed.), *The Summit of the City of David Excavations 2005–2008* (Jerusalem: Shoham Academic Research and Publication), 421–440.

Keel, Othmar and Mazar, Amihai (2009), 'Iron Age Seals and Seal Impressions from Tel Reḥov', *Eretz-Israel*, 29, 57*–69*. (Hebrew)

Keel, Othmar and Uehlinger, Christoph (1998), *Gods, Goddesses, and Images of God in Ancient Israel*, trans. Thomas H. Trapp (Minneapolis: Fortress Press).

Keel-Leu, Heidi (1990), *Vorderasiatische Stempelsiegel: Die Sammlung des Biblischen Instituts der Universität Freiburg Schweiz* (Orbis Biblicus et Orientalis 110; Fribourg and Göttingen: Academic Press, Vandenhoeck and Ruprecht).

Kempinski, Aaron (1974), 'Tell el-ʿAjjul, Beth Aglaim or Sharuḥen?', *Israel Exploration Journal*, 24, 148–149.

Kenyon, Kathleen M. (1960), *Archaeology in the Holy land* (London: E. Benn).

Kenyon, Kathleen M. (1973), 'Palestine in the Time of the Eighteenth Dynasty', in I.E.S. Edwards, Cyril J. Gadd, and Nicholas G.L. Hammond (eds.), *The Cambridge Ancient History Volume 2, Part 1: The Middle East and the Aegean Region, c.1800–1380 BC*, 526–556.

Khatchadourian, Lori (2016), *Imperial Matter: Ancient Persia and the Archaeology of Empires* (Oakland: University of California Press).

Kilani, Marwan (2020), *Byblos in the Late Bronze Age: Interactions between the Levantine and Egyptian World* (Studies in the Archaeology and History of the Levant 9; Leiden: Brill).

Killebrew, Ann E. (1996), *Tel Miqne-Ekron: Report of the 1985–1987 Excavations in Field INE: Areas 5, 6, 7—The Bronze and Iron Ages* (Jerusalem: Albright Institute of Archaeological Research).

Killebrew, Ann E. (1998), 'Ceramic Craft and Technology during the Late Bronze and Early Iron Ages: The Relationship between Pottery Technology, Style, and Cultural Diversity', Ph.D. Dissertation (The Hebrew University of Jerusalem).

Killebrew, Ann E. (2004), 'New Kingdom Egyptian-style and Egyptian Pottery in Canaan: Implications for Egyptian Rule in Canaan during the 19th and early 20th Dynasties', in Garry N. Knoppers and Antoine Hirsch (eds.), *Egypt, Israel, and the Ancient Mediterranean World: Studies in Honor of Donald B. Redford* (Probleme der Ägyptologie 20; Leiden and Boston: Brill), 309–343.

Killebrew, Ann E. (2005), *Biblical Peoples and Ethnicity: An Archaeological Study of Egyptians, Canaanites, Philistines, and Early Israel 1300–1100 B.C.E.* (SBL Archaeology and Biblical Studies; Atlanta: SBL).

Killebrew, Ann E. (2013), 'Early Philistine Pottery Technology at Tel Miqne-Ekron: Implications for the Late Bronze–Early Iron Age Transition in the Eastern Mediterranean', in Ann E. Killebrew and Gunnar Lehmann (eds.), *The Philistines and other "Sea Peoples" in Text and Archaeology* (Archaeology and Biblical Studies 15; Atlanta: SBL), 77–129.

Killebrew, Ann E., Goldberg, Paul, and Rosen, Arlene M. (2006), 'Deir el-Balah: A Geological, Archaeological, and Historical Reassessment of an Egyptianizing 13th and 12th Century B.C.E. Center', *Bulletin of the American Schools of Oriental Research*, 343, 97–119.

Killebrew, Ann E. and Lev-Tov, Justin (2008), 'Early Iron Age Feasting and Cuisine: An Indicator of Philistine-Aegean Connectivity', in Louise A. Hitchcock, Robert Laffineur, and Janice L. Crowley (eds.), *Dais—The Aegean Feast* (Aegaeum 29; Liège and Austin, Texas: Université de Liège; University of Texas at Austin), 339–346.

Killebrew, Ann E. and Lehmann, Gunnar (2013), 'Introduction', in Ann E. Killebrew and Gunnar Lehmann (eds.), *The Philistines and other "Sea Peoples" in Text and Archaeology* (Archaeology and Biblical Studies 15; Atlanta: SBL), 1–17.

Kisilevitz, Shua, et al. (2014), 'Moza, Tel Moza', *Hadashot Arkheologiyot: Excavations and Surveys in Israel*, 126. accessed 16 March 2016.

Kitchen, Kenneth A. (2012), 'Ramesses III and the Ramesside Period', in Eric H. Cline and David O'Connor (eds.), *Ramesses III: The Life and Times of Egypt's Last Hero* (Ann Arbor: University of Michigan Press), 1–26.

Kleiman, Sabine, Gadot, Yuval, and Lipschits, Oded (2016), 'A Snapshot of the Destruction Layer of Tell Zakarīye /Azekah Seen against the Backdrop of the Final Days of the Late Bronze Age', *Zeitschrift des Deutschen Palästina-Vereins*, 132 (2), 105–133.

Kleiman, Sabine, et al. (2019), 'Late Bronze Age Azekah—An Almost Forgotten Story', in Aren M. Maeir, Itzhaq Shai, and Chris McKinny (eds.), *The Late Bronze and Early Iron Ages of Southern Canaan* (Archaeology of the Biblical World 2; Berlin: De Gruyter), 37–61.

Knapp, A. Bernard (1992), 'Independence and Imperialism: Politico-economic Structures in the Bronze Age Levant', in A. Bernard Knapp (ed.), *Archaeology, Annales, and Ethnohistory* (Cambridge: Cambridge University Press), 83–98.

Knapp, A. Bernard (2012), 'Matter of Fact: Transcultural Contacts in the Late Bronze Age Eastern Mediterranean', in Joseph Maran and Philipp W. Stockhammer (eds.), *Materiality and Social Practice: Transformative Capacities of Intercultural Encounters* (Oxford: Oxbow Books), 32–50.

Knapp, A. Bernard and Manning, Sturt W. (2016), 'Crisis in Context: The End of the Late Bronze Age in the Eastern Mediterranean', *American Journal of Archaeology*, 120 (1), 99–149.

Koch, Ido (2012), 'The Geopolitical Situation in the Judean Lowland during the Iron Age I–IIa (1150–800 BCE)', *Cathedra: For the History of Eretz Israel and Its Yishuv*, 143, 45–64. (Hebrew)

Koch, Ido (2014), 'Goose Keeping, Elite Emulation and Egyptianized Feasting at Late Bronze Lachish', *Tel Aviv*, 41 (2), 161–179.

Koch, Ido (2016), 'Notes on Three South Canaanite Sites in the el-Amarna Correspondence', *Tel Aviv*, 43, 91–98.

Koch, Ido (2017a), 'Revisiting the Fosse Temple at Tel Lachish', *Journal of Ancient Near Eastern Religions*, 17, 64–75.

Koch, Ido (2017b), 'Settlements and Interactions in the Shephelah during the Late Second through Early First Millennia BCE', in Oded Lipschits and Aren M. Maeir (eds.), *The Shephelah during the Iron Age: Recent Archaeological Studies* (Winona Lake: Eisenbrauns), 181–207.

Koch, Ido (2018a), *The Shadow of Egypt: Colonial Encounters in Southwest Canaan during the Late Bronze Age and Early Iron Age* (Jerusalem: Yad Izhak Ben Zvi). (Hebrew)

Koch, Ido (2018b), 'The Egyptian-Canaanite Interface as Colonial Encounter: A View from Southwest Canaan', *Journal of Ancient Egyptian Interconnections*, 18, 24–39.

Koch, Ido (2018c), 'Late Iron Age I Southwestern Canaanite Multi-Facet Stamp-Amulets: Innovative Imagery and Interpreted Egyptian Heritage', in Itzhack Shai, et al. (eds.), *Tell it in Gath: Studies in the History and Archaeology of Israel Essays in Honor of Aren M. Maeir on the Occasion of his Sixtieth Birthday* (Ägypten und Altes Testament 90; Münster: Zaphon), 632–652.

Koch, Ido (2019), 'Southwestern Canaan and Egypt during the Late Bronze Age I–IIA', in Aren M. Maeir, Itzhaq Shai, and Chris McKinny (eds.), *The Late Bronze and Early Iron Ages of Southern Canaan* (Archaeology of the Biblical World 2; Berlin: De Gruyter), 262–282.

Koch, Ido (2020), 'On Philistines and Early Israelite Kings', in Joachim Krause, Omer Sergi, and Kristin Weingart (eds.), *Saul, Benjamin and the Emergence of Monarchy in Israel* (Ancient Israel and Its Literature 40; Atlanta: SBL), 7–31.

Koch, Ido, et al. (2017), 'Amulets in Context: A View from Late Bronze Age Tel Azekah', *Journal of Ancient Egyptian Interconnections*, 16, 9–24.

Kochavi, Moshe (1974), 'Khirbet Rabûd = Debir', *Tel Aviv*, 1 (1), 2–33.

Kochavi, Moshe and Beit-Arieh, Itzhaq (1991), *Archaeological Survey of Israel: Map of Rosh Ha-'Ayin—78* (Jerusalem: Israel Antiquities Authority).

Kolata, Alan L. (2006), 'Before and After Collapse: Reflections on the Regeneration of Social Complexity', in Glenn M. Schwartz and John J. Nichols (eds.), *After Collapse: the Regeneration of Complex Societies* (First paperback printing edn.; Tucson: University of Arizona press), 208–221.

Kopetzky, Karin (2011), 'The Southern Coastal Plain: Tell el-'Ajjul', in Mario A.S. Martin, *Egyptian-Type Pottery in the Late Bronze Age Southern Levant* (Contributions to the Chronology of the Eastern Mediterranean 29; Vienna: Verlag der Österreichischen Akademie der Wissenschaften), 201–209.

Kozloff, Arielle P. (2012), *Amenhotep III: Egypt's Radiant Pharaoh* (Cambridge: Cambridge University Press).

Kozloff, Arielle P. and Bryan, Betsy M. (1992), *Egypt's Dazzling Sun: Amenhotep III and His World* (Cleveland: Cleveland Museum of Art).

Lalkin, Nir (2006), 'The Scarabs', in Israel Finkelstein, David Ussishkin, and Baruch Halpern (eds.), *Megiddo IV: The 1998–2002 Seasons* (Monograph Series of the Institute of Archaeology of Tel Aviv University 24; Tel Aviv: Emery and Claire Yass Publications in Archaeology), 430–436.

Lalkin, Nir (2008), 'Late Bronze Age Scarabs from Eretz Israel', Ph.D. dissertation (Tel Aviv University).

Leclant, Jean (1960), 'Astarté a cheval d'après les représentations égyptiennes', *Syria*, 37, 1–67.

Lederman, Zvi and Bunimovitz, Shlomo (2014), 'Canaanites, "Shephelites" and Those who will become Judahites', in Guy Stiebel, et al. (eds.), *New Studies in the Archaeology of Jerusalem and Its Region 8* (Jerusalem), 61–71. (Hebrew with English summary)

Lehmann, Gunnar (2007), 'Decorated Pottery Styles in the Northern Levant during the Early Iron Age and Their Relationship with Cyprus and the Aegean', *Ugarit-Forschungen*, 39, 487–550.

Lehmann, Gunnar and Niemann, Hermann Michael (2014), 'When Did the Shephelah Become Judahite?', *Tel Aviv*, 41 (1), 77–94.

Lehmann, Gunnar, et al. (2010), 'Excavations at Qubur al-Walaydah, 2007–2009', *Welt des Orient*, 40, 137–159.

Leibowitz, Harold (1987), 'Late Bronze II Ivory Work in Palestine: Evidence of a Cultural Highpoint', *Bulletin of the American Schools of Oriental Research*, 265, 3–24.

Leonard, Albert (1994), *An Index to the Late Bronze Age Aegean Pottery from Syria-Palestine* (Studies in Mediterranean Archaeology 114; Jonsered: Åström).

Lev-Tov, Justin S.E. (2006), 'The Faunal Remains: Animal Economy in the Iron Age I', in Mark W. Meehl, Trude Dothan, and Seymour Gitin (eds.), *Tel Miqne-Ekron Excavations 1995–1996: Field INE East Slope Iron Age I (Early Philistine Period)* (Tel Miqne-Ekron Final Report Series; Jerusalem: W.F. Albright Institute of Archaeological Research and Institute of Archaeology, Hebrew University), 207–234.

Lev-Tov, Justin S.E. (2010), 'A Plebeian Perspective on Empire Economies: Faunal Remains from Tel Miqne-Ekron, Israel', in Douglas V. Campana, et al. (eds.), *Anthropological Approaches to Zooarchaeology: Colonialism, Complexity and Animal Transformations* (Oxford: Oxbow Books), 90–104.

Lev-Tov, Justin S.E. (2012), 'A Preliminary Report on the Late Bronze and Iron Age Faunal Assemblages from Tell es-Safi/Gath', in Aren M. Maeir (ed.), *Tell es-Safi/Gath I: Report on the 1996–2005 Seasons* (Ägypten und Altes Testament 64; Wiesbaden: Harrassowitz), 589–612.

Lev-Tov, Justin S.E. and Maher, Edward F. (2001), 'Food in Late Bronze Age Funerary Offerings: Faunal Evidence from Tomb 1 at Tell Dothan', *Palestine Exploration Quarterly*, 133 (2), 91–110.

Lev-Tov, Justin S.E. and McGeough, Kevin (2007), 'Examining Feasting in Late Bronze Age Syro-Palestine through Ancient Texts and Bones', in Katheryn C. Twiss (ed.), *The Archaeology of Food and Identity* (Center for Archaeological Investigations, Southern Illinois University Carbondale Occasional Paper 34; Carbondale: Center for Archaeological Investigations, Southern Illinois University), 85–111.

Lev-Tov, Justin S.E., Porter, Benjamin W., and Routledge, Bruce E. (2011), 'Measuring Local Diversity in Early Iron Age Animal Economies: A View from Khirbat al-'Aliya (Jordan)', *Bulletin of the American Schools of Oriental Research*, 361, 67–93.

Levy, Eythan (2017), 'A Note on the Geographical Distribution of New Kingdom Egyptian Inscriptions from the Levant', *Journal of Ancient Egyptian Interconnections*, 14, 14–21.

Liebmann, Matthew (2015), 'The Mickey Mouse Kachina and other "Double Objects": Hybridity in the Material Culture of Colonial Encounters', *Journal of Social Archaeology*, 15 (3), 319–341.

Lilyquist, Christine (1998), 'The Use of Ivories as Interpreters of Political History', *Bulletin of the American Schools of Oriental Research*, 310, 25–33.

Lipiński, Edward (1996), 'Egypto-Canaanite Iconography of Resheph, Ba'al, Ḥoron, and Anat', *Chronique D'Égypte*, 71, 254–262.

Lipschits, Oded, Gadot, Yuval, and Oeming, Manfred (2017), 'Four Seasons of Excavations at Tel Azekah: The Expected and (Especially) Unexpected Results', in Oded Lipschits and Aren M. Maeir (eds.), *The Shephelah during the Iron Age: Recent Archaeological Studies* (Winona Lake: Eisenbrauns), 1–25.

Lipschits, Oded, et al. (2019), 'The Last Days of Canaanite Azekah', *Biblical Archaeology Review*, 45 (1), 32–38, 70.

Lipton, Gary (2010), 'The Excavation of the Cemetery', in Trude Dothan and Baruch Brandl (eds.), *Deir el-Balaḥ: Excavations in 1977–1982 in the Cemetery and Settlement, Vol. 1: Stratigraphy and Architecture* (Qedem 49; Jerusalem: Institute of Archaeology, Hebrew University of Jerusalem), 3–46.

Loomba, Ania (2015), *Colonialism/Postcolonialism* (Third edn., The New Critical Idiom; London and New York: Routledge).

Loprieno, Antonio (1988), *Topos und Mimesis: zum Ausländer in der ägyptischen Literatur* (Ägyptologische Abhandlungen 48; Wiesbaden: Otto Harrassowitz Verlag).

Loud, Gordon (1948), *Megiddo II: Seasons of 1935–39* (Oriental Institute Publications 62; Chicago: University of Chicago Press).

Lucas, Gavin (2004), *The archaeology of time* (Routledge).

Lydon, Jane and Rizvi, Uzma Z. (2016), *Handbook of Postcolonial Archaeology* (World Archaeological Congress Research Handbooks in Archaeology 3; London and New York: Routledge).

Lyons, Claire L. and Papadopoulos, John K. (2002), *The Archaeology of Colonialism* (Issues and Debates, 9; Los Angeles: Getty Publications).

Macalister, R.A. Stewart (1914), *The Philistines: Their History and Civilization* (The Schweich Lecture 1911; London: Oxford University Press).

MacDonald, Eann, Starkey, James L., and Harding, Lankester (1932), *Beth-Pelet II* (Publications of the Egyptian Research Account 52; London: British School of Archaeology in Egypt).

Mączyńska, Agnieszka (ed.), (2014), *The Nile Delta as a Centre of Cultural Interactions Between Upper Egypt and the Southern Levant in the 4th millennium BC* (Studies in African Archaeology; Poznań: Poznań Archaeological Museum).

Maeir, Aren M. (2008), 'Aegean Feasting and other Indo-European Elements in the Philistine Household', in Louise A. Hitchcock, Robert Laffineur, and Janice L. Crowley (eds.), *Dais—The Aegean Feast* (Aegaeum 29; Liège and Austin, Texas: Université de Liège; University of Texas at Austin), 347–352.

Maeir, Aren M. (2011), 'The Archaeology of Early Jerusalem: From the Late Protohistoric Period (ca. 5th Millennium) to the End of the Bronze Age (ca. 1200 B.C.E.)', in Katharina Galor and Gideon Avni (eds.), *Unearthing Jerusalem: 150 Years of Archaeological Excavations in the Holy City* (Winona Lake: Eisenbrauns), 171–187.

Maeir, Aren M. (2012a), *Tell es-Safi/Gath 1: The 1996–2005 Seasons* (Ägypten und Altes Testament 69; Wiesbaden: Harrassowitz).

Maeir, Aren M. (2012b), 'Insights on the Philistine Culture and Related Issues: An Overview of 15 years of Work at Tell eṣ-Ṣafi/Gath', in Gershon Galil, et al. (eds.), *The Ancient Near East in the 12th–10th Centuries BCE Culture and History: Proceedings of the International Conference held at the University of Haifa, 2–5 May, 2010* (Alter Orient und Altes Testament 392; Münster: Ugarit-Verlag), 345–404.

Maeir, Aren M. and Uziel, Josef (2007), 'A Tale of Two Tells: A Comparative Perspective on Tel Miqne-Ekron and Tell es-Safi/Gath in Light of Recent Archaeological Research', in Shelly White Crawford (ed.), *"Up to the Gates of Ekron": Essays on the Archaeology and History of the eastern Mediterranean in Honor of Seymour Gitin* (Jerusalem: Albright Institute of Archaeological research), 29–42.

Maeir, Aren M. and Hitchcock, Louise A. (2011), 'Absence makes the "Hearth" grow Fonder: Searching for the Origins of the Philistine Hearth', *Eretz-Israel*, 30, 46*–64*.

Maeir, Aren M. and Hitchcock, Louise A. (2017a), 'Rethinking the Philistines: A 2017 Perspective', in Oded Lipschits, Yuval Gadot, and Matthew J. Adams (eds.), *Rethinking Israel: Studies in the History and Archaeology of Ancient Israel in Honor of Israel Finkelstein* (Winona Lake: Eisenbrauns), 247–266.

Maeir, Aren M. and Hitchcock, Louise A. (2017b), 'The Appearance, Formation and Transformation of Philistine Culture: New Perspectives and New Finds', in Peter M. Fischer and Teresa Bürge (eds.), *"Sea Peoples" Up-to-Date: New Research on Transformation in the Eastern Mediterranean in the 13th–11th Centuries BCE* (Contributions to the Chronology of Eastern Mediterranean 35; Vienna: Verlag der Österreichischen Akademie der Wissenschaften), 149–162.

Maeir, Aren M., Hitchcock, Louise A., and Horwitz, Liora Kolska (2013), 'On the Constitution and Transformation of Philistine Identity', *Oxford Journal of Archaeology*, 32 (1), 1–38.

Maeir, Aren M., et al. (2015), 'An Ivory Bowl from Early Iron Age Tell es-Safi/Gath (Israel): Manufacture, Meaning and Memory', *World Archaeology*, 47 (3), 414–438.

Maeir, Aren M., et al. (2019), 'The Late Bronze Age at Tell es-Safi/Gath and the Site's Rule in Southwestern Canaan', in Aren M. Maeir, Itzhaq Shai, and Chris McKinny (eds.), *The Late Bronze and Early Iron Ages of Southern Canaan* (Archaeology of the Biblical World 2; Berlin: De Gruyter), 1–18.

Magen, Yitzhak and Finkelstein, Israel (1993), *Archaeological Survey of the Hill Country of Benjamin* (Jerusalem: Israel Antiquities Authority).

Magrill, Pamela and Middleton, Andrew (2004), 'Late Bronze Age Pottery Technology: Cave 4034 Revisited', in David Ussishkin (ed.), *The Renewed Archaeological Excavations at Tel Lachish (1973–1994)* (Monograph Series of the Institute of Archaeology of Tel Aviv University 22; Tel Aviv: Emery and Claire Yass Publications in Archaeology), 2514–2549.

Maher, Edward (2005), 'The Faunal Remains', in Moshe Dothan and David Ben-Shlomo (eds.), *Ashdod VI: The Excavations of Areas H and K (1968–1969)* (Israel Antiquities Authority Reports 24; Jerusalem: Israel Antiquities Authority), 283–290.

Maisler, Benjamin (1952), 'Yurza: The Identification of Tell Jemmeh', *Palestine Exploration Quarterly*, 84 (1), 48–51.

Manassa, Colleen (2010), 'Defining Historical Fiction in New Kingdom Egypt', in Sarah C. Melville and Alice Slotsky (eds.), *Opening the Tablet Box: Near Eastern Studies in Honor of Benjamin R. Foster* (Culture and History of the Ancient Near East 42; Leiden: Brill), 245–269.

Manassa, Colleen (2013), 'Army, Pharaonic Egypt', *The Encyclopedia of Ancient History*.

Manassa Darnell, Colleen (2015), 'Transition 18th–19th dynasty', *UCLA Encyclopedia of Egyptology* (2 June 2015 edn., 1; UCLA: Department of Near Eastern Languages and Cultures).

Mann, Michael (1986), *The Sources of Social Power. Volume 1: A History of Power from the Beginning to A.D. 1760* (Cambridge: Cambridge University Press).

Manning, Sturt W. (2006–2007), 'Why Radiocarbon Dating 1200 BCE is Difficult: A Sidelight on Dating the End of the Late Bronze Age and the Contrarian Contribution', *Scripta Mediterranea*, 27–28, 53–80.

Maran, Joseph (2011), 'Lost in Translation: The Emergence of Mycenaean Culture as a Phenomenon of Glocalization', in Toby C. Wilkinson, Susan E. Sherratt, and John Bennet (eds.), *Interweaving Worlds: Systemic Interactions in Eurasia, 7th to 1st Millennia BC* (Oxford: Oxbow Books), 282–294.

Marcus, Ezra (2007), 'Amenemhet II and the Sea: Maritime Aspects of the Mit Rahina (Memphis) Inscription', *Egypt and the Levant*, 17, 137–189.

Margovsky, Yitzhak (1971), 'Three Temples in Northern Sinai', *Qadmoniot: A Journal for the Antiquities of Eretz-Israel and Bible Lands*, 4, 18–21. (Hebrew)

Martin, Mario A.S. (2004), 'Egyptian and Egyptianized Pottery in Late Bronze Age Canaan', *Ägypten und Levante/Egypt and the Levant*, 14, 265–284.

Martin, Mario A.S. (2005), 'The Egyptian and Egyptian-Style Pottery. Aspects of the Egyptian Involvement in Late Bronze and Early Iron Age Canaan. A Case Study.', Ph.D. dissertation (University of Vienna).

Martin, Mario A.S. (2007), 'A Collection of Egyptian and Egyptian-style Pottery at Beth Shean', in Manfred Bietak and Ernst Czerny (eds.), *The Synchronization of Civilisations in the Eastern Mediterranean in the Second Millennium B.C. III* (Contributions to the Chronology of the Eastern Mediterranean 9; Vienna: Verlag der Osterreichischen Akademie der Wissenschaften), 375–388.

Martin, Mario A.S. (2011), *Egyptian-Type Pottery in the Late Bronze Age Southern Levant* (Contributions to the Chronology of the Eastern Mediterranean 29; Vienna: Verlag der Österreichischen Akademie der Wissenschaften).

Martin, Mario A.S. (2017), 'The Provenance of Philistine Pottery in Northern Canaan, with a Focus on the Jezreel Valley', *Tel Aviv*, 44 (2), 193–231.

Martin, Mario A.S. and Finkelstein, Israel (2013), 'Iron IIA Pottery from the Negev Highlands: Petrographic Investigation and Historical Implications', *Tel Aviv*, 40 (1), 6–45.

Martin, Mario A.S., et al. (2013), 'Iron IIA slag-tempered pottery in the Negev Highlands, Israel', *Journal of Archaeological Science*, 40 (10), 3777–3792.

Maspero, Gaston (1875), *Histoire Ancienne des peuples de l'orient classique* (Paris: Librairie Hachette et Cie).

Master, Daniel M., Mountjoy, Penelope A., and Mommsen, Hans (2015), 'Imported Cypriot Pottery in Twelfth-Century B.C. Ashkelon', *Bulletin of the American Schools of Oriental Research*, 373, 235–243.

Mattingly, David J. (2014), *Imperialism, Power, and Identity: Experiencing the Roman Empire* (Second edn.; Princeton: Princeton University Press).

Mazar, Amihai (1980), *Excavations at Tell Qasile, Part 1: The Philistine Sanctuary: Architecture and Cult Objects* (Qedem 12; Jerusalem: Institute of Archaeology, Hebrew University of Jerusalem).

Mazar, Amihai (1985a), *Excavations at Tell Qasile, Part 2: The Philistine Sanctuary—Various Finds, the Pottery, Conclusions, Appendices* (Qedem 20; Jerusalem: Institute of Archaeology, Hebrew University of Jerusalem).

Mazar, Amihai (1985b), 'Pottery Plaques Depicting Goddesses Standing in Temple Facades', *Michmanim*, 2, 5–18.

Mazar, Amihai (1985c), 'The Emergence of the Philistine Material Culture', *Israel Exploration Journal*, 35 (2/3), 95–107.

Mazar, Amihai (1989), 'Features of Settlements in the Northern Shephelah during MB and LB in the Light of the Excavations at Tel Batash and Gezer', *Eretz-Israel*, 20, 58–67. (Hebrew)

Mazar, Amihai (1997), *Timnah (Tel Batash) 1: Stratigraphy and Architecture* (Qedem 37; Jerusalem: Institute of Archaeology, Hebrew University of Jerusalem).

Mazar, Amihai (1999), 'The 1997–1998 Excavations at Tel Reḥov: Preliminary Report', *Israel Exploration Journal*, 49 (1/2), 1–42.

Mazar, Amihai (2000), 'The Temples and Cult of the Philistines', in Eliezer D. Oren (ed.), *The Sea Peoples and Their World: A Reassessment* (University Museum Monograph 108; Philadelphia: University Museum, University of Pennsylvania), 213–232.

Mazar, Amihai (2003), 'Ritual Dancing in the Iron Age', *Near Eastern Archaeology*, 66 (3), 126–131.

Mazar, Amihai (2007), 'Myc IIIC in the Land of Israel: Its Distribution, Date and Significance', in Manfred Bietak and Ernst Czerny (eds.), *The Synchronization of Civilisations in the Eastern Mediterranean in the Second Millennium B.C. III* (Contributions to the Chronology of the Eastern Mediterranean 9; Vienna: Verlag der Osterreichischen Akademie der Wissenschaften), 571–582.

Mazar, Amihai (2009), 'The Iron Age Dwellings at Tell Qasile', in David J. Schloen (ed.), *Exploring the Longue Durée: Essays in Honor of Lawrence E. Stager* (Winona Lake: Eisenbrauns), 319–336.

Mazar, Amihai (2011), 'The Egyptian Garrison Town at Beth Shean', in Shai Bar, Dan'el Kahn, and J.J. Shirley (eds.), *Egypt, Canaan and Israel: History, Imperialism, Ideology and Literature: Proceedings of a Conference at the University of Haifa, 3–7 May 2009* (Culture and History of the Ancient Near East 52; Leiden and Boston: Brill), 155–189.

Mazar, Amihai (2015), 'Iron Age I: Northern Coastal Plain, Galilee, Samaria, Jezreel Valley, Judah, and Negev', in Seymour Gitin (ed.), *The Ancient Pottery of Israel and Its Neighbors: From the Iron Age through the Hellenistic Period* (1; Jerusalem: Israel Exploration Society), 5–70.

Mazar, Amihai and Panitz-Cohen, Nava (2001), *Timnah (Tel Batash) 2: The Finds from the First Millennium BCE* (Qedem 42; Jerusalem: Institute of Archaeology, Hebrew University of Jerusalem).

Mazar, Amihai and Panitz-Cohen, Nava (2007), 'It is the Land of Honey: Beekeeping at Tel Rehov', *Near Eastern Archaeology*, 70 (4), 202.

Mazar, Amihai and Panitz-Cohen, Nava (2019), 'Tel Batash in the Late Bronze Age—A Retrospect', in Aren M. Maeir, Itzhaq Shai, and Chris McKinny (eds.), *The Late Bronze and Early Iron Ages of Southern Canaan* (Archaeology of the Biblical World 2; Berlin: De Gruyter), 86–121.

Mazar, Amihai, et al. (2008), 'Iron Age Beehives at Tel Reḥov in the Jordan Balley', *Antiquity*, 82 (317), 629–639.

Mazar, Benjamin (1967), 'A Philistine Seal from Tel Qasile', *Yediot Bahaqirat Eretz-Israel Weatiqoteha*, 31, 64–67.

Mazow, Laura B. (2005), 'Competing Material Culture: Philistine Settlement at Tel Miqne-Ekron in the Early Iron Age', Ph.D. Dissertation (University of Arizona).

Mazow, Laura B. (2006–2007), 'The Industrious Sea Peoples: The Evidence of Aegean-style Textile Production in Cyprus and the Southern Levant', *Scripta Mediterranea*, 27–28, 291–321.

Mazow, Laura B. (2013), 'Throwing the Baby Out with the Bathwater: Innovations in Mediterranean Textile Production at the End of the 2nd/Beginning of the 1st Millennium BCE', in Marie-Louise Nosch, Henriette Koefoed, and Eva Anderson Strand (eds.), *Textile Production and Consumption in the Ancient Near East: Archaeology, Epigraphy, Iconography* (Ancient Textile Series 12; Oxford and Oakville: Oxbow Books), 215–223.

Mazow, Laura B. (2014), 'Competing Material Culture: Philistine Settlement at Tel Miqne-Ekron in the Early Iron Age', in John R. Spencer, Robert A. Mullins, and Aaron J. Brody (eds.), *Material Culture Matters: Essays on the Archaeology of the Southern Levant in Honor of Seymour Gitin* (Winona Lake, IN: Eisenbrauns), 131–163.

McAnany, Patricia A. and Yoffee, Norman (eds.) (2009), *Questioning Collapse: Human Resilience, Ecological Vulnerability, and the Aftermath of Empire* (Cambridge: Cambridge University Press).

McKinny, Chris, et al. (2018), 'Kiriath-Jearim (Deir el-ʿÂzar): Archaeological Investigations of a Biblical Town in the Judaean Hill Country', *Israel Exploration Journal*, 68, 30–49.

McNicoll, Anthony, Smith, Robert H., and Hennessy, Basil (1982), *Pella in Jordan 1: An Interim Report on the Joint University of Sydney and the College of Wooster Excavations at Pella 1979–1981* (1; Canberra: Australian National Gallery).

Meehl, Mark W., Dothan, Trude, and Gitin, Seymour (2006), *Tel Miqne-Ekron Excavations 1995–1996: Field INE East Slope Iron Age I (Early Philistine Period)* (Tel Miqne-Ekron Final Report Series 8; Jerusalem: W.F. Albright Institute of Archaeological Research and Institute of Archaeology, Hebrew University).

Meiri, Meirav, et al. (2013), 'Ancient DNA and Population Turnover in Southern Levantine Pigs—Signature of the Sea Peoples Migration?', *Scientific Reports*, 3.

Middleton, Guy D. (2015), 'Telling Stories: The Mycenaean Origins of the Philistines', *Oxford Journal of Archaeology*, 34 (1), 45–65.

Middleton, Guy D. (2017), 'The Show must go on: Collapse, Resilience, and Transformation in 21st-Century Archaeology', *Reviews in Anthropology*, 1–28.

Mierse, William E. (2012), *Temples and Sanctuaries from the Early Iron Age Levant: Recovery after Collapse* (History, Archaeology, and Culture of the Levant 4; Winona Lake: Eisenbrauns).

Millard, Alan (2009), 'The Armor of Goliath', in David J. Schloen (ed.), *Exploring the Longue Durée: Essays in Honor of Lawrence E. Stager* (Winona Lake: Eisenbrauns), 337–343.

Millek, Jesse Michael (2017), 'Sea Peoples, Philistines, and the Destruction of Cities: A Critical Examination of Destruction Layers "Caused" by the "Sea Peoples"', in Peter M. Fischer and Teresa Bürge (eds.), *"Sea Peoples" Up-to-Date: New Research on Transformation in the Eastern Mediterranean in the 13th–11th Centuries BCE* (Contributions to the Chronology of Eastern Mediterranean 35; Vienna: Verlag der Österreichischen Akademie der Wissenschaften), 113–140.

Millet, Martin (1990), *The Romanization of Britain: An Essay in Archaeological Interpretation* (Cambridge: Cambridge University Press).

Moreno Garcia, Juan Carlos (2014), 'Ancient Empires and Pharaonic Egypt: An Agenda for Future Research', *Journal of Egyptian History*, 7, 203–240.

Morkot, Robert G. (1990), 'Nb-Mʿt-Rʿ-United-with-Ptah', *Journal of Near Eastern Studies*, 49 (4), 323–337.

Morris, Ellen F. (2005), *The Architecture of Imperialism: Military Bases and the Evolution of Foreign Policy in Egypt's New Kingdom* (Probleme der Ägyptologie 22; Leiden and Boston: Brill).

Morris, Ellen F. (2006), 'Bowing and Scraping in the Ancient Near East: An Investigation into Obsequiousness in the Amarna Letters', *Journal of Near Eastern Studies*, 65 (3), 179–195.

Morris, Ellen F. (2018), *Ancient Egyptian Imperialism* (Hoboken, NJ: Wiley).

Mountjoy, Penelope A. (2010), 'A Note on the Mixed Origins of Some Philistine Pottery', *Bulletin of the American Schools of Oriental Research*, 359 () , 1–12.

Mountjoy, Penelope A. (2013), 'The Mycenaean IIIC Pottery at Tel Miqne-Ekron', in Ann E. Killebrew and Gunnar Lehmann (eds.), *The Philistines and other "Sea Peoples" in Text and Archaeology* (Archaeology and Biblical Studies 15; Atlanta: SBL), 53–75.

Mourad, Anna-Latifa (2015), *Rise of the Hyksos: Egypt and the Levant from the Middle Kingdom to the Early Second Intermediate Period* (Archaeopress Egyptology 11; Oxford: Holywell Press).

Müller, Miriam (2018), 'Foundation Deposits and Strategies of Place-Making at Tell el-Dab'ah/Avaris', *Near Eastern Archaeology*, 81, 182–190.

Mullins, Rubert A. (2006), 'A Corpus of Eighteenth Dynasty Egyptian-Style Pottery from Tel Beth-Shean', in Aren M. Maeir and Pierre de Miroschedji (eds.), *"I will Speak the Riddles of Ancient Times": Archaeological and Historical Studies in Honor of Amihai Mazar on the Occasion of His Sixtieth Birthday* (Winona Lake: Eisenbrauns), 247–262.

Mullins, Rubert A. (2007), 'The Late Bronze Age Pottery', in Amihai Mazar and Rubert A. Mullins (eds.), *Excavations at Tel Beth-Shean 1989–1996, Vol. 2: The Middle and Late Bronze Age Strata in Area R* (Jerusalem: Israel Exploration Society and the Institute of Archaeology, Hebrew University of Jerusalem), 390–547.

Münger, Stefan (2003), 'Egyptian Stamp-Seal Amulets and Their Implications for the Chronology of the Early Iron Age', *Tel Aviv*, 30 (1), 66–82.

Münger, Stefan (2005), 'Stamp-Seal Amulets and Early Iron Age Chronology—An Update', in Thomas E. Levy and Thomas Higham (eds.), *The Bible and Radiocarbon Dating—Archaeology, Text and Science* (London: Equinox), 381–404.

Münger, Stefan (2007a), 'Amulets in Context: Catalogue of Scarabs, Scaraboids and Stamp-seals from Tel Kinrot/Tell el-'Orēme (Israel)', in Susanne Biekel, et al. (eds.), *Bilder als Quellen Images as Sources: Studies on Ancient Near Eastern Artefacts and the Bible Inspired by the Work of Othmar Keel* (Orbis Biblicus et Orientalis Special Volume; Fribourg and Göttingen: Academic Press; Vandenhoeck & Ruprecht), 81–99.

Münger, Stefan (2007b), 'Stamp Seals and Seal Impressions', in Rudolph Cohen and Hannah Bernick-Greenberg (eds.), *Excavations at Kadesh Barnea (Tell el-Qudeirat) 1976–1982* (Israel Antiquities Authority Reports 34/1; Jerusalem: Israel Antiquities Authority).

Münnich, Maciej M. (2009), 'Two Faces of Resheph in Egyptian Sources', in Izaak J. De Hulster and Rüdiger Schmitt (eds.), *Iconography and Biblical Studies* (Alter Orient und Altes Testament 361; Münster: Ugarit-Verlag), 53–71.

Münnich, Maciej M. (2013), *The God Resheph in the Ancient Near East* (Orientalische Religionen in der Antike, 11; Tübingen: Mohr siebeck).

Mynářová, Jana (2007), *Language of Amarna—Language of Diplomacy. Perspectives on the Amarna Letters.* (Prague: Charles University in Prague, Faculty of Arts, Czech Institute of Egyptology).

Mynářová, Jana (2014), 'Egyptian State Correspondence of the New Kingdom. The Letters of the Levantine Client Kings in the Amarna Correspondence and Contemporary Evidence', in Karen Radner (ed.), *State Correspondence in the Ancient World. From New Kingdom Egypt to the Roman Empire* (Oxford Studies in Early Empires; Oxford: Oxford University Press), 10–31.

Nahshoni, Pirhiya, et al. (2013), 'A Thirteenth-Century BCE Site on the Southern Beach of Ashdod', *'Atiqot*, 74, 59–122.

Nakamura, Carolyn (2004), 'Dedicating Magic: Neo-Assyrian Apotropaic Figurines and the Protection of Assur', *World Archaeology*, 36 (1), 11–25.

Nayar, Pramond K. (2015a), *The Postcolonial Studies Dictionary* (Chichester: John Wiley & Sons).

Nayar, Pramond K. (ed.), (2015b), *Postcolonial Studies: An Anthology* (Chichester: Wiley Blackwell).

Na'aman, Nadav (1975), 'The Political Disposition and Historical Development of Eretz-Israel according to the Amarna Letters', Ph.D. dissertation (Tel Aviv University).

Na'aman, Nadav (1981), 'Economic Aspects of the Egyptian Occupation of Canaan', *Israel Exploration Journal*, 31 (3/4), 172–185.

Na'aman, Nadav (1986), 'Ḫabiru and Hebrews: The Transfer of a Social Term to the Literary Sphere', *Journal of Near Eastern Studies*, 45 (4), 271–288.

Na'aman, Nadav (1994), 'The Hurians and the End of the Middle Bronze Age in Palestine', *Levant*, 26, 175–187.

Na'aman, Nadav (1996), 'Sources and Composition in the History of David', in Volkmar Fritz and Philip R. Davies (eds.), *The Origin of the Ancient Israelite States* (Sheffield: Academic Press), 170–186.

Na'aman, Nadav (1997), 'The Network of Canaanite Late Bronze Kingdoms and the City of Ashdod', *Ugarit-Forschungen*, 29, 599–625.

Na'aman, Nadav (1999), 'Four Notes on the Size of Late Bronze Age Canaan', *Bulletin of the American Schools of Oriental Research*, 313, 31–37.

Na'aman, Nadav (2000), 'The Egyptian-Canaanite Correspondence', in Raymond Cohen and Raymond Westbrook (eds.), *Amarna Diplomacy: The Beginnings of International Relations* (Baltimore: Johns Hopkins University Press), 125–138.

Na'aman, Nadav (2002a), 'In Search of Reality Behind the Account of David's Wars with Israel's Neighbours', *Israel Exploration Journal*, 52 (2), 200–224.

Na'aman, Nadav (2002b), 'Dispatching Canaanite Maidservants to the Pharaoh', *Ancient Near Eastern Studies*, 39, 76–82.

Na'aman, Nadav (2004), 'The Boundary System and Political Status of Gaza under the Assyrian Empire', *Zeitschrift des Deutschen Palästina-Vereins*, 120, 55–72.

Na'aman, Nadav (2009), 'Ashkelon under the Assyrian Empire', in David J. Schloen (ed.), *Exploring the Longue Durée: Essays in Honor of Lawrence E. Stager* (Winona Lake: Eisenbrauns), 351–359.

Na'aman, Nadav (2010a), 'David's Sojourn in Keilah in Light of the Amarna Letters', *Vetus Testamentum*, 60 (1), 87–97.

Na'aman, Nadav (2010b), 'Khirbet Qeiyafa in Context', *Ugarit-Forschungen*, 42, 497–526.

Na'aman, Nadav (2011a), 'The Shephelah according to the Amarna Letters', in Israel Finkelstein and Nadav Na'aman (eds.), *The Fire Signals of Lachish* (Winona Lake: Eisenbrauns), 281–299.

Na'aman, Nadav (2011b), 'The Exodus Story: Between Historical Memory and Historiographical Composition', *Journal of Ancient near Eastern Religions*, 11 (1), 39–69.

Na'aman, Nadav (2017), 'Was Khirbet Qeiyafa a Judahite City? The Case against It', *Journal of Hebrew Scriptures*, 17, Article 7.

Na'aman, Nadav and Lissovsky, Nurit (2008), 'Kuntillet 'Ajrud, Sacred Trees and the Asherah', *Tel Aviv*, 35 (2), 186–208.

Niemann, Hermann Michael (2017), 'Comments and Questions about the Interpretation of Khirbet Qeiyafa: Talking with Yosef Garfinkel', *Zeitschrift für altorientalische und biblische Rechtsgeschichte*, 23, 245–262.

Nunn, John F. (2002), *Ancient Egyptian Medicine* (Norman, OK: University of Oklahoma Press).

O'Connor, David (1998), 'The City and the World: Worldwide and Built Forms in the Reign of Amenhotep III', in David O'Connor and Eric H. Cline (eds.), *Amenhotep III: Perspectives on His Reign* (Ann Arbor: University of Michigan Press), 125–172.

O'Connor, Kaori (2015), *The Never-Ending Feast: The Anthropology and Archaeology of Feasting* (London: Bloomsbury).

Ofer, Avi (1993), 'The Highland of Judah during the Biblical Period', Ph.D. dissertation (Tel Aviv University).

Oren, Eliezer D. (1973), *The Northern Cemetery of Beth Shean* (Museum Monograph of the University Museum of the University of Pennsylvania 33; Leiden: Brill).

Oren, Eliezer D. (1984), 'Governor's Residencies in Canaan under the New Kingdom: A Case Study of Egyptian Administration', *Journal of the Society for the Study of Egyptian Antiquities*, 14 (2), 37–56.

Oren, Eliezer D. (1992), 'Ashlar Masonry in the Western Negev in the Iron Age', *Eretz-Israel*, 23, 94–105. (Hebrew)

Oren, Eliezer D. (1993a), 'Haror, Tel', in Ephraim Stern (ed.), *New Encyclopedia of Archaeological Excavations in the Holy Land* (2; Jerusalem: Israel Exploration Society), 580–584.

Oren, Eliezer D. (1993b), 'Sera', Tel', in Ephraim Stern (ed.), *New Encyclopedia of Archaeological Excavations in the Holy Land* (4; Jerusalem: Israel Exploration Society), 1329–1335.

Oren, Eliezer D. (1993c), 'Northern Sinai', in Ephraim Stern (ed.), *New Encyclopedia of Archaeological Excavations in the Holy Land* (4; Jerusalem: Israel Exploration Society), 1386–1396.

Oren, Eliezer D. (1995), 'Tel Haror—1990', *Excavations and Surveys in Israel*, 13, 113–116.

Oren, Eliezer D. (2006a), 'An Egyptian Marsh Scene on Pottery from Tel Sera': A Case of Egyptianization in Late Bronze Age II Canaan', in Aren M. Maeir and P. de Miroschedji (eds.), *"I will Speak the Riddles of Ancient Times": Archaeological and Historical Studies in Honor of Amihai Mazar on the Occasion of His Sixtieth Birthday* (Winona Lake: Eisenbrauns), 263–275.

Oren, Eliezer D. (2006b), 'The Establishment of Egyptian Imperial Administration on the "Ways of Horus": An Archaeological Perspective from North Sinai', in Ernst Czerny (ed.), *Timelines: Studies in Honour of Manfred Bietak* (Orientalia Lovaniensia Analecta 149; Leuven: Peeters en Departement Oosterse Studies), 279–292.

Oren, Eliezer D. and Mazar, Amihai (1993), 'Ma'aravim, Tel', in Ephraim Stern (ed.), *New Encyclopedia of Archaeological Excavations in the Holy Land* (3; Jerusalem: Israel Exploration Society), 920–921.

Oren, Eliezer D. and Yekutieli, Yuval (1996), 'The Middle Bronze Age Defence System at Tel Haror', *Eretz-Israel*, 25, 15–26. (Hebrew)

Ornan, Tallay (2016), 'The beloved, Ne'ehevet, and Other Does: Reflections on the Motif of the Grazing or Browsing Wild Horned Animal', in Israel Finkelstein, Christian Robin, and T. Römer (eds.), *Alphabets, Texts and Artefacts in the Ancient Near East, Studies Presented to Benjamin Sass* (Paris: Van Dieren Éditeur), 279–302.

Ortiz, Steven M. and Wolff, Samuel R. (2012), 'Guarding the Border to Jerusalem: The Iron Age City of Gezer', *Near Eastern Archaeology*, 75 (1), 4–19.

Ortiz, Steven M. and Wolff, Samuel R. (2017), 'Tel Gezer Excavations 2006–2015: The Transformation of a Border City', in Oded Lipschits and Aren M. Maeir (eds.), *The Shephelah during the Iron Age: Recent Archaeological Studies* (Winona Lake: Eisenbrauns), 61–102.

Ortiz, Steven M. and Wolff, Samuel R. (2019), 'A Reevaluation of Gezer in the Late Bronze Age in Light of Renewed Excavations and Recent Scholarship', in Aren M. Maeir, Itzhaq Shai, and Chris McKinny (eds.), *The Late Bronze and Early Iron Ages of Southern Canaan* (Archaeology of the Biblical World 2; Berlin: De Gruyter), 62–85.

Ory, Jacob (1948), 'A Bronze-Age Cemetery at Dhahrat el Humriya', *Quarterly of the Department of Antiquities in Palestine*, 13, 75–89.

Palmié, Stephan (2006), 'Creolization and Its Discontents', *Annual Review of Anthropology*, 35, 433–456.

Panagiotopoulos, Diamantis (2011), 'The Stirring Sea: Conceptualising Transculturality in the Late Bronze Age Eastern Mediterranean', in Kim Duistermaat and Ilona Regulski (eds.), *Intercultural Contacts in the Ancient Mediterranean: Proceedings of the International Conference at the Netherlands-Flemish Institute in Cairo, 25th to 29th October 2008* (Orientalia Lovaniensia Analecta 202; Leuven, Paris and Walpole MA: Uitgeverij Peeters and Departement Oosterse Studies), 31–51.

Panagiotopoulos, Diamantis (2013), 'Material versus Design: A Transcultural Approach to the Two Contrasting Properties of Things', *Transcultural Studies*, 1, 145–176.

Panitz-Cohen, Nava (2006), 'Processes of Ceramic Change and Continuity: Tel Batash in the Second Millennium BCE as a Test Case', sPh.D. Dissertation (The Hebrew University of Jerusalem).

Panitz-Cohen, Nava (2009), 'The Organization of Ceramic Production during the Transition from the Late Bronze to the early Iron Ages: Tel Batash as a Test Case', in Christoph Bachhuber and R. Gareth Roberts (eds.), *Forces of Transformation: The End of the Bronze Age in the Mediterranean: Proceedings of an International Symposium Held at St. John's College, University of Oxford 25–6th March, 2006* (Oxford: Oxbow Books), 186–192.

Panitz-Cohen, Nava (2014), 'The Southern Levant (Cisjordan) during the Late Bronze Age', in Margarete L. Steiner and Ann E. Killebrew (eds.), *The Oxford Handbook of the Archaeology of the Levant c. 8000–332 BCE* (Oxford: Oxford University Press), 541–560.

Panitz-Cohen, Nava and Mazar, Amihai (2006), *Timnah (Tel Batash) 3: The Finds from the Second Millennium BCE* (Qedem 45; Jerusalem: Institute of Archaeology, Hebrew University of Jerusalem).

Panitz-Cohen, Nava and Mazar, Amihai (eds.) (2009), *Excavations at Tel Beth-Shean 1989–1996, Vol. 3, The 13th–11th Century BCE Strata in Areas N and S* (Jerusalem: Israel Exploration Society).

Parker, Bradley J. (2002), 'At the Edge of Empire: Conceptualizing Assyria's Anatolian Frontier ca. 700 B.C.', *Journal of Anthropological Archaeology*, 21 (3), 371–395.

Parker, Bradley J. (2003), 'Archaeological Manifestations of Empire: Assyria's Imprint on Southeastern Anatolia', *American Journal of Archaeology*, 107 (4), 525–557.

Parker, Bradley J. (2006), 'Toward an Understanding of Boundary Processes', *American Antiquity*, 71 (1), 77–100.

Parker, Bradley J. (2011), 'The Construction and Performance of Kingship on the New-Assyrian Empire', *Journal of Anthropological Research*, 67, 357–386.

Parker, Bradley J. (2013), 'Geographies of Power: Territoriality and Empire during the Mesopotamian Iron Age', *Archeological Papers of the American Anthropological Association*, 22 (1), 126–144.

Parker, Bradley J. (2015), 'Hegemony, Power and the Use of Force in the Neo Assyrian Empire', in Bleda S. Düring (ed.), *Understanding Hegemonic Practices in the Early Assyrian Empire: Essays Dedicated to Frans Wiggermann* (Leiden: Nederlands Instituut voor Nabije Oosten), 287–299.

Peden, Alexander J. (1994), *Egyptian Historical Inscriptions of the Twentieth Dynasty* (Documenta mundi. Aegyptiaca 3; Jonsered: P. Astroms Forlag).

Pedrazzi, Tatiana (2010), 'Globalization Versus Regionalism: LB II/Iron I Transition in Coastal Syria from the Storage Jars Point of View', in Fabrizio Venturi (ed.), *Societies in Transition Evolutionary Processes in the Northern Levant between Late Bronze Age II and Early Iron Age. Papers Presented on the Occasion of the 20th Anniversary of the New Excavations in Tell Afis Bologna, 15th November* (Studi e testi orientali 9; Bologna: CLUEB), 53–64.

Peilstöcker, Martin and Kapitaikin, Arieh (2000), 'Bet Dagan', *Excavations and Surveys in Israel*, 20, 59*–60*. (Hebrew)

Petrie, William M.F. (1890), 'The Egyptian Bases of Greek History', *Journal of Hellenic Studies*, 11, 271–277.

Petrie, William M.F. (1891), *Tell el Ḥesy (Lachish)* (London: A.P. Watt).

Petrie, William M.F. (1906), *Researches in Sinai* (London: J. Murray).

Petrie, William M.F. (1928), *Gerar* (British School of Archaeology in Egypt 43; London: British School of Archaeology in Egypt).

Petrie, William M.F. (1930), *Beth-Pelet I (Tell Fara)* (British School of Archaeology in Egypt 48; London: British School of Archaeology in Egypt).

Petrie, William M.F. (1931), *Ancient Gaza I* (British School of Archaeology in Egypt 53; London: British School of Archaeology in Egypt).

Petrie, William M.F. (1932), *Ancient Gaza II* (British School of Archaeology in Egypt 54; London: British School of Archaeology in Egypt).

Petrie, William M.F. (1933), *Ancient Gaza III* (British School of Archaeology in Egypt 55; London: British School of Archaeology in Egypt).

Petrie, William M.F. (1934), *Ancient Gaza IV* (British School of Archaeology in Egypt 56; London: British School of Archaeology in Egypt).

Petrie, William M.F. (1937), *Anthedon Sinai* (British School of Archaeology in Egypt 58; London: British School of Archaeology in Egypt).

Pfoh, Emanuel (2016), *Syria-Palestine in the Late Bronze Age: An Anthropology of Politics and Power* (Copenhagen International Seminar; London and Ney York: Routledge).

Pfoh, Emanuel (2019), 'Prestige and Authority in the Southern Levant during the Amarna Age', in Aren M. Maeir, Itzhaq Shai, and Chris McKinny (eds.), *The Late Bronze and Early Iron Ages of Southern Canaan* (Archaeology of the Biblical World 2; Berlin: De Gruyter), 247–261.

Phythian-Adams, William J. (1923), 'Reports on Sounding at Gaza, etc.', *Palestine Exploration Quarterly Statement*, 55 (1), 11–30.

Pierce, Krystal V.L. (2013), 'Living and Dying Abroad: Aspects of Egyptian Cultural Identity in Late Bronze Age and Early Iron Age Canaan', Ph.D. dissertation(UCLA).

Pinch, Geraldine (1993), *Votive Offerings to Hathor* (Oxford: Griffith Institute, Ashmolean Museum).

Porter, Anne (2014), 'When the Subject is the Object: Relational Ontologies, the Partible Person and Images of Naram-Sin', in Brian A. Brown and Marian H. Feldman (eds.), *Critical Approaches to Ancient Near Eastern Art* (Boston and Berlin: De Gruyter), 597–617.

Pratt, Mary Louise (2008), *Imperial Eyes: Travel Writing and Transculturation* (Second edn.; London and New York: Routledge).

Press, Michael D. (2012), *Ashkelon 4: The Iron Age Figurines of Ashkelon and Philistia* (Winona Lake: Eisenbrauns).

Quack, Joachim Friedrich (2015), 'Importing and Exporting Gods? On the Flow of Deities between Egypt and its Neighboring Countries', in Antje Flüchter and Jivanta Schöttli (eds.), *The Dynamics of Transculturality. Concepts and Institutions in Motion* (Cham, Heidelberg and New York: Springer), 255–277.

Rahmstorf, Lorenz (2005), 'Ethnicity and Changes in Weaving Technology in Cyprus and the Eastern Mediterranean in the 12th Century BC', in Vassos Karageorghis, Hertmut Matthäus, and Sabine Rogge (eds.), *Cyprus: Religion and Society from the Late Bronze Age to the End of the Archaic Period: Proceedings of an International Symposium on Cypriote Archaeology, Erlangen, 23–24 July 2004* (Bialystock: Bibliopolis), 143–169.

Rahmstorf, Lorenz (2011), 'Handmade Pots and Crumbling Loomweights: "Barbarian" Elements in the Eastern Mediterranean in the Last Quarter of the 2nd millennium BC', in Vassos Karageorghis and Ourania Kouka (eds.), *On Cooking Pots, Drinking Cups, Loomweights and Ethnicity in Bronze Age Cyprus and Neighbouring Regions: An International Archaeological Symposium Held in Nicosia, November 6th–7th 2010* (Nicosia: A.G. Leventis Foundation), 315–330.

Rainey, Anson F. (1993), 'Sharḫân/Sharuhen—The Problem of Identification', *Eretz-Israel*, 24, 178*–187*.

Rainey, Anson F. (1996), 'Who is a Canaanite? A Review of the Textual Evidence', *Bulletin of the American Schools of Oriental Research*, 304, 1–15.

Rainey, Anson F. (1999), 'Taanach Letters', *Eretz-Israel*, 26, 153*–162*.

Rainey, Anson F. (2003), 'Some Amarna Collations', *Eretz-Israel*, 27, 192*–202*.

Ravikovitch, Shlomo (1969), *Manual and Map of Soils of Israel* (Jerusalem: Magnes). (Hebrew).

Re'em, Amit (2010), 'Yafo, the French Hospital, 2007–2008', *Hadashot Arkheologiyot: Excavations and Surveys in Israel*, 120.

Reade, Wendy J., Barag, Dan, and Oren, Eliezer D. (2017), 'Glass Vessels and Beads from the Late Bronze Age Temple at Tel Sera', Israel', *Journal of Glass Studies*, 59, 11–21.

Rebillard, Eric (2015), 'Material Culture and Religious Identity in Late Antiquity', in Rubina Raja and Jörg Rüpke (eds.), *A Companion to the Archaeology of Religion in the Ancient World* (Blackwell Companions to the Ancient World; Chichester, West Sussex; John Wiley & Sons Inc), 427–436.

Redford, Donald B. (1979), 'A Gate Inscription from Karnak and Egyptian Involvement in Western Asia during the early 18th Dynasty', *Journal of the American Oriental Society*, 99, 270–287.
Redford, Donald B. (1992), *Egypt, Canaan, and Israel in Ancient Times* (Princeton: Princeton University Press).
Redford, Donald B. (2003), *The Wars in Syria and Palestine of Thutmose III* (Culture and History of the Ancient Near East 16; Leiden: Brill).
Ristvet, Lauren (2012), 'Resettling Apum: Tribalism and Tribal States in the Tell Leilan Region, Syria', in N. Laneri, P. Pflzner, and S. Valentini (eds.), *Looking North: the Socioeconomic Dynamics of Northern Mesopotamian and Anatolian Regions during the Late Third and Early Second Millennium BC* (Wiesbaden: Harrassowitz), 37–50.
Römer, Thomas C. (2005), *The So-Called Deuteronomistic History: A Sociological, Historical and Literary Introduction* (London: T&T Clark).
Roux, Valentine (2013), 'Spreading of Innovative Technical Traits and Cumulative Technical Evolution: Continuity or Discontinuity?', *Journal of Archaeological Method and Theory*, 20 (2), 312–330.
Rüpke, Jörg (2015), 'Religious agency, identity, and communication: reflections on history and theory of religion', *Religion*, 45 (3), 344–366.
Rüpke, Jörg (2016), *On Roman Religion: Lived Religion and the Individual in Ancient Rome* (Ithaca and London: Cornell University Press).
Russell, Anthony (2009), 'Deconstructing Ashdoda', *BABesch*, 84, 1–15.
Rutter, Jeremy B. (2013), 'Aegean Elements in the Earliest Philistine Ceramic Assemblage: A View from the West', in Ann E. Killebrew and Gunnar Lehmann (eds.), *The Philistines and other "Sea Peoples" in Text and Archaeology* (Archaeology and Biblical Studies 15; Atlanta: SBL), 543–561.
Said, Edward (1978), *Orientalism* (New York: Pantheon Books).
Saller, Sylvester J. (1964), *The Excavations at Dominus Flevit (Mount Oliveto-Jerusalem) II: The Jebusite Burial Place* (Jerusalem: Franciscan Printing Press).
Sapir-Hen, Lidar (2019), 'Food, Pork Consumption, and Identity in Ancient Israel', *Near Eastern Archaeology*, 82 (1), 52–59.
Sapir-Hen, Lidar, Gadot, Yuval, and Finkelstein, Israel (2014), 'Environmental and Historical Impacts on Long Term Animal Economy: The Southern Levant in the Late Bronze and Iron Ages', *Journal of the Economic and Social History of the Orient*, 57, 703–744.
Sapir-Hen, Lidar, Meiri, Meirav, and Finkelstein, Israel (2015), 'Iron Age Pigs: New Evidence on Their Origin and Role in Forming Identity Boundaries', *Radiocarbon*, 57 (2), 307–315.
Sapir-Hen, Lidar, et al. (2013), 'Pig Husbandry in Iron Age Israel and Judah New Insights Regarding the Origin of the "Taboo"', *Zeitschrift des Deutschen Palästina-Vereins*, 129 (1), 1–20.

Sass, Benjamin (2002), 'Wenamun and His Levant—1075 BC or 925 BC?', *Egypt and the Levant*, 12, 247–255.
Sass, Benjamin, et al. (2015), 'The Lachish Jar Sherd: An Early Alphabetic Inscription Discovered in 2014', *Bulletin of the American Schools of Oriental Research*, 374, 233–245.
Savage, Stephen G. and Falconer, Steven E. (2003), 'Spatial and Statistical Inference of Late Bronze Age Polities in the Southern Levant', *Bulletin of the American Schools of Oriental Research*, 330, 31–45.
Schipper, Bernd U. (2005), *Die Erzählung des Wenamun* (Orbis Biblicus et Orientalis 209; Fribourg and Göttingen: Academic Press; Vandenhoeck and Ruprect).
Schloen, David J. (2001), *The House of the Father as Fact and Symbol: Patrimonialism in Ugarit and the Ancient Near East* (Studies in the Archaeology and History of the Levant 2; Winona Lake: Eisenbrauns).
Schneider, Thomas (2003a), 'Foreign Egypt: Egyptology and the Concept of Cultural Appropriation', *Ägypten und Levante/Egypt and the Levant*, 13, 155–161.
Schneider, Thomas (2003b), 'Texte über den syrischen Wettergott aus Ägypten', *Ugarit-Forschungen*, 35, 605–627.
Schneider, Thomas (2010a), 'Foreigners in Egypt: Archaeological Evidence and Cultural Context', in Willeke Wendrich (ed.), *Egyptian Archaeology* (Blackwell Studies in Global Archaeology 13; Chichester, U.K. and Malden, MA: Wiley-Blackwell), 143–163.
Schneider, Thomas (2010b), 'Contributions to the Chronology of the New Kingdom and the Third Intermediate Period', *Egypt and the Levant*, 20, 373–409.
Schneider, Thomas (2012), 'The Philistine Language: New Etymologies and the Name David', *Ugarit-Forschungen*, 43, 569–580.
Schneider, Thomas (2015), 'The Old Kingdom Abroad: An Epistemological Perspective. With Remarks on the Biography of Iny and the Kingdom of Dugurasu', in Peter Der Manuelian and Thomas Schneider (eds.), *Towards a New History of the Old Kingdom: Perspectives on the Pyramid Age. Proceedings of the Conference at Harvard University, April 26th, 2012* (Harvard Egyptological Studies 1; Leiden and Boston: Brill), 425–451.
Schortman, Edward M. (2014), 'Networks of Power in Archaeology', *Annual Review of Anthropology*, 43, 167–182.
Schoske, Sylvia (2008), 'At the Center of Power: Tiye, Ahhotep and Hatshpsut', in Christiane Ziegler (ed.), *Queens of Egypt: From Hetepheres to Cleopatra* (Monaco and Paris: Grimaldi Forum; Somogy editions d'art), 188–199.
Schroer, Silvia (1989), 'Die Göttin aus den Stempelsiegeln aus Palästina/Israel', in Othmar Keel, Heidi Keel-Leu, and Silvia Schroer (eds.), *Studien zu den Stempelsiegel aus Palästina/Israel 2* (Orbis Biblicus et Orientalis 88; Fribourg and Göttingen: Academic Press, Vandenhoeck and Ruprecht), 89–207.
Schroer, Silvia (2008), *Die Ikonographie Palästinas/Israels und der Alte Orient 2: Die Mittelbronzezeit* (Fribourg: Academic Press).

Schroer, Silvia (2011), *Die Ikonographie Palästinas/Israels und der Alte Orient 3: Die Spätbronzezeit* (Fribourg: Academic Press).

Schroer, Silvia and Keel, Othmar (2005), *Die Ikonographie Palästinas/Israels und der Alte Orient 1: Von ausgehenden Mesolithikum bis zur Frühbronzezeit* (Fribourg: Academic Press).

Schulman, Alan R. (1988), 'Catalogue of Egyptian Finds', in Benno Rothenberg (ed.), *The Egyptian Mining Temple at Timna (Researches in the Arabah 1959–1984)* (London: Institute for Archaeo-Metallurgical Studies and Institute of Archaeology, University College London), 114–147.

Schwartz, Glenn M. (2006), 'From Collapse to Regeneration', in Glenn M. Schwartz and John J. Nichols (eds.), *After Collapse: the Regeneration of Complex Societies* (First paperback printing edn.; Tucson: University of Arizona press), 3–17.

Schwartz, Glenn M. and Nichols, John J. (2006), *After Collapse: the Regeneration of Complex Societies* (First paperback printing edn.; Tucson: University of Arizona press).

Seger, Joe D. (1983), 'Investigations at Tell Halif, Israel, 1976–1980', *Bulletin of the American Schools of Oriental Research*, 252, 1–23.

Seger, Joe D. (1992), 'Limping about the Altar', *Eretz-Israel*, 23, 120*–127*.

Seger, Joe D. and Lance, Hubert D. (1988), *Gezer V: The Field I Caves* (Annual of the Nelson Glueck School of Biblical Archaeology 5; Jerusalem: Nelson Glueck School of Biblical Archaeology).

Seger, Joe D., et al. (1990), 'The Bronze Age Settlements at Tell Halif: Phase II Excavations, 1983–1987', *Bulletin of the American Schools of Oriental Research. Supplementary Studies*, 26, 1–32.

Sellers, Ovid R. (1968), *The 1957 Excavations at Beth-Zur* (Annual of the American Schools of Oriental Research; Cambridge: American Schools of Oriental Research).

Sergi, Omer (2015a), 'State Formation, Religion and "Collective Identity" in the Southern Levant', *Hebrew Bible and Ancient Israel*, 4 (1), 56–77.

Sergi, Omer (2015b), 'The Emergence of Judah between Jerusalem and Benjamin', *New Studies in the Archaeology of Jerusalem and its Region*, 9, 50–73. (Hebrew with English Summary)

Shai, Itzhaq, Uziel, Joe, and Chadwick, Jeffery R. (2017), 'Late Bronze Age Canaanite Gath', *Near Eastern Archaeology*, 80, 292–295.

Shai, Itzhaq, et al. (2011), 'Differentiating between Public and Residential Buildings: A Case Study from Late Bronze Age II Tell es-Safi/Gath', in Assaf Yasur-Landau, Jennie Ebeling, and Laura B. Mazow (eds.), *Household Archaeology in Ancient Israel and Beyond* (Culture and History of the Ancient Near East 50; Leiden and Boston: Brill), 107–131.

Shalvi, Golan, et al. (2020), 'Pigments on Late Bronze Age painted Canaanite Pottery at Tel Esur: New Insights into Canaanite–Cypriot Technological Interaction', *Journal of Archaeological Science: Reports*, 30, 102212.

Sharon, Ilan (2001), 'Philistine Bichrome Painted Pottery: Scholarly Ideology and Ceramic Typology', in Samuel R. Wolf (ed.), *Studies in the Archaeology of Israel and Neighboring Lands in Memory of Douglas L. Esse* (Chicago: University of Chicago), 555–609.

Sharp, Joanne P. (2009), *Geographies of Postcolonialism: Spaces of Power and Representation* (London: Sage).

Sharratt, Nicola (2016), 'Collapse and Cohesion: Building Community in the Aftermath of Tiwanaku State Breakdown', *World Archaeology*, 48 (1), 144–163.

Shavit, Alon (2003), 'Settlement Patterns in Israel's Southern Coastal Plain during the Iron Age II', Ph.D. dissertation (Tel Aviv University).

Shavit, Alon (2008), 'Settlement Patterns of Philistine City-States', in Alexander Fantalkin and Assaf Yasur-Landau (eds.), *Bene Israel: Studies in the Archaeology of Israel and the Levant during the Bronze and Iron Ages in Honour of Israel Finkelstein* (Culture and History of the Ancient Near East 31; Leiden and Boston: Brill), 135–164.

Shavit, Alon and Yasur-Landau, Assaf (2005), 'A Bronze and Iron Age Settlement at Netiv Ha-'Asara', *Salvage Excavation Reports*, 2, 59–92.

Shaw, Julia (2013), 'Archaeology of Religious Change: Introduction', *World Archaeology*, 45 (1), 1–11.

Sherratt, Susan E. (1998), '"Sea Peoples" and the Economic Structure of the late Second Millennium in the Eastern Mediterranean', in Seymour Gitin, Amihai Mazar, and Ephraim Stern (eds.), *Mediterranean Peoples in Transition: Thirteenth to Early Tenth Centuries BCE, In Honor of Trude Dothan* (Jerusalem: Israel Exploration Society), 292–313.

Sherratt, Susan E. (2003), 'The Mediterranean Economy: "Globalization" at the End of the Second Millennium B.C.E.', in William G. Dever and Seymour Gitin (eds.), *Symbiosis, Symbolism, and the Power of the Past* (Winona Lake: Eisenbrauns), 37–62.

Sherratt, Susan E. (2006), 'The Chronology of the Philistine Monochrome Pottery—An Outsider's View', in Aren M. Maeir and P. de Miroschedji (eds.), *"I will Speak the Riddles of Ancient Times": Archaeological and Historical Studies in Honor of Amihai Mazar on the Occasion of His Sixtieth Birthday* (Winona Lake: Eisenbrauns), 361–374.

Sherratt, Susan E. (2011), 'Between Theory, Texts and Archaeology: Working with the Shadows', in Kim Duistermaat and Ilona Regulski (eds.), *Intercultural Contacts in the Ancient Mediterranean: Proceedings of the International Conference at the Netherlands-Flemish Institute in Cairo, 25th to 29th October 2008* (Orientalia Lovaniensia Analecta 202; Leuven, Paris and Walpole MA: Uitgeverij Peeters and Departement Oosterse Studies), 3–29.

Sherratt, Susan E. (2013), 'The Ceramic Phenomenon of the "Sea Peoples": An Overview', in Ann E. Killebrew and Gunnar Lehmann (eds.), *The Philistines and other "Sea Peoples" in Text and Archaeology* (Archaeology and Biblical Studies 15; Atlanta: SBL), 619–644.

Shuval, Menakhem (1990), 'A Catalogue of Early Iron Stamp Seals from Israel', in Othmar Keel, Menakhem Shuval, and Christoph Uehlinger (eds.), *Studien zu den Stempelsiegeln aus Palästina/Israel, III* (Orbis Biblicus et Orientalis 100; Fribourgh and Göttingen: Academic Press, Vandenhoeck and Ruprecht), 67–161.

Silberman, Neil A. (1998), 'The Sea Peoples, the Victorians, and Us: Modern Social Ideology and Changing Archaeological Interpretations of the Late Bronze Age Collapse', in Seymour Gitin, Amihai Mazar, and Ephraim Stern (eds.), *Mediterranean Peoples in Transition: Thirteenth to Early Tenth Centuries BCE, In Honor of Trude Dothan* (Jerusalem: Israel Exploration Society), 268–275.

Silberman, Neil A. (1999), 'Petrie's Head: Eugenics and Near Eastern Archaeology', in Alice B. Kehoe and Mary B. Emmerichs (eds.), *Assembling the Past: Studies in the Professionalization of Archaeology* (Albuquerque: University of New Mexico Press), 69–79.

Silliman, Stephen W. (2015), 'A Requiem for Hybridity? The Problem with Frankensteins, Purées, and Mules', *Journal of Social Archaeology*, 15 (3), 277–298.

Singer, Itamar (1985), 'The Beginning of Philistine Settlement in Canaan and the Northern Boundary of Philistia', *Tel Aviv*, 12 (2), 109–122.

Singer, Itamar (1986), 'An Egyptian "Governor's Residency" at Gezer?', *Tel Aviv*, 13 (1), 26–31.

Singer, Itamar (1988), 'Merneptah's Campaign to Canaan and the Egyptian Occupation of the Southern Coastal Plain of Palestine in the Ramesside Period', *Bulletin of the American Schools of Oriental Research*, 269, 1–10.

Singer, Itamar (1988–1989), 'The Political Status of Megiddo VIIA', *Tel Aviv*, 15 (1), 101–112.

Singer, Itamar (2013a), 'Hittite Gods in Egyptian Attire', in David Vanderhooft and Abraham Winitzer (eds.), *Literature as Politics, Politics and Literature: Essays on the Ancient Near East in Honor of Peter Machinist* (Winona Lake: Eisenbrauns), 433–457.

Singer, Itamar (2013b), 'The Philistines in the Bible: A Short Rejoinder to a new Perspective', in Ann E. Killebrew and Gunnar Lehmann (eds.), *The Philistines and other "Sea Peoples" in Text and Archaeology* (Archaeology and Biblical Studies 15; Atlanta: SBL), 19–27.

Singer-Avitz, Lily (2004), 'The Pottery of the Late Bronze I phase', in David Ussishkin (ed.), *The Renewed Archaeological Excavations at Tel Lachish (1973–1994)* (Monograph Series of the Institute of Archaeology of Tel Aviv University 22; Tel Aviv: Emery and Claire Yass Publications in Archaeology), 1012–1031.

Sinopoli, Carla M. (1994), 'The Archaeology of Empires', *Annual Review of Anthropology*, 23 (1), 159–180.

Sinopoli, Carla M. (2001), 'Empires', in Gary M. Feinman and T. Douglas Price (eds.), *Archaeology at the Millennium* (New York: Kluwer Academic), 439–471.

Smith, Mark S. (2010), *God in Translation: Deities in Cross-Cultural Discourses in the Biblical World* (Grand Rapids MI and Cambridge UK: Eerdmans).

Smith, Michael E. (2017), 'Bounding Empires and Political/Military Networks Using Archaeological Data', *Journal of Globalization Studies*, 8 (1), 30–47.
Smith, Monica L. (2005), 'Networks, Territories, and the Cartography of Ancient States', *Annals of the Association of American Geographers*, 95 (4), 832–839.
Smith, Monica L. (2007), 'Territories, Corridors, and Networks: A Biological Model for the Premodern State', *Complexity*, 12 (4), 28–35.
Smith, Stuart T. (2003), *Wretched Kush: Ethnic Identities and Boundaries in Egypt's Nubian Empire* (London and New York: Routledge).
Smith, Stuart T. (2013), 'Revenge of the Kushites: Assimilation and Resistance in Egypt's New Kingdom Empire and Nubian Ascendancy over Egypt', in Gregory E. Areshian (ed.), *Empires and Diversity: On the Crossroads of Archaeology, Anthropology, and History* (Ideas, Debates, and Perspectives; Los Angeles: Cotsen Institute of Archaeology University of California), 84–107.
Snape, Steven R. (2012), 'The Legacy of Ramesses III and the Libyan Ascendancy', in Eric H. Cline and David O'Connor (eds.), *Ramesses III: The Life and Times of Egypt's Last Hero* (Ann Arbor: University of Michigan Press), 404–441.
Sommer, Michael (2012), 'Heart of Darkness? Post-colonial Theory and the Transformation of the Mediterranean', *Ancient West & East*, 11, 235–245.
Sowada, Karin (2009), *Egypt in the Eastern Mediterranean during the Old Kingdom: An Archaeological Perspective* (Orbis Biblicus et Orientalis 237; Fribourg and Göttingen: Academic Press and Vandenhoeck & Ruprecht).
Spalinger, Anthony J. (2003), 'The Battle of Kadesh: The Chariot Frieze at Abydos', *Ägypten und Levante/Egypt and the Levant*, 13, 163–199.
Spalinger, Anthony J. (2005), *Warfare in Ancient Egypt: The New Kingdom* (A Companion to the Ancient Near East; Malden MA: Blackwell Publishing).
Sparks, Rachael T. (2004), 'Canaan in Egypt: Archaeological Evidence for a Social Phenomenon', in Janine Bourriau and Jacke Phillips (eds.), *Invention and Innovation: The Social Context of Technological Change 2: Egypt, the Aegean and Near East 1650–1150 BC: Proceedings of a Conference Held at the McDonald Institute for Archaeological Research, Cambridge, 4–6 September 2002* (Oxford: Oxbow Books), 25–54.
Sparks, Rachael T. (2005), 'The Lost Loci of Tell EL-'Ajjul: Petrie's Area C', *Palestine Exploration Quarterly*, 137 (1), 23–29.
Spencer, Neal, Macklin, Mark G., and Woodward, Jamie C. (2012), 'Re-assessing the Abandonment of Amara West: The Impact of a Changing Nile?', *Sudan & Nubia*, 16, 37–43.
Spencer, Neal, Stevens, Anna, and Binder, Michaela (eds.) (2017), *Nubia in the New Kingdom: Lived Experience, Pharaonic Control and Indigenous Traditions* (British Museum Publications in Egypt and Sudan 3; Leuven, Paris and Bristol, CT: Peeters).
Stadelmann, Rainer (1967), *Syrisch-palästinensische Gottheiten in Ägypten* (Probleme der Ägyptologie, 5; Leiden: Brill).

Stager, Lawrence E. (1985), 'Merneptah, Israel and the Sea Peoples: New Light on an Old Relief', *Eretz-Israel*, 18, 56*–64*.

Stager, Lawrence E. (1995), 'The Impact of the Sea Peoples in Canaan (1185–1050 BCE)', in Thomas E. Levy (ed.), *The Archaeology of Society in the Holy Land* (London: Leicester University), 332–348.

Stager, Lawrence E. (2002), 'The MBIIA Ceramic Sequence at Tel Ashkelon and its Implications for the "Port Power" Model of Trade', in Manfred Bietak (ed.), *The Middle Bronze Age in the Levant* (Contributions to the Chronology of the Eastern Mediterranean 3; Vienna: Verlag der Osterreichischen Akademie der Wissenschaften), 353–362.

Stager, Lawrence E. (2006), 'Biblical Philistines: A Hellenistic Literary Creation?', in Aren M. Maeir and Pierre de Miroschedji (eds.), *"I will Speak the Riddles of Ancient Times": Archaeological and Historical Studies in Honor of Amihai Mazar on the Occasion of His Sixtieth Birthday* (Winona Lake: Eisenbrauns), 375–384.

Stager, Lawrence E., Schloen, David J., and Master, Daniel M. (2008), *Ashkelon 1: Introduction and Overview (1985–2006)* (Winona Lake: Eisenbrauns).

Staubli, Thomas (2009), 'Bull Leaping and other Images and Rites of the Southern Levant in the Sign of Scorpius', *Ugarit-Forschungen*, 41, 611–630.

Stavi, Boaz (2015), *The Reign of Tudhaliya II and Šuppiluliuma I: The Contribution of the Hittite Documentation to a Reconstruction of the Armana Age* (Texte der Hethiter: Philologische und historische Studien zur Altanatolistik 31; Heidelberg Universitätsverlag).

Stein, Gil (2005a), *The Archaeology of Colonial Encounters* (Santa Fe: School of American Research Press).

Stein, Gil (2005b), 'Introduction', in Gil Stein (ed.), *The Archaeology of Colonial Encounters* (Santa Fe: School of American Research Press), 3–31.

Steinmetz, George (2014), 'The Sociology of Empires, Colonies, and Postcolonialism', *Annual Review of Sociology*, 40 (1), 77–103.

Stieglitz, Robert R. (1974), 'Ugaritic Mḫd—the Harbor of Yabne-Yam?', *Journal of the American Oriental Society*, 94 (1), 137–138.

Stockhammer, Philipp W. (2011), 'An Aegean Glance at Megiddo', in Walter Gauß, et al. (eds.), *Our Cups Are Full: Pottery and Society in the Aegean Bronze Age, Papers presented to Jeremy B. Rutter on the occasion of his 65th birthday* (Oxford: Archaeopress), 282–296.

Stockhammer, Philipp W. (2012), 'Performing the Practice Turn in Archaeology', *Transcultural Studies*, 1, 7–42.

Stockhammer, Philipp W. (2013), 'From Hybridity to Entanglement, From Essentialism to Practice', *Archaeological Review from Cambridge*, 28 (1), 11–28.

Stockhammer, Philipp W. (2019), 'Shifting Meanings and Values of Aegean-type Pottery in the Late Bronze Age Southern Levant', in Aren M. Maeir, Itzhaq Shai, and Chris McKinny (eds.), *The Late Bronze and Early Iron Ages of Southern Canaan* (Archaeology of the Biblical World 2; Berlin: De Gruyter), 233–246.

Strandberg, Åsa (2009), *The Gazelle in Ancient Egyptian Art Image and Meaning* (Uppsala Studies in Egyptology 6; Uppsala: Uppsala University).

Strandsbjerg, Jeppe (2010), *Territory, Globalization and International Relations: The Cartographic Reality of Space* (New York and Basingstoke: Palgrave Macmillan).

Strawn, Brent (2005), *What is Stronger than a Lion? Leonine Image and Metaphor in the Hebrew Bible and the Ancient Near East* (Orbis Biblicus et Orientalis 212; Fribourg and Göttingen: Academic Press, Vandenhoeck and Ruprecht).

Streit, Katharina, et al. (2018), 'Between Destruction and Diplomacy in Canaan: The Austrian-Israeli Expedition to Tel Lachish', *Near Eastern Archaeology*, 81 (4), 259–268.

Sugandi, Namita (2013), 'Conquests of Dharma: Network Models and the Study of Ancient Polities', *Archeological Papers of the American Anthropological Association*, 22 (1), 145–163.

Survey, The Epigraphic (1930), *Medinet Habu I: Earlier Historical Records of Ramesses III* (Oriental Institute Publications 8; Chicago: Oriental Institute).

Survey, The Epigraphic (1932), *Medinet Habu II: Later Historical Records of Ramesses III* (Oriental Institute Publications 9; Chicago: Oriental Institute).

Survey, The Epigraphic (1996), *The Battle Reliefs of King Sety I* (Oriental Institute Publications 170; Chicago: Oriental Institute).

Suter, Claudia E. and Uehlinger, Christoph (2005), 'Introduction', in Claudia E. Suter and Christoph Uehlinger (eds.), *Crafts and Images in Contact* (Orbis Biblicus et Orientalis 210; Fribourg and Göttingen: Academic Press, Vandenhoeck and Ruprecht), XVII–XXXI.

Sweeney, Deborah (2003), 'A Lion-Hunt Scarab and Other Egyptian Objects from the Late Bronze Fortress at Jaffa', *Tel Aviv*, 30 (1), 54–65.

Sweeney, Deborah (2004), 'The Hieratic Inscriptions', in David Ussishkin (ed.), *The Renewed Archaeological Excavations at Tel Lachish (1973–1994)* (Monograph Series of the Institute of Archaeology of Tel Aviv University 22; Tel Aviv: Emery and Claire Yass Publications in Archaeology), 1601–1617.

Sweeney, Deborah, et al. (2018), 'A Triad Amulet from Tel Azekah', *Israel Exploration Journal*, 68, 129–149.

Tamar, Karin, et al. (2015), 'Geography and Economic Preferences as Cultural Markers in a Border Town: The Faunal Remains from Tel Beth-Shemesh, Israel', *International Journal of Osteoarchaeology*, 25 (4), 414–425.

Tappy, Ron E. (2008), 'Zayit, Tel', in Ephraim Stern (ed.), *New Encyclopedia of Archaeological Excavations in the Holy Land* (5; Jerusalem and Washington, DC: Israel Exploration Society and Biblical Archaeological Society), 2082–2083.

Tazawa, Keiko (2009), *Syro-Palestinian Deities in New Kingdom Egypt. The Hermeneutics of Their Existence* (BAR International Series 1965; Oxford: Archaeopress).

Thiersch, Hermann (1908), 'Die neueren Ausgrabungen in Palästina', *Archäologischer Anzeiger*, 23, 344–413.

Toffolo, Michael B., et al. (2014), 'Absolute Chronology of Megiddo, Israel, in the Late Bronze and Iron Ages: High-Resolution Radiocarbon Dating', *Radiocarbon*, 56.

Toffolo, Michael B., et al. (2018), 'Microarchaeology of a Grain Silo: Insights into Stratigraphy, Chronology and Food Storage at Late Bronze Age Ashkelon, Israel', *Journal of Archaeological Science: Reports*, 19, 177–188.

Torgë, Hagit and Avner, Rina (2018), 'Rosh Ha-'Ayin, Qurnat Haramiya', *Hadashot Arkheologiyot: Excavations and Surveys in Israel*, 130. <http://www.hadashot-esi.org.il/Report_Detail_Eng.aspx?id=25463&mag_id=126>.

Trigger, Bruce G. (2006), *A History of Archaeological Thought* (Second edition edn.; New York: Cambridge University Press).

Troy, Lana (2008), 'The Queen as a Female Counterpart of the Pharaoh', in Christiane Ziegler (ed.), *Queens of Egypt: From Hetepheres to Cleopatra* (Monaco and Paris: Grimaldi Forum; Somogy editions d'art), 154–170.

Tufnell, Olga (1953), *Lachish (Tell ed Duweir) III: The Iron Age* (London: Oxford University Press).

Tufnell, Olga (1958), *Lachish (Tell ed Duweir) IV: The Bronze Age* (London: Oxford University Press).

Tufnell, Olga, Inge, Charles H., and Harding, Lester (1940), *Lachish (Tell ed Duweir) II: The Fosse Temple* (London: Oxford University Press).

Tweed, Thomas A. (2015), 'After the Quotidian Turn: Interpretive Categories and Scholarly Trajectories in the Study of Religion since the 1960s', *The Journal of Religion*, 95 (3), 361–385.

Twiss, Katheryn (2012), 'The Archaeology of Food and Social Diversity', *Journal of Archaeological Research*, 20 (4), 357–395.

Uehlinger, Christoph (1988), 'Der Amun-Tempel Ramses' III. in p3-Kn'n, seine südpalästinischen Tempelgüter und der Übergang von der Ägypter—zur Philisterherrschaft. Ein Hinweis auf einige wenig beachtete Skarabäen', *Zeitschrift des Deutschen Palästina-Vereins*, 104, 6–25.

Uehlinger, Christoph (2000), 'Introduction', in Christoph Uehlinger (ed.), *Images as Media: Sources for the Cultural History of the Near East and the Eastern Mediterranean (1st Millennium BCE)* (Orbis Biblicus et Orientalis 175; Fribourg and Göttingen: Academic Press, Vandenhoeck and Ruprecht), XV–XXXII.

Ussishkin, David (1985), 'Level VII and VI at Tel Lachish and the End of the Late Bronze Age in Canaan', in Jonathan N. Tubb (ed.), *Palestine in the Bronze and Iron Ages: Papers in Honour of Olga Tufnell* (London: The Institute of Archaeology), 213–230.

Ussishkin, David (2004), *The Renewed Archaeological Excavations at Tel Lachish (1973–1994)* (Monograph Series of the Institute of Archaeology of Tel Aviv University 22; Tel Aviv: Emery and Claire Yass Publications in Archaeology).

Ussishkin, David (2005), 'The Fortifications of Philistine Ekron', *Israel Exploration Journal*, 55 (1), 35–65.

Ussishkin, David (2007), 'Lachish and the Date of the Philistine Settlement in Canaan', in Manfred Bietak and Ernst Czerny (eds.), *The Synchronization of Civilisations in the Eastern Mediterranean in the Second Millennium B.C. III* (Contributions to the Chronology of the Eastern Mediterranean 9; Vienna: Verlag der Osterreichischen Akademie der Wissenschaften), 601–607.

Uziel, Josef (2008), 'The Southern Coastal Plain of Canaan during the Middle Bronze Age', Ph.D. dissertation (Bar Ilan University).

Uziel, Josef (2010), 'Middle Bronze Age Ramparts: Functional and Symbolic Structures', *Levant*, 142 (1), 24–30.

Uziel, Josef and Avissar-Lewis, Rona (2013), 'The Tel Nagila Middle Bronze Age Homes: Studying Household Activities and Identifying Children in the Archaeological Record', *Palestine Exploration Quarterly*, 145 (4), 268–293.

Uziel, Josef, Shai, Itzhaq, and Cassuto, Deborah R. (2014), 'Ups and Downs of Settlement Patterns: Why Sites Fluctuate', in John R. Spencer, Rubert A. Mullins, and Aaron J. Brody (eds.), *Material Culture Matters: Essays on the Archaeology of the Southern Levant in Honor of Seymour Gitin* (Winona Lake, IN: Eisenbrauns), 295–308.

Van Andringa, William (2015), 'The Archaeology of Ancient Sanctuaries', in Rubina Raja and Jörg Rüpke (eds.), *A Companion to the Archaeology of Religion in the Ancient World* (Blackwell Companions to the Ancient World; Chichester, West Sussex: John Wiley & Sons Inc), 30–40.

Van den Brink, Edwin C.M., et al. (2017), 'A Late Bronze Age II clay coffin from Tel Shaddud in the Central Jezreel Valley, Israel: context and historical implications', *Levant*, 49 (2), 105–135.

Van den Brink, Edwin C.M. and Levy, Thomas E. (eds.) (2001), *Egypt and the Levant: Interrelations from the 4th through the Early 3rd Millennium B.C.E.* (New Approaches to Anthropological Archaeology; London and New York: Leicester University Press).

Van Dommelen, Peter (1997), 'Colonial Constructs: Colonialism and Archaeology in the Mediterranean', *World Archaeology*, 28 (3), 305–323.

Van Dommelen, Peter (1998), *On Colonial Grounds: A Comparative Study of Colonialism and Rural Settlement in First Millennium BC West Central Sardinia* (Archaeological Studies Leiden University 2; Leiden: Faculty of Archaeology, Leiden University).

Van Dommelen, Peter (2005), 'Colonial Interactions and Hybrid practices: Phoenician and Carthaginian Settlement in the Ancient Mediterranean', in Gil Stein (ed.), *The*

Archaeology of Colonial Encounters (Santa Fe: School of American Research Press), 109–141.

Van Dommelen, Peter (2011), 'Postcolonial Archaeologies between Discourse and Practice', *World Archaeology*, 43 (1), 1–6.

Van Dommelen, Peter (2012), 'Colonialism and Migration in the Ancient Mediterranean', *Annual Review of Anthropology*, 41 (1), 393–409.

Van Dommelen, Peter (2014a), 'Fetishizing the Romans', *Archaeological Dialogues*, 21 (1), 41–45.

Van Dommelen, Peter (2014b), 'Moving On: Archaeological Perspectives on Mobility and Migration', *World Archaeology*, 46 (4), 477–483.

Van Dommelen, Peter and Rowlands, Michael (2012), 'Material Concerns and Colonial Encounters', in Joseph Maran and Philipp W. Stockhammer (eds.), *Materiality and Social Practice: Transformative Capacities of Intercultural Encounters* (Oxford: Oxbow Books), 20–31.

Van Seters, John (2009), *The Biblical Saga of King David* (Winona Lake: Eisenbrauns).

Van Valkenburgh, Parker and Osborne, James F. (2013), 'Home Turf: Archaeology, Territoriality, and Politics', *Archeological Papers of the American Anthropological Association*, 22 (1), 1–27.

Versluys, Miguel John (2014), 'Understanding Objects in Motion. An Archaeological Dialogue on Romanization', *Archaeological Dialogues*, 21 (1), 1–20.

Vidal, Jordi (2006), 'Ugarit and the Southern Levantine Sea-Ports', *Journal of the Economic and Social History of the Orient*, 49 (3), 269–279.

Vita, Juan-Pablo (2015), *Canaanite Scribes in the Amarna Letters* (Alter Orient und Altes Testament; Münster: Ugarit-Verlag).

Vitto, Fanny and Edelstein, Gershon (1993), 'Ridan, Tel', in Ephraim Stern (ed.), *New Encyclopedia of Archaeological Excavations in the Holy Land* (4; Jerusalem: Israel Exploration Society), 1283.

Von Hesberg, Henner (2015), 'Temples and Temple Interiors', in Rubina Raja and Jörg Rüpke (eds.), *A Companion to the Archaeology of Religion in the Ancient World* (Blackwell Companions to the Ancient World; Chichester, West Sussex: John Wiley & Sons Inc), 320–332.

Voskos, Ioannis and Knapp, A. Bernard (2008), 'Cyprus at the End of the Late Bronze: Crisis and Colonization or Continuity and Hybridization?', *American Journal of Archaeology*, 112, 659–684.

Waiman-Barak, Paula, Gilboa, Ayelet, and Goren, Yuval (2014), 'A Stratified Sequence of Early Iron Age Egyptian Ceramics at Tel Dor, Israel', *Ägypten und Levante*, 24, 315–342.

Webster, Jane and Cooper, Nicholas J. (eds.) (1996), *Roman Imperialism: Post-Colonial Perspectives (A Collection of Papers Originally presented to a Symposium held at Leicester University in November 1994)* (Leicester: Leicester University Press).

Webster, Lyndelle, et al. (2019), 'Identifying the Lachish of Papyrus Hermitage 1116a Verso and the Amarna Letters: Implications of New Radiocarbon Dating', *Journal of Ancient Egyptian Interconnections*, 21, 88–99.

Webster, Lyndelle C., et al. (2017), 'Preliminary Radiocarbon Results for Late Bronze Age Strata at Tel Azekah and Their Implications', *Radiocarbon*, 1–23.

Weinstein, James M. (1981), 'The Egyptian Empire in Palestine: A Reassessment', *Bulletin of the American Schools of Oriental Research*, 241, 1–28.

Weinstein, James M. (1991), 'Egypt and the Middle Bronze IIC/Late Bronze IA Transition in Palestine', *Levant*, 23 (1), 105–115.

Weinstein, James M. (1992), 'The Collapse of the Egyptian Empire in the Southern Levant', in William A. Ward and Martha S. Joukowsky (eds.), *The Crisis Years: The 12th Century BC: From beyond the Danube to the Tigris* (Dubuque: Kendall Hunt), 99–110.

Weinstein, James M. (2001), 'Foundation Deposits', in Donald B. Redford (ed.), *The Oxford Encyclopedia of Ancient Egypt* (1; New York: Oxford University Press), 559–561.

Weinstein, James M. (2012), 'Egypt and the Levant in the Reign of Ramesses III', in Eric H. Cline and David O'Connor (eds.), *Ramesses III: The Life and Times of Egypt's Last Hero* (Ann Arbor: University of Michigan Press), 160–180.

Weiss, Ehud, et al. (2019), 'Foreign Food Plants as Prestigious Gifts: The Archaeobotany of the Amarna Age Palace at Tel Beth-Shemesh, Israel', *Bulletin of the American Schools of Oriental Research*, 381 (1), 83–105.

Wilson-Wright, Aren M. (2016), *Athtart* (Forschungen zum Alten Testament 2. Reihe; Tübingen: Mohr Siebeck).

Wimmer, Stefan J. (1990), 'Egyptian Temples in Canaan and Sinai', in Sarah Israelite-Groll (ed.), *Studies in Egyptology Presented to Miriam Lichtheim* (Jerusalem: Magnes), 1065–1106.

Wimmer, Stefan J. (2008), 'A New Hieratic Ostracon from Ashkelon', *Tel Aviv*, 35 (1), 65–72.

Wimmer, Stefan J. (2010), 'A Hieratic Inscription', in Trude Dothan and Baruch Brandl (eds.), *Deir el-Balaḥ: Excavations in 1977–1982 in the Cemetery and Settlement* (Qedem 50; Jerusalem: Institute of Archaeology, Hebrew University of Jerusalem), 225–228.

Wimmer, Stefan J. and Maeir, Aren M. (2007), '"The Prince of Safit"? A Late Bronze Age Hieratic Inscription from Tell eṣ-Ṣāfi/Gath', *Zeitschrift des Deutschen Palästina-Vereins*, 123 (1), 37–48.

Wimmer, Stefan J. and Lehmann, Gunnar (2014), 'Two Hieratic Inscriptions from Qubur el-Walayda', *Egypt and the Levant*, 24, 343–348.

Wimmer, Stefan J. (2019), 'Lachish is Lachish on the Lachish Bowl: An Object Lesson for Reading Hieratic, with Little Surprising Results', in Aren M. Maeir, Itzhaq Shai, and Chris McKinny (eds.), *The Late Bronze and Early Iron Ages of Southern Canaan* (Archaeology of the Biblical World 2; Berlin: De Gruyter), 136–147.

Winter, Holly A. (2018), 'Tell el-'Ajjul Palaces I and II: Context and function', *Palestine Exploration Quarterly*, 150 (1), 4–33.

Woolf, Greg (2014), 'Romanization 2.0 and its alternatives', *Archaeological Dialogues*, 21 (1), 45–50.

Wright, Ernest G. (1966), 'Fresh Evidence for the Philistine Story', *Biblical Archaeologist*, 29 (3), 70–86.

Yannai, Eli (1994), 'A Late Bronze Age Gate at Gezer?', *Tel Aviv*, 21 (2), 283–287.

Yannai, Eli (2002), 'A Stratigraphic and Chronological Reappraisal of the "Governor's Residence" at Tell el-Far'ah (South)', in Eliezer D. Oren and S. Aḥituv (eds.), *Aaron Kempinski Memorial Volume* (Beer-Sheva 15; Beer-Sheva: Ben Gurion University Press), 368–376.

Yannai, Eli, et al. (2013), 'A Late Bronze Age Cemetery on the Coast of Palmaḥim', *'Atiqot* 74, 9–57.

Yassine, Khair N. (1975), 'Anthropoid Coffins from Raghdan Royal Palace Tomb in Amman', *Annual of the Department of Antiquities of Jordan*, 20, 57–68.

Yasur-Landau, Assaf (2001), 'The Mother(s) of All Philistines? Aegean Enthroned Deities of the 12th–11th Century Philistia', in Robert Laffineur and Robin Hagg (eds.), *Potnia* (Aegaeum 22; Liège: Universite de Liège, Histoire de l'art et archeologie de la Grece antique; University of Texas at Austin: Program in Aegean Scripts and Prehistory), 329–343.

Yasur-Landau, Assaf (2005), 'Old Wine in New Vessels: Intercultural Contact, Innovation and Aegean, Canaanite and Philistine Foodways', *Tel Aviv*, 32 (2), 168–191.

Yasur-Landau, Assaf (2006), 'A LHIIIC Stirrup Jar from Area K', in Israel Finkelstein, David Ussishkin, and Baruch Halpern (eds.), *Megiddo IV: The 1998–2002 Seasons* (Monograph Series of the Institute of Archaeology of Tel Aviv University 24; Tel Aviv: Emery and Claire Yass Publications in Archaeology), 299–302.

Yasur-Landau, Assaf (2007), 'Let's Do the Time Warp Again: Migration Processes and the Absolute Chronology of the Philistine Settlement', in Manfred Bietak and Ernst Czerńy (eds.), *The Synchronization of Civilisations in the Eastern Mediterranean in the Second Millennium B.C. III* (Contributions to the Chronology of the Eastern Mediterranean 9; Vienna: Verlag der Osterreichischen Akademie der Wissenschaften), 609–620.

Yasur-Landau, Assaf (2009), 'Behavioral Patterns in Transition: 11th-Century BCE Innovation in Domestic Textile Production', in David J. Schloen (ed.), *Exploring the Longue Durée: Essays in Honor of Lawrence E. Stager* (Winona Lake: Eisenbrauns), 507–515.

Yasur-Landau, Assaf (2010a), *The Philistines and Aegean Migration at the End of the Late Bronze Age* (New York: Cambridge University Press).

Yasur-Landau, Assaf (2010b), 'On Birds and Dragons: A Note on the Sea Peoples and Mycenaean Ships', in Yoram Cohen, Amir Gilan, and Jared L. Miller (eds.), *Pax Hethitica. Studies on the Hittites and Their Neighbours in Honor of Itamar Singer* (Studien zu den Bogazköy-Texten 51; Wiesbaden: Harrassowitz), 399–410.

Yasur-Landau, Assaf (2011), 'Deep change in Domestic Behavioural Patterns and Theoretical Aspects of Interregional Interaction in the 12th Century Levant', in Vassos Karageorghis and Ourania Kouka (eds.), *On Cooking Pots, Drinking Cups, Loomweights and Ethnicity in Bronze Age Cyprus and Neighbouring Regions: An International Archaeological Symposium Held in Nicosia, November 6th–7th 2010* (Nicosia: A.G. Leventis Foundation), 245–255.

Yasur-Landau, Assaf (2012a), 'The Role of the Canaanite Population in the Aegean Migration to the Southern Levant in the late Second Millennium BCE', in Joseph Maran and Philipp W. Stockhammer (eds.), *Materiality and Social Practice: Transformative Capacities of Intercultural Encounters* (Oxford: Oxbow Books), 191–197.

Yasur-Landau, Assaf (2012b), 'Chariots, Spears and Wagons: Anatolian and Aegean Elements in the Medinet Habu Land Battle Relief', in Gershon Galil, et al. (eds.), *The Ancient Near East in the 12th–10th Centuries BCE Culture and History: Proceedings of the International Conference held at the University of Haifa, 2–5 May, 2010* (Alter Orient und Altes Testament 392; Münster: Ugarit-Verlag), 549–567.

Yasur-Landau, Assaf (2013), 'The "Feathered Helmets" of the Sea Peoples: Joining the Iconographic and Archaeological Evidence', *TALANTA*, 44, 27–40.

Yasur-Landau, Assaf, et al. (2014), 'A Rare Cypriot Krater of the White Slip II Style from Azekah', *Israel Exploration Journal*, 64 (1), 1–8.

Yellin, Joseph and Gunneweg, Jan (1985), 'Provenience of Pottery from Tell Qasile Strata VII, X, XI and XII', in Amihai Mazar (ed.), *Excavations at Tell Qasile, Part 2: The Philistine Sanctuary—Various Finds, the Pottery, Conclusions, Appendices* (Qedem 20; Jerusalem: Institute of Archaeology, Hebrew University of Jerusalem), 111–117.

Yisraeli, Yael (1993), 'Far'ah, Tell el- (South)', in Ephraim Stern (ed.), *New Encyclopedia of Archaeological Excavations in the Holy Land* (2; Jerusalem: Israel Exploration Society), 441–444.

Yoffee, Norman (2009), 'Making Ancient Cities Plausible', *Reviews in Anthropology*, 38, 264–289.

Young, Robert J.C. (2001), *Postcolonialism: An Historical Introduction* (Oxford, UK and Malden, MA Blackwell).

Young, Robert J.C. (2005), *Colonial Desire: Hybridity in Theory, Culture and Race* (Second edn.; London and New York: Routledge).

Zernecke, Anna (2013), 'The Lady of the Titles: The Lady of Byblos and the Search for her "True Name"', *Die Welt des Orients*, 43 (2), 226–242.

Ziffer, Irit (2005), 'From Acemhöyük to Megiddo: The Banquet Scene in the Art of the Levant in the Second Millennium BCE', *Tel Aviv*, 32 (2), 133–167.

Ziffer, Irit, Bunimovitz, Shlomo, and Lederman, Zvi (2009), 'Divine or Human? An Intriguing Late Bronze Age Plaque Figurine from Tel Beth-Shemesh', *Egypt and the Levant*, 19, 333–341.

Zivie-Coche, Christiane (1994), 'Dieux autres, dieux des autres: Identite culturelle et alterite dans l'Egypte ancienne', in I. Alon, I. Gruenwald, and Itamar Singer (eds.), *Concepts of the Other in Near Eastern Religions* (Israel Oriental Studies 14; Leiden: Brill), 39–79.

Zori, Colleen, Brant, Erika, and Rodríguez, Mauricio Uribe (2017), 'Empires as Social Networks: Roads, Connectedness, and the Inka Incorporation of Northern Chile', *Ñawpa Pacha*, 37 (1), 1–23.

Zorn, Jeffrey R. (2010), 'Reconsidering Goliath: An Iron Age I Philistine Chariot Warrior', *Bulletin of the American Schools of Oriental Research*, 360, 1–22.

Zuckerman, Sharon (2007), '"... Slaying Oxen and Killing Sheep, Eating Flesh and Drinking Wine ...": Feasting in Late Bronze Age Hazor', *Palestine Exploration Quarterly*, 139 (3), 186–204.

Zuckerman, Sharon (2012), 'The Temples of Canaanite Hazor', in Jens Kamlah (ed.), *Temple Building and Temple Cult: Architecture and Cultic Paraphernalia of Temples in the Levant (2.-1. Mill. B.C.E.)* (Abhandlungen des Deutschen Palästina-Vereins 41; Wiesbaden: Harrassowitz), 99–125.

Zukerman, Alexander (2009), 'Notes on Pottery with Philistine, Cypriot and Aegean Affinities', in Nava Panitz-Cohen and Amihai Mazar (eds.), *Excavations at Tel Beth-Shean, 1989–1996 Vol. 3: The 13th–11th Centuries BCE Strata in Areas N and S* (Jerusalem: Israel Exploration Society and the Institute of Archaeology, Hebrew University of Jerusalem), 500–509.

Index of Place Names

Acre 64. *See also* Akko
Abu Salima, Tell 121
Adorayim, Naḥal 88
Aegean 10, 61, 73–76, 78–79, 96–101, 124, 128
Ajjul, Tell el- 14–24, 28–31, 33, 43, 69, 115, 119, 123, 125
Akko 64, 96, 110–111, 121–122. *See also* Acre
Amarna, el- 27–28, 30–31, 35, 37–38, 40, 42–43, 68, 72, 126
Anatolia 25, 52, 64, 65, 74, 79, 94, 128
Aphek, Tel 13, 15, 42, 55, 58, 68, 81, 84–85, 93–94
Arabah 90
Arish, al- 23, 55
Ashdod, Tel 10, 14, 35–36, 75, 77, 87, 89, 93, 96, 99, 128
Ashdod-Yam 36
Ashkelon 13–14, 22, 28, 32–35, 38, 42–43, 54–56, 67, 75, 77, 85, 87, 93, 98–99, 103, 106–109, 114–116, 118, 126–127
Ayalon Valley 36, 39–40
Ayalon, Naḥal 40–41, 85
Azekah, Tel 16, 56, 80–82, 86, 103, 110, 127
Azor, Tel 15, 85

Batash, Tel 15–17, 19, 21, 64, 87, 93
Beersheba Valley 28, 36
Beit-Mirsim, Tell 16, 38–39
Besor Basin 16, 89–90
Besor, Naḥal Ha- 90
Besor region 28–30, 42, 89–90, 127
Beth-Dagan 85
Beth-Horon 88
Beth-Shean, Tel 17, 19–20, 22, 32, 50, 55–56, 62, 66, 90, 94–96, 106
Beth-Shemesh, Tel 13, 15–16, 21, 33, 38, 50, 55–57, 65, 87, 89, 91, 94, 98–99, 101, 109–111, 114, 117, 123, 126, 128
Bethlehem 88
Bir el-Abd 23
Burak, Tel 13
Burg, Tell el- 66

Burna, Tel 16
Byblos 12, 50, 110

Canaan 2, 4–5, 7, 9–10, 12, 14, 16–17, 19–20, 23–24, 27–28, 30, 32, 43–45, 48–49, 52, 55–56, 58, 61–62, 64, 69, 71–78, 91–92, 94–96, 98–100, 102–106, 108–109, 112, 114–115, 118, 120–121, 123–128
Cyprus 50, 79, 84, 95–96, 98–103, 128

Dabaʿ, Tell ed- 13
Deir el-ʿAzar 88
Deir el-Balaḥ 31–32, 55, 61, 90, 111–112, 116, 119–120
Deir el-Medina 65
Dothan, Tel 58, 113, 119
Duwer, Tell ad- 37. *See also* Lachish, Tel

Egypt 1, 5–8, 12, 16, 20, 23, 27, 30, 40, 43–44, 48–49, 52–54, 57, 59, 61, 64–69, 71, 74, 76–77, 79, 84, 100, 102–103, 106, 121–123, 125, 127–128
'Elah, Naḥal Ha- 36, 37, 88
Elah Valley 38, 40
Eton, Tel 88, 123

Farʿah (S), Tell el- 8, 21, 31–33, 59–62, 79–80, 89–90, 106, 106–119, 121, 123

Gath 32–33, 36–38, 40, 80, 81, 89, 106, 117, 126, 128. *See also* Ṣafi, Tell eṣ-
Gath-Carmel 40. *See also* Jatt
Gaza 1, 8, 28–33, 35, 43, 69, 77, 80, 81, 89–90, 99, 108, 124, 125, 128
Gerar, Naḥal 28, 30
Gerisa, Tel 15, 55, 84, 106–115, 117
Gezer, Tel 15–16, 19, 21, 24, 35, 37, 39–40, 43, 54, 56, 67, 72, 81, 87, 91, 98, 101, 110, 114, 117–119, 122, 126–127

Habua, Tell el- 23
Ḥalif, Tel 14–17, 58, 88, 115
Ḥamid, Tel 94

INDEX OF PLACE NAMES   193

Ḥarasim, Tel   15, 64, 93
Ḥaror, Tel   14, 24, 30–33, 81, 90, 109, 126
Ḥaruva   23, 55
Hayyat, Tell el-   13
Hazor   45, 49, 58, 61
Hebron Hills   28, 38, 88
Hesban, Tel   58
Ḥesi, Tell el-   14, 31–32, 43, 56

Ifshar, Tel   13
Izbeth Ṣarṭa   84

Jaffa   1, 15, 17, 22–24, 32, 35, 40–43, 49–51, 81, 83, 85, 91, 119, 125, 127
Jemmeh, Tell   14, 16, 30–32, 56, 89, 96, 110, 118
Jerusalem   35, 37–38, 40, 88, 99, 110, 112
Jezreel Valley   5, 62, 96
Jib, al- Plateau   39, 88
Judean Highland   36

Kabri, Tel   13
Kadesh   12, 54, 120
Kadesh Barnea   123
Keilah   37
Keisan, Tell   121

Lachish, Tel   14–17, 19, 21, 24, 28, 32–33, 35–39, 43, 45–46, 49–50, 52–53, 55–56, 58–59, 61–63, 66, 80, 81–82, 86, 93, 95, 99, 108–109, 115–118, 121–123, 126–127. *See also* Duwer, Tell ad-
Lachish, Naḥal   36, 37
Lahav Hills   28
Levant   1, 4–10, 12–13, 16–17, 20, 23–24, 26, 28, 30, 43, 45, 47, 50, 54, 57–58, 61, 64–67, 69, 72–74, 76–77, 79, 92, 94–95, 100–104, 115, 122, 124–125

Maaravim, Tel   90
Maḥoz   126
Malkata   51
Masos, Tel   90
Medinet Habu   77, 79
Mediterranean   6, 8, 26, 73–76, 79–80, 93, 99, 102, 104, 124
Megiddo, Tel   10, 12, 17, 19–20, 57–61, 72, 82, 94, 96, 113, 117

Memphis   51, 65
Mesopotamia   59
Michal, Tel   15, 17, 58
Miqne, Tel   15, 22, 36, 56, 58, 75, 83, 85–89, 91, 92–99, 101, 103, 112–116, 121, 128
Mor, Tel   14, 36, 81, 95
Muḫḫazu   33, 35, 40

Nagila, Tel   14
Naṣbeh, Tell en-   96, 121
Negev Highlands   28, 90
Netiv Ha'Asarah   16, 31–32, 90
Nile Delta   16, 52, 77, 99
Nile Valley   1, 12, 26, 59
Nubia   6, 8, 26, 51, 71, 79

Palestine   5, 74
Pella   49, 55–56, 62. *See also* Ṭabaqat Faḥl
Pr-Ramesses   54

Qalunia   88
Qaneh, Naḥal   40
Qarnayim, Tel   66
Qashish, Tel   58
Qasile, Tel   72, 84–85, 91, 96–99, 106–110, 112, 116–118, 120–121, 128
Qeiyafa, Khirbet   88–89, 91
Qila, al-   37
Qubur al-Walaydah   32, 81
Qurnat el-Haramiya   84

Rabba, Naḥal   40
Rabud, Khirbet   88
Rafah   23, 32. *See also* Raphia
Ramallah   39
Raphia   30. *See also* Rafah
Reḥov, Tel   55–56, 94, 123
Ridan, Tel   32
Rumeida, Tell er-/Hebron   88

Ṣafi, Tell eṣ-   15, 24, 32–33, 36–37, 55, 58, 81, 87, 89, 91, 93–94, 96, 101, 106, 111–112, 117, 128. *See also* Gath
Sharḥan   12, 23, 27
Sedinga   51
Seraʿ, Tel   14, 17, 31–33, 56, 81, 89–90, 95
Serabit el-Khadim   50–51, 72
Sharon Plain   40

Shechem   40
Shephelah   16, 34, 36, 38–39, 86, 88, 97, 99–100
Shiloh   58
Shiloh, Naḥal   40
Shiqma Basin   38
Shiqma, Naḥal   28, 32–33, 36, 88, 90
Sinai Peninsula   9, 23, 30, 33, 55
Soleb   51
Sorek, Naḥal   36, 39–40, 87
Sorek Valley   38

Taanach   17, 30
Ṭabaqat Faḥl   56, 62. *See also* Pella
Tanis   72, 106
Thebes   51, 72

Timna   49, 72
Tubeiqa, Khirbet   88

Ugarit   52, 102

Ways of Horus   30, 55, 69

Yarkon Basin   16, 33, 40–42, 83–85, 91, 99, 128
Yarkon River   40–41, 84
Yarmout, Tel   88–89
Yavneh-Yam   14, 34–35, 87, 126
Yenoam   54
Yoqneam, Tel   58, 94
Yurza   27–28, 30–33, 81, 126

Zayit, Tel   16

Index of Historical Figures

Abdi-Ḫeba   35, 37–38, 40
Abdi-na[...]   38
Ahmose   12, 16, 23, 131
Amenemope   77
Amenhotep I   12, 131
Amenhotep II   12, 35, 131
Amenhotep III   12, 28, 49–53, 65, 126, 131
Amenhotep IV/Akhenaten   28, 131
Ashur-bel-kala   72

Harihor   72
Hatshepsut   12, 131
Horemheb   54, 131

Kamose   23

Lab'ayu   44

Merneptah   35, 40, 54, 67, 131
Milki-Ilu   37, 40
Muwatalli II   54

Ramesses I   54, 131
Ramesses II   30, 35, 41, 54–55, 67, 109–110, 114, 119, 131
Ramesses III   30, 71–73, 77, 79, 131
Ramesses IV   71–73, 131
Ramesses V   72, 132
Ramesses VI   72, 132
Ramesses VIII   71, 132
Ramesses IX   71–72, 132
Ramesses X   71, 132
Ramesses XI   71–72, 132

Sennacherib   42
Seti I   23, 30, 54–55, 67, 131
Setnakhte   71, 131
Shuwardata   37

Thutmose I   12, 131
Thutmose II   12, 131
Thutmose III   6, 12, 17, 23–24, 27, 29–31, 35, 40, 42, 68, 125, 131
Thutmose IV   12, 40, 131
Tiglath-pileser I   72
Tutankhamun   28, 59, 131

Yaḫzib-Hadda   38

Printed in the United States
by Baker & Taylor Publisher Services